MW01257786

JOY UNSPEAKABLE

JOY UNSPEAKABLE

Finding Joy in Christ-like Suffering

PETER Y. LEE

Foreword by Scott Redd

WIPF & STOCK · Eugene, Oregon

JOY UNSPEAKABLE
Finding Joy in Christ-like Suffering

Wipf & Stock
An Imprint of Wipf and Stock Publishers
199 W. 8th Ave., Suite 3
Eugene, OR 97401

www.wipfandstock.com

PAPERBACK ISBN:978-1-5326-6453-3
HARDCOVER ISBN: 978-1-5326-6454-0
EBOOK ISBN: 978-1-5326-6455-7

Manufactured in the U.S.A.   12/14/18

Dedicated with love,

To my daughter, Kara Ruth Lee

And to my family
Clara, Caleb, Jeremiah, Micah, Tabitha, and Priscilla
All of you bring me nothing but *joy*

In loving memory of my beloved father,
Sepoong Samuel Lee
And to my mother, Soonsill Lee
Greater parents a son could not have

In loving memory of Kaitlyn In-Kyung Yoon
And to the Yoon family
Sam, Cassie, Andrew, Sophie, and Matthew
I have no doubt that Kaitlyn is amazingly proud of all of you

Beloved, do not be surprised at the fiery trial when it comes upon you to test you, as though something strange were happening to you. But rejoice insofar as you share Christ's sufferings, that you may also rejoice and be glad when his glory is revealed.

1 PETER 4:12–13

Contents

Foreword

THERE IS A PERSISTENT double vision to the Christian experience of suffering and joy. In the case of each, we tend to see both what is and what will be simultaneously—the focal points of each pushing to crowd out the other. We find suffering's double vision in the moment beside the hospital bed that speaks to the despair of this present condition and the human affliction of Christ with whom we are united. We find joy's double vision in the healing, the reconciliation, the unexpected laugh with a friend, and the image of a new world in which all healings, reconciliations, and laughter finds their culmination and nexus.

To complicate things, we also tend to keep our own counsel in both experiences. In suffering, we come to fear the salutation, "How are you?" because, "You couldn't handle it if I told you," and all that. In joy, the experience might be so sublime, so unspeakable, the mere report of it would seem glib and cheapening. And yet endless movies, songs, and art explore both experience with scientist-like zeal, in which they establish set pieces that evoke the pure feeling, the exact experience, of suffering or joy—it doesn't matter which—without the distractions of real life. The simulacrum is so much easier than the actual thing.

In reality, after the loved one passes away, you still have to pay the bills and perhaps even rush off to keep an appointment or pick up a kid from school. Joy, too, is often interrupted by the tyrannical, urgent task, so that it is lost to memory and space. The scriptures speak of actual human suffering. Perhaps nowhere else in ancient literature do we find such rounded characters as Abraham, the doubting patriarch, Moses, the reluctant lawgiver, and David, the impulsive king—not to mention Peter, Paul, and John. Biblical suffering often resists the easy dignity of the movies, and biblical joy comes and goes in a flash. This is because it is true and inspired by the same God who sustains us today, and it was given to humans whose experiences are remarkably similar to ours.

For the believer united with Christ, perhaps no other experiences give expression to the place of the Christian in the story of redemption than both suffering and joy. By our union with Christ the two are intertwined. He suffered that we might have joy. We are united with him in his suffering, and that union is a source of joy for us. We can persevere in our suffering, knowing that it will not stand forever, but is incomparable to the joy to come (Rom 8:18). In fact, we can persevere in all things, knowing that the joy of the Lord is the source of our strength (Neh 8:10). One reminds us of what our savior has accomplished while the other ensures us that his promises will be fulfilled, and hence the double vision of those united with Christ.

Furthermore, the experiences of suffering and joy resist easy justification. For what are not entirely obvious reasons, the skeptic usually only considers the problem of suffering, not the problem of joy. If one is interested in questioning God's character and existence in light of present suffering, it is only fair to include joy in the investigation. Doesn't joy tell us something of God? And shouldn't that influence our reasoning?

As you work your way through this book, I would encourage you to pay as close attention to what Dr. Peter Lee says of suffering and joy as to what he does not say. You are in the hands of a skilled biblical interpreter who is not interested in selling books with shallow, reductionistic explanations of safe, abstract problems. In this book, you will find relevant biblical passages that address important aspects of suffering and joy, but you will also find a perspective that is informed by a close reading of the whole scriptural account, even those passages that are not obviously relevant to the question. This is where the answers will be found, not in disconnected, decontextualized texts but rather in the broad sweep of the holy word of God. Yes, the doctrine of union with Christ will provide much of the bedrock of Dr. Lee's perspective, but such a topic is notoriously broad in its application. The New Testament tends to traffic in superlatives when our Lord is the subject.

The trick is that suffering and joy are not moments of the Christian life; rather, they are the substance of the Christian life. We grow, struggle, and repent into our suffering and joy, and because we are united with Christ, all of it, the whole messy process, is unto life and glory, forever and ever.

Dr. Scott Redd
President
Reformed Theological Seminary, Washington DC

Preface

THIS BOOK DEALS WITH two biblical themes that most people do not naturally associate with each other—suffering and joy. I have written this book for the *suffering* Christian so that they may not be defeated or overwhelmed by the sorrows they endure for the sake of Christ. My hope is for them to find a surprising yet astonishing *joy*—a joy that can only be found by faith in Jesus Christ.

We usually think of suffering and joy as polar opposites and cannot fathom that they may have anything in common. When we suffer, joy seems to be a distant dream. We hope for it, pray for it, and long for it, but it seems unreachable. I wish to show you that suffering and joy are not mutually exclusive; that Christian suffering can be the *source* of Christian joy. Joy can be found in even the most gut-wrenching situations. The kind of biblical suffering at the source of this joy, however, is "suffering for righteousness' sake" (Matt 5:10–12). Chapters 1 to 3 address this "Christ-like suffering." Chapters 4 to 8 address the extraordinary joy that can stem from this suffering. In hopes that this book can be useful for smaller groups in church (or school) settings, I have included reading questions as an appendix. These questions are designed to summarize major points within each chapter and stimulate discussion.

To demonstrate the integration of suffering and joy, I try to bring together two other apparently conflicting concepts: theology and prac-ticality. Among the numerous books on Christian suffering, the most helpful books show that a solid understanding of God comforts us in our sufferings. I have taken a similar approach. For that reason, there is a heavy dependence upon the Bible throughout these chapters.

During an independent study on the life and theology of the great Protestant theologian John Calvin, I used Calvin's *The Institutes of the Christian Religion* as my primary text. Anyone familiar with Calvin's work cannot but be impressed with his brilliance as a theologian and systematician. This, I expected. What I did not expect was his pastoral heart. Those who view Calvin as a cold-hearted theologian who majors on minors and lacks sensitivity for God's people have clearly not read him. Calvin shows the importance of biblical faithfulness—and that faithful and meaningful pastoral ministry cannot be done without it. He is a champion and the standard for intellectual rigors as a necessary component to effective and godly ministry. Christians in our contemporary society have much to gain from him.

The impact of that study has had a lasting effect on me. Ever since, I have attempted to show that theological knowledge has direct benefits on the Christian life. During my time in ministry, I preached the thoughts and principles from Calvin on many Sunday mornings, and the fruits have been extraordinary. Despite my personal ineptitude, these sermons provided comfort for many. Early in my church planting years, I had to wear many hats. I was the church administrator, events coordinator, publisher, setup crew for Sunday services, worship leader, and more. In addition to all of this, I preached every Lord's Day. In those days, I ran out of time in my preparations more often than I care to remember. In addition to the regular chores, crises arose without warning: violation of marital vows, a young woman diagnosed with brain cancer, and the death of a young child. What possible words could a mere man share to minister to the emotional storm that rages in the hearts of God's people in the middle of such trials? I knew of none, but as a pastor, I had to share something on Sunday mornings. I preached Christ and the grace that he provides from sharing in his sufferings, because I did not know what else to share. If any good came from my ministry of the word, it was solely due to the power of the truths found in Scripture, because nothing but the life-changing power of God's word can deal with those circumstances.

I believe that theological truths have life-changing power because I have seen their fruits. The unfortunate misconception currently rampant within the church is that theology cannot offer words of comfort during times of distress. Nothing could be further from the truth. In times of suffering, we need more than superficial prattle about the goodness of God. This shallow understanding cannot withstand the chaos that suffering brings to God's people. We need a clear, complete biblical foundation that is centered upon the person and work of Jesus Christ.

Although both suffering and joy are the themes addressed, this book is really more about Christian joy than suffering. One (suffering) is a means to the other (joy). I mention painful situations because these are the adversities that frequently burden the lives of God's people. I cannot change them, nor can I offer any promises that the sufferings will soon come to an end. The unfortunate reality is that they may not. What we need is not necessarily a change in our situation, but a change in our worldview—to see our suffering not always as a curse, but as a blessing, a source of joy. The Word of God is greater than any meager words I can offer, but I pray that if you are suffering, this book may help you to find a joy that cannot be described with human words: *A Joy Unspeakable*.

Acknowledgments

No PROJECT IS THE work of one person. The publication of this work is a testament to this fact, and I had an army of people who supported and encouraged me through many years of writing, editing, and refining. The end result is not only a finished product that I pray will touch the hearts of many but also my realization that because of these people, I am the most blessed man on the face of the earth. If permitted to do so, I could write an entire volume that describes the grace they extended to me. Although I alone will know the value of their amazing care, the world needs to know who they are and their never-ending encouragement to this humbled servant.

Harlan Shiau and Justin Parke, you are two dear brothers in the Lord. I thank you for the time and care that you took to comment on the early draft of this work.

Leah Hamilton and Zack Marin, your writing and editing skills are a gift, and I was witness to the tender ways in which you improved my flow of thought.

Dr. Tremper Longman, you have become an endearing friend over the years. Thank you for taking time to read an early version of this work. Your endorsement warmed my heart and blessed me to no end. I will remain forever grateful for the time that you took to encourage a junior colleague.

Dr. Scott Redd, thank you for all our times of discussion on this subject and your constant words of support. There were moments when I wanted to give up this project. It was your friendship and kind words that nurtured my soul and stirred me to press on. In you, the Lord has blessed me with more than an inspiring leader and a fellow scholar-in-arms, but also a gracious friend. I can think of no one else to write the "foreword" for this book other than you.

Dr. Howard Griffith, you have been an amazing and faithful friend. Thank you for all your wise and insightful words. Every time we discuss Scripture, theology, ministry, and life, I am humbled by your wisdom, blessed by your insight, and inspired by your dedication to the truths of Scripture.

Dr. Tommy Keene, thank you for reading and commenting on several early chapters of this work. Attending your lectures on Hebrews–Revelation clarified my thoughts on certain key ideas.

Mr. Geoff Sackett, thank you for your kind words of endorsement of the early draft of this work. You have been and remain a good friend, and I was a direct beneficiary of your ministry at the seminary.

Matthew Wimer and the staff of Wipf & Stock publishers, thank you for all your patience and help through the entire publishing process. Thank you for answering all my questions and taking me through the complexities of publication. You made this entire process extremely rewarding.

A special word of gratitude to Dr. Chad Van Dixhoorn. You have done more for me than I can say, professionally and personally. It was your comments that brought a clear focus to the book and helped me to think of others before myself. Because of your remarks, this final version is by far better than the original draft. Your friendship surpasses institutions and geographies, and I pray that I was as much a blessing to you as you have been to me.

Another special word of gratitude to Dr. Paul Jeon, thank you for constantly encouraging me to seek the publication of this project and endorsing this work to others. Not only are you an outstanding scholar but also a loving pastor. Our growing friendship means the world, and you helped me to never feel alone.

Living Hope Presbyterian Church, as you read this book, you may find the content familiar. They were once sermons which were preached to you. It was our ministry together that refined my thoughts on this subject. Thank you for being such an open, vulnerable, and loving people.

Sam, Cassie, the Yoon children, and the entire Yoon family, your friendship means more to me than all the riches of this world. During some of the hardest days, it was your trust in the Lord that inspired me to strive to be a better pastor and friend. I can only hope that the dedication of this book in the memory of your beloved Kaitlyn will continue to heal your deep wounds and turn them into a "joy unspeakable."

Clara, my dearest wife and the greatest blessing a man could have, thank you. You are truly one of the most gifted people I know. Not only have you been the rock-solid "suitable helper," your skills as an editor are unsurpassed. I could not imagine life without you. You are a daily reminder of the grace of God in my life.

My children—Caleb, Jeremiah, Kara, Micah, Tabitha, and Priscilla—you are all a "joy" to your father and continue to bless me every day of my life.

I

Introduction

A Layout of the Land

Though you have not seen him, you love him. Though you do not now see him, you believe in him and rejoice with joy that is inexpressible and filled with glory.

1 Peter 1:8[1]

It was the winter of 1994, and I was going through one of the most difficult times of my life. My maternal grandmother, the prayer-warrior who had supported me stalwartly through all my life, had suddenly passed, and I felt like a ship that had lost its rudder. I was twenty-four years old—young, eager, and enthusiastic with many hopes and dreams. My entire life was ahead of me, and yet, for that brief time, my future looked uncertain. I was gripped with fear. Feeling isolated and at a loss, I needed time away from the world to pray, to meditate, and to heal.

At the time, I was just beginning my studies at Westminster Seminary in California. It was the winter term and the only class offered was "Preaching Christ in 1 Peter," taught by the late Dr. Edmund P. Clowney. This was not a required class for my degree program, but I knew I needed something—anything—that could bring me hope and provide some perspective on my life. So I sat in that class and listened to Dr. Clowney's lectures. Those who were fortunate enough to sit under the instruction

1. Unless otherwise stated, all Scriptural quotations are from the English Standard Version (ESV).

and ministry of Dr. Clowney know that he had an extraordinary way of
revealing the beauty of the glory of Christ. In fact, he made a career of
doing this in all of the Scripture, including 1 Peter. Those few days were a
time of spiritual renewal and emotional healing. Thus began my lifelong
journey of reflection of this amazing epistle. Through those studies, the
Lord taught me a profound understanding of how to experience "joy that
is inexpressible" (1 Pet 1:8) in the midst of Christian suffering.

My experience is not different than anyone else. Everyone goes
through trials at some point in their lives—times of agony and pain so
overwhelming that no hope seems in sight. You may be reading this book
because you are in search of the same thing I sought so many years ago: an
answer to the pain. This book is neither the first treatment on the subject
of Christian suffering nor will it be the last. The quest for the resolution
to suffering has been going on ever since the fall of humanity in the book
of Genesis. It is one of the hallmark traits of man. This quest has recently
been intensified due to the tragic events of September 11, 2001. Beyond
just looking for answers to difficult theological and philosophical questions (e.g., existence of pain and suffering in light of a good God), this
has been a desperate search for comfort and joy in the midst of tragedy.

First Peter is an epistle that directly addresses this question. Consider the following passages:

- "In this you rejoice, though now for a little while, as was necessary,
  you have been grieved by various trials." (1 Pet 1:6)

- "For this is a gracious thing, when, mindful of God, one endures
  sorrows while suffering unjustly. For what credit is it if, when you
  sin and are beaten for it, you endure? But if when you do good and
  suffer for it you endure, this is a gracious thing in the sight of God."
  (1 Pet. 2:19–20)

- "But even if you should suffer for righteousness' sake, you will be
  blessed." (1 Pet 3:14)

- "And after you have suffered a little while, the God of all grace, who
  has called you to his eternal glory in Christ, will himself restore,
  confirm, strengthen, and establish you." (1 Pet 5:10)

The hardship that Peter's readers faced is obvious, but so is the hope
that can be gained amid this hardship. Peter is the only biblical author to
describe this hope as a "living hope" (1 Pet 1:3). This life of hope is also
described as one filled with a "joy that is inexpressible and filled with

glory" (1 Pet 1:8). These are extraordinary descriptions for seemingly abstract concepts like "hope" and "joy." Peter's readers were suffering tremendously. It is ironic that an existence so consumed with agony and defeat could be described as a life filled with a "living hope," a life marked with a "joy that is inexpressible." How can we gain such blessing? I don't know about you, but this is something that I want. That is a question 1 Peter answers.

A Layout of the Biblical Landscape

Many find comfort knowing that our God is sovereignly in control of all things in our lives. When difficult times arise, we are assured that this is not beyond the powers of our sovereign God, who divinely orchestrated this scenario for our well being (Rom 8:28). Knowing that God is sovereign assures us that there is purpose for my suffering, but we are still left pondering, "why?" This is the question I have faced repeatedly, both in pastoral ministry and in my personal life.

The people of God can take comfort in this fact: the Holy Scriptures are saturated with answers to the question of "why." They explain why suffering seems to be a regular part of the daily lives of God's people and also gives the reasons for the trials that they face. Listed below are brief summaries of several of those reasons. The compilation of these various themes provides a layout of the biblical landscape, which shows a broad, panoramic response to the reason(s) *why* God appoints suffering for His people.[2]

1. *Suffering is a result of sin.* The Scriptures make it clear that sin is the primary reason for suffering. We suffer because we have sinned. In the garden of Eden, humanity lived at peace with God and with each other. All that changed when sin entered our world (Gen 3), and now we live in a constant state of tension. For example, envy, pride, hatred—sins of the heart—have historically led to violent outbreaks, causing many to suffer. Competition, racism, and murder; as bad as these conflicts with our fellow men are, what is worse is the effect of sin on our relationship with God. Because of sin, we are distant

---

2. The following list is a compilation from the following books: Carson, *How Long, O Lord*; Piper and Taylor, *Suffering and the Sovereignty of God*; McCartney, *Why Does It Have to Hurt?*; Currid, *Why do I Suffer?*; Keller, *Walking with God*; and Sproul, *Surprised by Suffering*.

from our blessed creator and king. We now suffer the "wages of sin" which is "death" (Rom 6:23; cf. Gen 2:17), both physical death as well as spiritual death, meaning suffering eternal condemnation (Heb 9:27; Rev 20:6). If it were not for the redemptive work of Jesus Christ, in His death on the cross and resurrection from the grave, there would be no hope for any form of reconciliation at all. However, because of Christ, "we have peace with God" (Rom 5:1). Through Christ, God has "reconciled us to himself" and given to us the message of the gospel so that everyone can know that there is reconciliation with God through Jesus Christ (2 Cor 5:18–19; cf. Rom 5:11). Only by understanding the amazing love of God for us can we love each other and overcome our sinful desires to harm each other (Matt 18:21–35). Although the sufferings of Christians and non-Christians may look the same outwardly, they are decidedly different. For Christians, the suffering that results from their sin leads to the softening of a hardened heart, which brings about genuine repentance and restoration before God (2 Cor 7:8–11). For non-Christians, suffering is part of the penalty and punishment from God as their judge, which leads to the ever-hardening of their heart and their ultimate condemnation for eternity—something believers will never know or experience (Rom 8:1).

2. *Suffering teaches us to trust in God and not in ourselves.* The apostle Paul describes this reality in his own life when he says, "For we do not want you to be unaware, brethren, of our affliction which came to us in Asia, that we were burdened excessively, beyond our strength, so that we despaired even of life; indeed, we had the sentence of death within ourselves *in order that we should not trust in ourselves, but in God who raises the dead*" (2 Cor 1:8–9). Paul acknowledges that his suffering is a regular reminder that he should not trust in himself, but in God. In the midst of such crisis, it becomes abundantly clear that any resolution cannot be brought about by mere mortal man. The only person to whom we can turn is God himself "who raises the dead." If He can bring life back to the dead, then is there anything that He cannot do (Rom 8:31–32)? The proper response for believers is to turn to their gracious Heavenly Father in humble prayer.

3. *Suffering leads us to the Word of God.*[3] In times of despair, the believer searches for a message that can provide insight into the nature of their struggle and how they can endure through it. But from where will such a message come? It comes from the Word of God, the Holy Scriptures. When facing adverse struggles, the people of God are to turn to the Word of God, which is the only inspired source of teaching on matters of faith and life (2 Tim 3:16–17). The previous section established that suffering leads the believer to the presence of the Lord in prayer. Dr. Clowney was fond of reminding his students that the biblical psalter is not only a magnificent collection of songs and poems, but also prayers.[4] Through the words of these inspired poems, we can "call to the Lord when my heart is faint" even if we are at the "ends of the earth" (Ps 61:2). We want to understand the nature of these hardships, but this can be found only in the Scriptures. Only through the Scriptures can we find hope (Rom 15:4), restoration and renewal (Ps 119:50), and an accurate understanding of the nature of our affliction and hardship. It is through the Scriptures that we can make sense of all our sufferings. One of the many reasons why believers struggle with their suffering is because they seek worldly wisdom to cope with their pain instead of seeking counsel from the divine Word. For example, when facing a crisis, the wisdom of this world tells us to look to ourselves, to believe in ourselves even when no one else does. This is the gospel according to American Idol. The Word of God, however, teaches us to seek out the Lord who is "my strength . . . my rock and my fortress and my deliverer, my God, my rock, in whom I take refuge, my shield, and the horn of my salvation, my stronghold (Ps 18:2; see also section 2 above).

3. In this section, I am indebted to John Currid, *Why do I Suffer?*, 59–60. Dr. Currid provides four reasons on why believers should turn to the Word in times of hardship. First, the Word provides comfort and hope. Second, the Word restores the discouraged believer who finds restoration and renewal through the Scriptures (Ps 119:50, 93). Third, the Word strengthens the believer. Fourth, the Scripture teaches the true nature of suffering. Interestingly, he is the only author to explicitly state what many others (including myself) presume, namely that our suffering is to lead us to the Scriptures. He correctly reminds us of a necessity that can often be overlooked. At the same time, however, we must wisely minister to the wounded with the Word and avoid quoting Scripture after Scripture in a way that batters one who is already downtrodden. Often, the best ministry is a listening ear with a prayerful heart, not one with many words of instruction. We should be "quick to listen and slow to speak" (Jas 1:19).

4. See chapter 4, "Joy in Singing Songs of Lament" for more details.

4. *Suffering is the result of fatherly discipline.* This teaching is explicitly clear in passages such as Hebrews 12:5–12, where the suffering of believers is a result of God the father's acts of loving chastisement of his children. The purpose of this chastisement is for our growth and maturity in the faith. As Hebrews states, "Besides this, we have had earthly fathers who disciplined us and we respected them. Shall we not much more be subject to the Father of spirits and live? For they disciplined us for a short time as it seemed best to them, but he [God] disciplines us for our good, that we may share his holiness" (Heb 12:9–10). God disciplines us "for our good" when we stray. He also disciplines us so that we may share in his holiness. If God does not discipline us when we stray, it is because he is not our father and we are not his children. Non-Christians also suffer, but only the suffering of a Christian can be understood as an act of gracious discipline. God does not discipline those whom He does not love. To these, "God gave them up in the lusts of their hearts to impurity" (Rom 1:24) and "to a debased mind to do what ought not to be done" (Rom 1:28). As a result, they suffer all the negative consequences that come from such a destructive lifestyle. Parents correct their children out of undying love, not out of judicial punishment. This is an axiomatic truth that any parent would affirm. How much more, then, would God the perfect, heavenly father do the same for his beloved children?

5. *Suffering produces Christian virtues.* Paul says in Romans: "More than that, we rejoice in our sufferings, knowing that suffering produces endurance, and endurance produces character, and character produces hope" (Rom 5:3–4). In verse 2, Paul says that we rejoice in the *future* hope of the glory of God. In verse 3, however, he says that we can also rejoice in the *present* day. Even if our present reality is marred with suffering, Paul says that we can still find joy. As Peter does in 1 Peter 4:12–13, Paul encourages believers to rejoice because of their suffering.[5] For Paul, suffering triggers the development of Christ-like virtues in the believer. James 1:2–4 says the same: "Count it all joy, my brothers, when you meet trials of various kinds, for you know that the testing of your faith produces steadfastness. And let steadfastness have its full effect, that you may be perfect and

---

5. 1 Peter 4:12–13 is the passage upon which this book is based. Therefore, it will be given thorough treatment in chapters 2 and 3.

complete, lacking in nothing." In 2 Corinthians 12:7, Paul says that God would not remove his personal suffering caused by a "thorn in the flesh" because it kept him humble. Suffering, therefore, seems necessary to sanctify us, to help us conform ever more so to the image of Christ and reflect these Christ-like virtues (Rom 8:29).

6. *Suffering demonstrates the power of God.* John 9 begins with an encounter between a man born blind and the disciples of Jesus. Having seen firsthand the hardships that this man endured, the disciples turned to their teacher and asked: "Who sinned, this man or his parents, that he was born blind?" (John 9:2). Jesus replies that the suffering of this man was not due to any sin committed by the man himself or his parents; rather, his blindness and his subsequent healing was ordained by God "that the work of God might be demonstrated in him" (John 9:3). Jay Adams, in his book *The Grand Demonstration: A Biblical Study of the So-Called Problem of Evil,* says this theme of a *grand demonstration* singlehandedly offers the loud, resounding biblical answer to the question of the problem of evil so that there is no longer any problem.[6] Although he oversimplifies the problem of evil, there is little doubt that one reason why God brings suffering upon his people is to use it as a means to declare His glory to an anxious world.

7. *Suffering ignites missionary zeal.*[7] The apostle Paul speaks about the zeal and boldness of fellow servants of the gospel when they heard of his imprisonment in Philippians: "And most of the brothers, having become confident in the Lord by my imprisonment, are much more bold to speak the word without fear" (Phil 1:14). With Paul imprisoned and out of commission, the Christian community could have easily grown discouraged and overcome with fear. The Spirit of God, however, used Paul's suffering to ignite within them zeal so that instead of being frightened and becoming spiritual invalids, they continued preaching the gospel with boldness and faithful courage.

8. *Suffering is a witness to the Gospel.* The trials that believers face are powerful opportunities to share the hope that we have in Christ. This is the instruction that Peter gives us: "But in your hearts honor

6. See Adams, *Grand Demonstration.*

7. For a wonderful description of this point, see Piper, "Why God Appoints Suffering," 100–6.

Christ the Lord as holy, always being prepared to make a defense to anyone who asks you for a reason for the hope that is in you" (1 Pet 3:15). Paul says as much when he tells the Philippians that he was suffering "for the sake of the gospel" (Phil 1:16). Pain and agony are real experiences in a fallen world, and they do not only target believers. Suffering is neither discriminatory nor is it prejudicial; Christians and non-Christians alike experience trials of all sorts for various reasons. Suffering reveals the harsh realities of life in a fallen world and everyone is forced to struggle through it. Only Christians, however, can speak of hope in the midst of suffering since they are the only ones who worship a God who has the sovereign power to transform it into something good. Although non-Christians may speak of the hope and purpose of trials, they do so without any foundation or substance. According to their own worldview, there is either no God to whom they can turn or the god they believe in is such a weak being that he is unable to help them. Their only source of hope is the strength of humanity itself. Can this guarantee hope or joy? Even if humanity were able to fight through one instance of suffering, can they endure a relentless siege of pain on their own? Even if they can endure all this, how can such a life be viewed as good or beneficent? Where can joy be found? It is at such times that the reality of life with a non-Christian worldview reveals its logical and genuine end—hopelessness. True hope for resolution of suffering can only be found by faith in the resurrected Christ.

9. *Suffering demonstrates the genuineness of our faith in Christ.* First Peter is filled with extraordinary words of encouragement for the Christian sufferer. Peter says, "In this you rejoice, though now for a little while, as was necessary, you have been grieved by various trials, so that the tested genuineness of your faith—more precious than gold that perishes though it is tested by fire—may be found to result in praise and glory and honor at the revelation of Jesus Christ" (1 Pet 1:6–7). Peter describes the refining process in which gold is placed in fire to burn away any impurities. In the same way, "various trials" serve to purify faith from any doubt within and without the believer. Trials force Christians to turn to the only person who can help them, namely Jesus Christ. It purges them from any false sense of self-confidence or misguided faith in any person or thing other than Jesus. The end result of these trials is a pure and undefiled

faith.[8] Peter is eager to help his readers understand that their suffering is not due to their lack of faith. Suffering purifies their faith so that it has an unobstructed God-centered focus. Insofar as we turn our attentions to God, suffering is for our good.

10. *Suffering manifests the supreme suffering of Christ.* Pastor John Piper describes what he calls "the ultimate biblical explanation for the existence of suffering."[9] He says that Jesus Christ lived a perfectly obedient life in every way possible. He should have received countless blessings, but instead he received a death sentence on the cross. His crucifixion was unjust and the result of the evil schemes of sinful men. Yet his death on the cross was also the highest and purest expression of the grace of God. What makes his suffering so glorious is that it was so unjust. In spite of his perfect obedience, he willingly gave himself to death on the cross for the salvation of his elect. Suffering, therefore, is necessary, so that the glory of Christ can reach its apex. Without it, the world would not be able to recognize how gracious the suffering of Christ is for the believer—and thus not fully glorify and magnify him.

11. *Suffering prepares us for the glory of eternity.* Perhaps no word of comfort can be more meaningful for Christian sufferers than this: we are called to patiently endure difficult times of suffering because they prepare us for an eternal inheritance. Consider the words of Paul when he says: "For this slight momentary affliction is preparing for us an eternal weight of glory beyond all comparison, as we look not to the things that are seen but to the things that are unseen. For the things that are seen are transient, but the things that are unseen are eternal" (2 Cor 4:17–18). Paul admonishes his readers that the afflictions of this life, which are visible to them, do not compare with that which is not visible: the boundless riches of the blessings of eternal glory. As our peace of mind is more often determined by what we see or experience—as opposed to what we know to be true as our future hope—Paul compares the brevity of the present

8. The Greek word for "genuineness" (*dokimion*) in verse 7 can be understood as "proof," which would suggest that the purpose of these trials is to *prove* that there is indeed true saving faith, rather than the view that suggests that trials are a purifying agent of faith. What is "found," then, is an existing faith, not a refined faith. Although I lean towards the former, one cannot rule out the interpretative possibility of the latter. See chapter 2 for further details on these options.

9. Piper and Taylor, *Suffering and the Sovereignty of God*, 82.

agonies of the believer with the future glory and joy that awaits them for eternity. Regarding that suffering, Paul literally says it is "a momentary lightness of our affliction." Compared to the "eternal weight of glory," our present sufferings are "light" and only for a "moment." For Paul, suffering is not something believers can avoid. Rather, he encourages us to view suffering in light of the richness of the eternal bliss that awaits us. In this way, suffering is "preparing" us for that overwhelming weight of glory. The Greek word for "prepare" is *katergazetai*, meaning "to work out, produce." Suffering "works out" an eternal glory for us. It is the path through which we are called to journey in order to reach the glorious life. It is difficult for Paul's readers, as it is for us, to persevere through such times, where the "outer man is wasting away" (2 Cor 4:16), but this will eventually "produce" glory for us. Paul says similarly in Romans: "If [we are] children, then [we are] heirs—heirs of God and fellow heirs with Christ, provided we suffer with him in order that we may also be glorified with him. For I consider that the sufferings of this present time are not worth comparing with the glory that is to be revealed to us" (Rom 8:17–18).

Each view described above can instill a sense of genuine hope within the heart of believers. In fact, I can envision a series of sermons or Sunday school lessons where each of the themes mentioned above are addressed with greater detail.[10] They should not be viewed, however, as isolated approaches, independent of each other, from which we pick and choose during times of suffering. Rather, they should be viewed as a collection of shining stars of glorious hope that together form a heavenly constellation, providing a radiant light by which we can properly view and understand the darkness of suffering that so frequently clouds our vision.

Theme passage of 1 Peter 4:12–13

As encouraging as the list is above, one view is missing. That is the one this book describes, the view taken from 1 Peter 4:12–13:

---

10. I would give this series the title "An Anthology of Hope." This instills the comfort that we can gain through the suffering that we are to endure.

Beloved, do not be surprised at the fiery trial when it comes upon you to test you, as though something strange were happening to you. But rejoice insofar as you share Christ's sufferings, that you may also rejoice and be glad when his glory is revealed.

From a quick reading of this passage, these words may not seem the most encouraging or helpful for the suffering Christian. After all, it sounds as if Peter is saying that suffering is inevitable and unavoidable, so we are doomed to experience it. Despite this, we as Christians are called to rejoice in the middle of all this suffering. If that is indeed what Peter is saying, then yes, this would be extremely discouraging, to say the least. The original readers of his epistle may have even fallen into depression, wondering whether the life of following Christ was really what they bargained for.

A proper understanding of these words, however, will give hope to believers in a way that is truly refreshing and meaningful—hope that differs drastically from any of the approaches mentioned earlier. This understanding gives profound insight into the Christian life and magnificently portrays Christ as both our righteous Savior and our righteous Sufferer. The majority of the views above encourage suffering believers with a future confidence that will either remove their current suffering or transform it into a great blessing. Peter, however, encourages us to see that there is a certain kind of suffering that is part of the Christian life. To suffer in this way is to *share in the sufferings of Christ*, which is the very foundation of a joy that the believer can now have. In other words, Christian suffering is the source of Christian joy!

We live in a world where the health-and-wealth gospel is alive and well, which is ironic given the clear instructions in Scripture that informs us otherwise. It is easy to conclude that, as a Christian, we should be freed of suffering—when the exact opposite is true. Without this understanding of the function of suffering in the Christian life, we can become disillusioned with Christianity. If you are struggling with such thoughts, I urge you to cling onto Jesus.

He endured excruciating suffering for our sins, and through his powerful resurrection, we have been transformed into a new humanity. It was our violation of the law of God that made Jesus go to the cross as our substitute. He suffered the wrath of God not because of any crime or sin that he committed but because his people "were straying like sheep" (1 Pet 2:25). He took upon himself our penalty and transferred to us his perfect obedience so that we now have the "righteousness of God" that comes by faith (Rom 3:21–22). The reason he suffered so unjustly was for us. For this reason, we love him wholeheartedly.

Although we steadily grow in our sanctification, we will continue to struggle with sin internally until we reach glory. That is the life of a Christian. However, a Christian's struggle also comes from living among other morally corrupt people. We are abused both verbally and physically—and this is often the case because we strive to live a life that follows the teachings of the Bible. Such a life of suffering gives us an insight into the life of our Savior. To know Jesus is not only to know that he saved us from divine condemnation and death but also that he saved us from a meaningless life of agony. And to know Jesus is our greatest joy.

You can know such joy only if you see Christ as your Savior. It is not enough to share an outward similarity; you must also experience an inward, Spirit-induced transformation. Only when we are renewed by the Spirit can we appreciate the value of our unjust suffering as *fellowship with Christ*. Without it, any external resemblance with Jesus's sufferings cannot be a source of joy. Instead, it will only cultivate frustration. And if Christ cannot bring you joy in the midst of your suffering, then I do not know who (or what) can.

Many have sought this joy outside of Christ; they have exhausted all options without success. We have more knowledge now than ever before in the history of humanity. We know more about our ever-expanding universe, the nature of our world, and even ourselves—through discoveries in genetic research and the social and life sciences. We have access to all this knowledge through the internet in ways that were unfathomable in prior generations. In spite of all this, humanity is neither any happier nor more content. It seems the more knowledge we accumulate about our world, the cosmos, and ourselves, the more that true joy and contentment is illusive and unattainable. There is wisdom and truth in such a conclusion. True joy is not gained from increased knowledge of our world, from solving the unknown mysteries of our universe, or from knowing oneself. It is much simpler, yet much more profound. It comes from knowing Jesus Christ, in his sufferings as well as his glory.

In the context of 1 Peter, this joy is not typical: it is described as a "joy that is inexpressible and filled with glory" (1 Pet 1:8). I love the old KJV translation, which states that you rejoice with "*joy unspeakable* and full of glory." This is a joy that cannot be described with mere words; this is a joy that is a product of the eternal kingdom. That is what you, O

Christian, can have now. Not in the future—now! This does not require a change in your current circumstance nor is it dependent on a future glory. In that sense, these words of the apostle Peter are indeed wondrous.

2

The Inconvenient Truth

The Biblical Foundation for Christ-Centered Suffering, Part 1

> *Beloved, do not be surprised at the fiery ordeal among you, which comes upon you for your testing, as though some strange thing were happening to you.*

1 Peter 4:12

"LIFE IS PAIN! ANYONE who tells you otherwise is trying to sell you something!" That is one of many memorable lines from the classic movie *The Princess Bride*. Although it occurs in a fantasy tale, it expresses an intuition that we all have about life—everyone will experience times of suffering. This is one of the lessons that children inevitably learn as they grow into adulthood. As much as parents may desire to shield their kids from the harsh realities of life, children are incredibly observant and know when their friends or family members are hurting. Many children thus fear the future since they know that they will be adults one day and eventually face similar hardships. If they can, they will avoid it at any cost.

This may be the reason for the popularity of children's characters such as "Peter Pan," a young boy who never grows into adulthood and, as a result, avoids all the pains and agonies of it. The 1991 movie *Hook* portrays this Peter Pan as a grown man in the real world. He reunites with his longtime friend Tinkerbell, who tries to bring out a "happy thought"

from Peter so that he can fly. Sadly, he is now an adult who has experienced abandonment, brokenness, and pain. So Tinkerbell concludes, "I
can see why you can't find a happy thought. So many sad memories!"

I recall a similar moment with my children who sensed my distress
during pastoral ministry, which caused them to dread their inescapable
ascent into adulthood. It pains me to realize that my lack of faith and
trust in the Lord during those times caused my children to fear for their
own futures. They saw adulthood as a series of stress-filled events that
they wanted nothing to do with. I was hardly in a position to disagree
with them.

Such a message is depressing, to say the least. If everyone's life is
inundated with suffering, then what is the point of life? One could easily
accept the message of the book of Ecclesiastes and conclude that "everything is meaningless" (Eccl 1:2) and a "chasing after the wind" (Eccl 1:17).
One very vivid image in Ecclesiastes captures this point well:

> Again I saw all the oppressions that are done under the sun.
> And behold, the tears of the oppressed, and they had no one to
> comfort them! On the side of their oppressors there was power,
> and there was no one to comfort them. And I thought the dead
> who are already dead more fortunate than the living who are
> still alive. But better than both is he who has not yet been and
> has not seen the evil deeds that are done under the sun. (Eccl
> 4:1–3)

What a shocking statement! Or is it? Can't we all remember a
time in life when we could have echoed the same sentiment? Perhaps
the struggles of those in the ancient world were not that different from
contemporary struggles. Can we even find a bit of joy that will last, or is
life nothing more than a morass of dark times, of peril, with only brief,
momentary blips of relief?

The readers of 1 Peter may have thought otherwise. In earlier portions of his letter, Peter spends a great deal of time describing the rich
and abundant blessings that believers have in Christ. He says that they are
sanctified by his blood (1 Pet 1:2) and newly born into a life of hope (1 Pet
1:3). He also says that the precious message of the gospel—something for
which the Old Testament prophets "searched and inquired carefully" (1
Pet 1:10) and into which "angels long to look" (1 Pet 1:12)—is the good
news that was preached to them. Peter even refers to his readers as "living
stones," who make up God's New Covenant temple (1 Pet 2:5), and that
they are "a chosen race, a royal priesthood, a holy nation, a people for

God's own possession" (1 Pet 2:9) who have received the "great mercy" of God (1 Pet 1:3; 2:10). The more Peter established their hope upon these vivid blessings in Christ, the stranger it may have seemed to his readers that they must suffer.

Peter's audience may have concluded, as with many Christians today, that suffering is unexpected. That is not the conclusion that Peter reaches, and it is certainly not the conclusion of Christ Jesus himself.

1 Peter 4:12–13 overflows with words of encouragement that the inspired apostle offers to his readers. The first is found in verse 12, where Peter encourages them to understand that the trials they are enduring are not out of the norm for the Christian life. What they are experiencing is to be expected and should not catch them off guard. We will focus our thoughts on this initial point before moving onto verse 13, where Peter helps us to see another extraordinary truth: not only are these hardships to be *expected* but they are in fact also the *source* of a "joy unspeakable." Suffering is necessary for joy.

Don't Be Surprised

Peter begins this section of his epistle with these astonishing, yet wise and comforting words:

> Beloved, do not be surprised at the fiery ordeal among you, which comes upon you for your testing, as though some strange thing were happening to you. (1 Pet 4:12)

There is little doubt that his readers were feeling vulnerable and in desperate need of words of hope that could provide some rationale for the "fiery ordeal" they were enduring. Peter demonstrates his pastoral heart when he addresses his readers as "beloved." He approaches them as a caring overseer who is eager for their spiritual well being, so his words must be understood to reflect his pastoral intent. He does not communicate a sense of inevitability and doom. He does not tell them, "You better buckle down and suck it up because that is just the way that things are!"

The harsh, suffering characteristic of the Christian life is not a predator which stalks believers until their inevitable death. That is not the way Peter portrays the life of a disciple of Christ. Instead, Peter awakens his readers to a sobering reality, an *inconvenient truth*: "Expect the fiery ordeal among you, which proves your faith to be genuine, since that is characteristic of the Christian life." He urges his readers to prepare for the coming trials that await them to gain a proper understanding of their current suffering.

At this point, Peter is consistent with the general depiction of the life of a Christian disciple as found in other passages of Scripture. Jesus himself teaches that "a servant is not greater than his master" (John 15:20). He immediately interprets this phrase by saying: "If they persecuted me, they will also persecute you." Later in John, he also says: "In the world you will have tribulation" (John 16:33). Although Christ adds that we can "take heart"—because our faith is in him who "has overcome the world"—this does not negate the fact that hardship is coming our way. Consider also what Paul says: "Indeed, all who desire to live a godly life in Christ Jesus will be persecuted" (2 Tim 3:12) and "For we who live are always being given over to death for Jesus's sake" (2 Cor 4:11). In Acts, Luke teaches that "through many tribulations we must enter the kingdom of God" (Acts 14:22).

This is a small sample of New Testament texts that say the same thing about the nature of the Christian life that 1 Peter 4:12 does: suffering is to be expected. But why must this be so? What is the underlying principle of these hardships? At the end of the day, this is the question that haunts God's people and keeps us up many sleepless nights. Throughout his epistle, Peter offers four reasons to explain why these painful trials are to be expected:

1. They prove the genuineness of our faith.

2. As those "born again" in Christ, we are at odds with the world in which we live.

3. We are spiritual sojourners in a world hostile to Christ.

4. We are in spiritual warfare.

Understanding why suffering must come not only helps us to accept it, but it also gives us the hope to rejoice in it. We will explore each below.

1) Suffering Proves the Genuineness of Faith

In verse 12, Peter provides an encouraging purpose for suffering—to test our faith. Of course, this does not undermine the fact that suffering is painful. Yet, according to Peter, we need to undergo this pain if only to keep our faith focused upon Christ. In a society filled with so many distractions, it is easy to lose focus upon the crucified and resurrected Savior. If not for the trials that come upon us, we would forget the Lord and his divine presence in our lives. Worse yet, we may even have the audacity to believe that we can live without him. How many days go by in the pleasant lives of Christians in the western world without the thought of God entering into our psyche?

The Screwtape Letters and Christian Suffering

The Screwtape Letters is one of my favorite books by the great Christian author, C. S. Lewis. In it, Lewis takes the viewpoint of a senior demon, Screwtape, who writes a collection of letters to his nephew and junior demon, Wormwood, on strategic ways to secure the eternal condemnation of an unnamed British man, who is simply referred to as "the patient." As fictitious as these satirical accounts are, they do provoke thoughts about satanic tactics in spiritual warfare. One issue that Lewis (that is, Screwtape) raises is the need to drag the man's attention away from God (who is referred to as "The Enemy") at all cost. Indeed, he suggests that it would be ideal for the church itself to become a distraction. When the patient is in church, Screwtape encourages Wormwood to divert the attention of the patient to the unusual people who are there, to the bad (or good) singing, or to the old building in which they meet. Anything short of prayer and attention to the Word of God would serve as an effective distraction. He says: "Whenever they [Christians] are attending to the Enemy [God] himself, we are defeated."[1]

According to Lewis, demons look upon something as horrible as war with ambivalence. Demons may enjoy the sheer extent of destruction and death war brings upon beloved image bearers of God, but suffering caused by war can be disastrous to the demonic agenda since it renders one of their best weapons useless—complacency and lackadaisical contentment. Screwtape says, "In wartime, not even a human can believe that he is going to live forever," thus redirecting man's attention to matters of spiritual life or death.[2] In one of his explicit statements, Screwtape boldly declares, "All extremes, except devotion to the Enemy [God], are to be encouraged."[3] I imagine Satan and his demonic legions trying to do just

---

1. Lewis, *Screwtape*, 25.
2. Lewis, *Screwtape*, 32.
3. Lewis, *Screwtape*, 40.

this—drawing the church's attention away from Jesus Christ. Suffering, at least, reminds us that we need Jesus every day.

The True Reality of Life

Consider this question: what is the true reality of life? Is it consistent with reality to suggest that we can live a single day, a single hour, a single minute, or even a single second without the providential power of the Almighty God in our lives? Do we genuinely believe that Hebrews 1:3 is true when it teaches us that God is the one who "upholds all things by the power of his word"? Or do we live from day to day in a fantasy, thinking that we can indeed get through the day without him? Harsh difficulties bring us back to the *reality* of life: without the living God, we cannot survive for a single moment.

It does not take suffering to teach us this truth since this is one of the dominant themes in Scripture. Regular studies in the Word of God remind us of our frailties, the unstable characteristics of this fallen world, and thus our need for something or someone (that is, Someone) greater than ourselves, our situations, and our suffering. The wise person grows through his study of the Word. Most of us, however, are not so wise. We need adversity to remind us of the simple truth that we need Jesus. This alone makes our sufferings a blessing in disguise.

Peter uses the image of a fiery ordeal to illustrate this point. He seems to suggest that one of the purposes of Christian suffering is to cause a refining effect upon us and, more specifically, upon our faith. After enduring the anguish of suffering, what results is a purified faith in Christ. The image of fire is frequently used in Scripture to describe the cleansing effect that suffering has upon the faith of the believer. As gold is refined and purged of every impurity that is found within it, so suffering cleanses all impurities that hinder a pure faith in Christ. Proverbs 27:21 also uses similar imagery of a purifying fire that refines various precious metals.

It is hard not to think of other passages in Scripture, such as Malachi 3:2–3, which describes the Lord as a "refiner's fire" who will come to purify the priesthood of Israel just as fire purifies gold and silver. Peter may have even thought of the account in Daniel 3, in which three young men of Judah are thrown into a "furnace of burning fire" because of their unwillingness to bow to a pagan idol in the image of a Babylonian king.

They suffered because of their faith to the one and true God. Suffering brings us to the stark reality of the necessity of Christ in our lives. At the same time, it refines our faith so that our hearts may be focused upon him who is the author and perfecter of our faith (Heb 12:3). In him, we have a "new birth into a living hope" (1 Pet 1:3) and a "joy unspeakable" (1 Pet 1:8).

Real or False Faith

One may understand this imagery of suffering as a fiery ordeal in yet another way. Not only does suffering purify our faith, it reveals the presence or absence of a "genuine" faith in Christ. 1 Peter 1:6–7 says that Christians will be grieved by various trials in order to reveal a "genuineness of your faith which is more precious than gold that perishes." The apostle seems to assert that suffering discloses the true spiritual status of the individual—either he possesses a true faith or he does not. There are other passages in Scripture that confirm this purpose of suffering.

In Matthew, Jesus teaches, "Not everyone who says to me, 'Lord, Lord,' will enter the kingdom of heaven" (Matt 7:21). In the following verses, he goes on to say that in the last days, many will call upon him, such as those who had done wondrous deeds, prophesied in his name, cast out demons, and performed all sorts of other mighty works. Further, all this miraculous work was done "in the name of the Lord." Yet, the sober response of Christ is to declare to them, "I never knew you; depart from me, you workers of lawlessness" (Matt 7:23).

Suffering burns away any presence of spiritual pretense or religious formalism and reveals professing believers for who they genuinely are: either they are ones who have a *true and real* faith in Christ, or they are ones who have the *appearance* of faith in Christ. Some may mistakenly take this to mean that a true believer can lose their faith due to suffering. However, the supernatural origin of a true saving faith makes it invincible and permanent (1 Pet 1:4; Eph 2:8–9). Instead, the person who abandons the Lord due to suffering reveals himself to be someone who had never possessed true saving faith in Christ at all. This person is a hypocrite, and the suffering simply reveals his actual identity as a reprobate.

Jesus teaches a similar understanding of faith in the famous Parable of the Sower in Matthew 13:3–8. In that parable, there is a sower who plants seeds in a field. The seeds, however, land in various locations that directly impact their growth. Some seeds land on the hard road, where there is no soil for them to take root; these seeds lie bare and are eaten by birds (Matt 13:3–4). A second group falls upon rocky ground, where there is little soil. For a brief time, the seeds are able to show some beginnings of life, but they are vulnerable to the heat of the sun, so they wither and die (Matt 13:5–6). A third falls among thorns that choke the vegetation from the seeds (Matt 13:7). Only the seeds that land on good soil yield a multi-fold crop (Matt 13:8).

In his interpretation of this parable, Jesus explains how each scenario represents a type of listener of his gospel message (Matt 13:18–23). For our purposes, it is the second type that is of interest here. In verses 20–21, Jesus says that this second kind (i.e., the seed planted in rocky soil) represents the man "who hears the word and immediately receives it with joy, yet he has no root in himself, but endures for a while, and when tribulation or persecution arises on account of the word, immediately he falls away."

What he means is this: there are many who come to a superficial appreciation of the gospel where its message is heard and initially taken with eager enthusiasm. The gospel is indeed an amazing and beautiful message that many wish could be true. Although there are those who find it appealing at the outset, faith in Christ comes at a price, since the sinful world has rejected it and thus rejects those who follow it. Those who face such trials find their superficial faith tested by the fires of godless persecution. Such "faith," according to Jesus, is not genuine, and the person who abandons the faith during these trials was never a true disciple of Christ to begin with. Those who endure are the ones who possess a truly saving faith in Christ, and the fiery persecution around them only demonstrates the *fact* that true saving faith has been present all along.[4]

Although "the testing of faith," mentioned in 1 Peter 4:12, can refer to the refining and purifying of faith, in light of 1 Peter 1:6–7, it seems more likely that the apostle suggests that suffering reveals the "genuineness" or the reality of our faith in Christ.[5]

Regardless of how "the testing of faith" is understood, it is absolutely necessary to accept that faith is essential in the Christian life. Not only is

---

4. The book of Hebrews expounds more upon this subject of persevering faith in the face of trials.

5. Certainly, suffering serves to accomplish both. It refines our faith and thus demonstrates it as genuine. Peter, however, leans towards the latter. See above for the implications of this view.

it by faith that we are saved (i.e., justified, adopted, sanctified, and glorified), it is also by faith that we can overcome the sufferings that burden us in this fallen world.

Faith Must Always Be "in Christ"

It is crucial, however, to remember that it is not faith *per se* that saves us, nor is it what helps us in times of trials. Faith is not a unique virtue, exclusive to Christianity. Other world religions also teach about faith. In some way, shape, or form, all religious teachings involve some call to faithful trust in their respective deities. Whereas the act of faith is a virtue in itself in other world religions, it is the *object* of Christian faith that sets it apart as unique. The faith that can withstand the harshest trials is the one that has *Jesus Christ alone as its object*.

According to Peter, what we need in the midst of intense suffering is not a great quantity of faith. After all, even if you have "faith like a grain of mustard seed, you could say to this mulberry tree, 'Be uprooted and planted in the sea,' and it would obey you" (Luke 17:6). What we need is the object of our faith, namely Jesus Christ. John Murray eloquently states thus:

> It is to be remembered that the efficacy of faith does not reside in itself. Faith is not something that merits the favour of God. All the efficacy unto salvation resides in the Saviour. As one has aptly and truly stated the case, it is not faith that saves but faith in Jesus Christ; strictly speaking, it is not even faith in Christ that saves but Christ that saves through faith.[6]

Simply put, Christian faith is invincible, not because of the nature of faith, but because of the object of our faith, Jesus. Because *he* is strong, Christian faith is strong. Because *he* is powerful, Christian faith is powerful. Because *he* is unshakable, Christian faith is unshakable. This is the reason why the Holy Scriptures cannot speak about faith without also presuming the object of our faith. Biblical faith, therefore, is never just "faith," but always "faith in Christ," even when "Christ" is not explicitly mentioned. It is Christ who saves us, not our faith. It is Christ who is stronger than our suffering, not our faith. For that reason, Christian faith

6. Murray, *Redemption*, 112.

is always *extraspective*.[7] It is a virtue that requires the individual to redirect one's focus outside of oneself, towards Jesus.

The *Westminster Confession of Faith* says that faith is "the alone instrument of justification."[8] Not only is it the "alone instrument" in our justification, it is also the "alone instrument" in overcoming suffering because it alone turns our attention to Christ. If we were to look inwardly to our own abilities for our salvation, we would find nothing but a dead-end and utter failure. This same principle applies when we try to overcome suffering. We can try to whip ourselves into an emotional frenzy to overcome times of intense agony by our own strength of will, but this will ultimately fail. What we need is someone greater than ourselves and our suffering. We need a biblically grounded faith because faith is the only virtue that points us to that greater someone who is our only hope and source of joy. This is why Paul can say: "That is why it depends on faith, in order that the promise may rest on grace" (Rom 4:16).

It is extraordinary how much comfort the risen Christ brings to those who believe. The agony of suffering burns away any confidence we may have had in material things or idols. There is wisdom in recognizing that it is faith in Jesus that we need in the midst of suffering—not faith in man, in the world, or even in ourselves. In the midst of devastating grief, what in this world can offer any solace? Can all the money in the world bring healing to the young mother who persistently miscarries at twenty weeks in each of her five pregnancies? Can any single human being return health to those who are terminal with an incurable disease? What about ourselves? Is there anything that we can do to bring back our deceased loved ones? Of course not. Cancer is not impressed with our professional or academic accomplishments. Disease is not intimidated by the abundance of our wealth. Death is not threatened by the number of graduate degrees we possess. These fiery trials are a constant reminder that our ultimate solution is not found in the dross of this world (Phil 3:8).[9] Our only hope is found in the living Christ.

7. My teacher of theology at Westminster Seminary in California, Dr. Robert Strimple, says this term "extra-spective" was most likely coined by his teacher, Professor John Murray.

8. *WCF*, 11.2

9. This is a significant message in the book of Ecclesiastes.

Psalm 73: From Hopeless Intro-spection to
Comforting Extra-spection

Psalm 73 provides an example of someone who moved from hopeless
intro-spection to comforting *extra*-spection. The psalmist struggled intensely because of the apparent prosperity of the wicked while he experienced nothing but suffering. He was confused when he contemplated
why the wicked prosper and the righteous suffer. Initially, he did not look
outside of himself and unto the Lord; he attempted to comprehend this
apparent injustice using his own reasoning. Humanity has a history of
using God-given gifts to establish our autonomy from God, and human
reason is no different. If we were honest with ourselves, we would have to
acknowledge that there is little within the human heart that gives us any
significant hope. When the psalmist used his own intellect to discern this
problem, he was left in a state of utter despair. He nearly stumbled (Ps
73:2), he found himself engaged in a wearisome task (Ps 73:16), he saw
his previous obedience and pursuit of holiness as vain and meaningless
(Ps 73:13), and he realized that he was nothing more than a brute and
ignorant fool (Ps 73:22).

It was only when he looked outside of himself, when he "went into
the sanctuary of God" (Ps 73:17), that he found the resolution to this
dilemma. He realized that he was not to envy the wicked because they
were in "slippery places" and that eventually the Lord would "make them
fall to ruin" (Ps 73:18). They had been prosperous during their brief time
in this earthly life, but their ultimate end would be their destruction in
judgment (Ps 73:19). While the righteous are beloved of the Lord, the
wicked are "despised like a passing phantasm" (Ps 73:20). The psalmist
found the answer only when he realized that the Lord was ever present
with him—this Lord was the "God of my strength, my portion forever"
(Ps 73:26).

Suffering causes us to lift our eyes to the hill from where our help
comes (Ps 121:1). "The hill" is a reference to Zion, so the psalmist looks
to the temple, which is the dwelling place of God. We find help only by
looking towards the Lord, "the maker of heaven and earth" (Ps 121:2), in
faith. In these psalms, the suffering of the psalmists has neither changed
nor ended. They are still in the midst of hardship. What has changed
is their focus; they are no longer dominated by the circumstances that
caused their suffering, but are now content because they look beyond

their immediate troubling situation and turn, by faith, to the one who is greater than the suffering.

2) The Suffering from Our Spiritual Birth

Early in his letter, Peter says that "according to his great mercy, [God] has caused us to be born again" (1 Pet 1:3). This notion of being "born again" is relevant to our current discussion of why Christians should expect to endure suffering.

The great reformed theologian B. B. Warfield describes this new birth as follows:

> This conception [of a new birth] is that salvation in Christ involves a radical and complete transformation wrought in the soul (Rom 12:2; Eph 4:23) by God the Holy Spirit (Tit 3:5; Eph 4:24), by virtue of which we become "new men" (Eph 4:24; Col 3:10), no longer conformed to this world (Rom 12:2; Eph 4:22; Col 3:9), but in knowledge and holiness of the truth created after the image of God (Eph 4:24; Col 3:10; Rom 12:2).[10]

I love this idea. It emphasizes the most fundamental and important truth of Scripture—*God must save us because we cannot save ourselves*! This is what reformed theologians call the *sovereignty of God* in salvation. Just as we cannot bring about our earthly birth, so also we cannot cause our "new birth."

We Are "Dead in Sin"

Prior to this new birth, Scripture teaches us that we were "dead in sin" (Eph 2:1). This issue was not limited just to those whom Paul had ministered. Human sin is present throughout the entire biblical narrative. Even during the days of Noah, the Bible says: "The LORD saw that the wickedness of man was great in the earth, and that every intention of the thoughts of his heart was only evil continually" (Gen 6:5). This was the reason for the flood-waters that devastated the "world that then existed" (2 Pet 3:6).

Even someone as great as David, the author of many of the psalms that we love and sing today, realized that he could easily commit horrible

10. Warfield, "On the Biblical Notion of 'Renewal,'" 439.

acts of sin against those close to him and against the Lord. The narrative of the sins of David is recorded in 2 Samuel 11–12. While his faithful and dedicated soldier Uriah was risking his life by fighting for his king, David steals his wife Bathsheba, violates her, and impregnates her with his illegitimate child. To cover up his sin, he calls Uriah back from battle so that Uriah might sleep with his wife and thus give the impression that Bathsheba became pregnant by her husband. However, Uriah, the ever-faithful soldier, cannot bear the thought of resting comfortably at home with his wife while his fellow soldiers are in harm's way, so he decides to sleep outside with all the other servants of the king. When Uriah does not fall for his ploy, David sees no alternative but to get rid of this loyal servant. He commands his general Joab to place Uriah in the frontlines of battle, where he is killed as a casualty of war. David then takes Bathsheba as his wife as a way to comfort her while she mourns. David conspired to cover up his sin, and he succeeded. Or so it seemed.

David is then confronted by Nathan, the prophet who exposes his cover-up in a way that startles David with the horrifying degree of his sins. David realizes that he is capable of adultery, conspiracy, and murder, all without blinking an eye. What frightens David more than the actual sinful acts is the shocking reality that he did not struggle at all with any guilt before his encounter with Nathan. That had been the extent of his sinful heart. Once he comes to realize that this is possible, he cries out in one of the most famous psalms of repentance known in Scripture, Psalm 51. In that psalm, he comes face to face with the magnitude of his sin: "For I know my transgressions, and my sin is ever before me" (Ps 51:3). He realizes that this sin is symptomatic of a much deeper issue—that his nature is sinful and the reason why he could commit such atrocities was due to his fallen nature: "Behold, I was brought forth in iniquity, and in sin did my mother conceive me" (Ps 51:5). What he needed was nothing short of a radical, new transformation of his heart: "Create in me a clean heart, O God, and renew a right spirit within me" (Ps 51:10). The Lord answers his prayer. In fact, because the Lord "created" him anew, he was able to face the depth of his sin and do so with humility and contrition.

What does it mean to be "born again"? It means that we have been radically transformed. We were once "dead in our transgressions," but because we have been given this new birth we are now a "new creation" (2 Cor 5:17).

New Birth Is Necessary to Believe

I emphasized the importance of faith earlier because it is completely true. Our sinful nature is so powerful that we cannot do anything to overcome it; we are "slaves to sin" (Rom 6:17, 20; cf. John 8:32). This means that on our own, we cannot even turn to God and believe in his only son for our salvation (John 3:16). We would rather choose our own desires. In order for us to believe, we need divine intervention. We must *first* be given a new nature—we must *first* be "born again." And, praise God, that is exactly what God does for us! This is why Peter stresses that our new birth is "according to his great mercy" (1 Pet 1:3). God does not give us this new birth because we first chose to follow him. Again, on our own, we would never make such a choice. He gives us this precious gift because of his sovereign mercy.

I find it ironic, even troubling, when the term "born-again Christian" is often used to describe a mere type of Christianity. Perhaps you know of such "born-again Christians." They read their Scriptures regularly, attend Bible studies, and faithfully worship the Lord. These are the Christians who live their lives fully and solely for the glory of God and desire to grow in closer and deeper intimacy with their Savior. If that is what it means to be "born again," then I pray that I will be such a Christian. The truth of the matter is that Scripture does not teach that there are various degrees or types of Christianity. Either you are a Christian or you are not. For that reason, there is no other kind of Christian than one who is "born again," thus making the subcategory of "born-again Christian" superfluous. New birth is not an option—it is a necessity for all who would seek eternal life in Jesus Christ.

New Identity in the New Birth

One of these blessings that Peter describes in detail is that believers are now a holy temple where the glory presence of God dwells (1 Pet 2:4–8). The significance of this cannot be overstated. When the construction of the first temple was completed, the Scriptures say that "a cloud filled the house of the LORD, so that the priests could not stand to minister because of the cloud, for the glory of the LORD filled the house of the LORD" (1 Kgs 8:10–11). In the New Testament, the true temple of God is Jesus Christ (John 2:19–21). According to Peter, once we have been "born again," each individual believer becomes part of a large construction project, the New Covenant temple. The glory presence of the Lord that had overwhelmed the Aaronic priesthood now dwells within us! In Christ, we are the temple of the Lord.

Peter does not stop here. In light of this reality of being "born again," Peter parades a list of glorious titles that the church can claim for herself. He says we are "a chosen race, a royal priesthood, a holy nation, a people for his own possession" (1 Pet 2:9).

In 1 Peter 2:10, he also alludes to the writings of the prophet Hosea, that we were once "not a people" but now we are "the people of God"; that we were once a people without mercy but now we have received mercy. Hosea was called by the Lord to give rather eccentric names to his children, names that reflected God's acts of pending judgment against the Israelite community for their violation of the Mosaic covenant.[11] Thus, Hosea's daughter was named Lo-Ruhamah, which means "no mercy," and his son Lo-Ammi, which means "not my people." But because of the amazing grace of God, Israel does not remain as the recipients of covenant curse; rather they have the blessings of the New Covenant. They will be called "Mercy" and "My people." By alluding to this prophetic text, Peter seems to apply a similar type of name change upon the church. As rebellious sinners, our names were once "No mercy" and "Not my people," but because of the death and resurrection of Jesus Christ, our name has been changed. We can now be called "Mercy" and "My people." We can claim all these blessings and titles for ourselves because "he has caused us to be born again" (1 Pet 1:3).

Spiritual Virtues in a Hostile World

Because we are now born anew, we are called to live by the specific moral standard that is consistent with our new identity as citizens of a "holy nation," where Christ is seated as the king. One example of this standard is that believers are not to fight with each other within the Christian community, but rather to "love one another earnestly from a pure heart" (1 Pet 1:22). According to Peter, the foundation of this godly love is that "you have been born again" (1 Pet 1:23).

In this world, feuds, factions, and unhealthy competition, fueled by animosity, permeate every aspect of life. In the church, however, we are to live together in Christ-like love out of our new status as "born-again"

11. See chapter 7, "Joy of a Broken Marriage/Family" for more details.

children of God. Since we are dead to this fallen world, we are not to live according to its moral standard. This is why Peter calls us to put aside "all malice and all deceit and hypocrisy and envy and all slander" (1 Pet 2:1). Instead, we are called to live a life of heartfelt love for fellow Christians and in humility towards various authorities and institutions in society (1 Pet 2:13–3:7).

Peter warns his readers that as newly born citizens of the kingdom of God, the values of this world will conflict with their new values. He admonishes us "to abstain from the passions of the flesh, which *wage war against your soul*" (1 Pet 2:11). He sees a clash of virtues between the newborn Christian believers and the antagonistic and rebellious world around them. Due to the nature of such a conflict, the church is bound to suffer spiritual damage. If the world hated Christ, then it most definitely will hate those who bear his name.

We can live in peace with this sinful world around us, but do we really want to? Consider this for a moment. Jesus says, "If you were of the world, the world would love you as its own" (John 15:19). If the world saw the "believer" as a like-minded friend, then it would not hate him. It would welcome him as one who is in allegiance with its own sinful, rebellious agenda. Such a "believer" does not love the things of God but hates him as the world does because "whoever wishes to be a friend of the world makes himself an enemy of God" (Jas 4:4). Any respite that this so-called "believer" may experience is only temporary and ultimately ends with the wrath of God being poured out upon them (Ps 73:17–20).

Jesus then sets up the following contrast: *follow Christ and be in conflict with the world, or follow the world and be in conflict with Christ.* Both John and Peter reiterate this teaching of Jesus in their respective texts.

God has chosen us from this world. We who were once rebels against the will of God are now born anew into a community that conforms to the good and pleasing will of God. Because of our new identity—as disciples of Christ, who join in his condemnation of the values of the fallen world—the world now sees us in the same way that it perceived Jesus. The end result: we are persecuted and rejected by this world. That is the price that we pay, the cost of discipleship. That is why we are to expect suffering in our lives.

3) The Suffering of Spiritual Sojourners

In addition to being "born again" in 1 Peter 1:3, Peter uses several titles that portray how we, as believers, are to view ourselves in relation to the fallen world around us. The first is found in 1 Peter 1:1 where Peter calls us "foreigners." [12] Later, in 1 Peter 2:11, he repeats the term "foreigner" but also adds the new title of "resident alien." Although there has been a mild dispute among commentators on the nature of these designations, the general consensus is that they serve as metaphors to describe the Christian's spiritual identity during his time in this world. [13] We are journeymen who are roaming through this earthly world as we wait patiently for the new heavens and new earth to come.

Each of these terms has its own specific nuance, but together they teach a significant lesson that is critical to understanding Peter's whole letter. We have already seen how our "new birth" leads to hostility from the sinful world around us. Peter uses the image of sojourners and aliens to further explain the suffering and persecution that Christians will face. As a result of the "new birth" that Christ accomplished on our behalf, we are given a new status as spiritual "foreigners" and "resident aliens." Since we are now pilgrims with a new, spiritual identity in Christ, we are to see ourselves as spiritual sojourners who are traveling through a hostile world that will not hesitate to mock and ridicule us because of our faith in Christ. The end of our journey, however, will be our entrance into our true heavenly homeland that is "imperishable" (1 Pet 1:4, 23).

12. 1 Peter begins with three theological titles to describe believers: the "elect," "foreigners," and "the dispersions." It was "according to his great mercy" (1 Pet 1:3) that God "elected" (1 Pet 1:1) them. Those whom He "elected" are those whom God "caused to be born again." As a result of this new birth, the elect-newborns have become spiritual "foreigners" of the "dispersion," who are "exiles" (1 Pet 2:11) in this world. The doctrine of election, therefore, is the first of the "spiritual blessings in the heavenly places" (Eph 1:3), the one from which all other spiritual blessings flow, including the doctrine of regeneration (new birth). It is worth noting that Peter opens his epistle with a doctrine that has caused so much apprehension in the church. The doctrine of election reminds us God is sovereign in our salvation as well as our lives. Because he is the God of election, we can have hope in the midst of current trials, and eternal security in our "great salvation" (1 Pet 1:10). When the doctrine of election is properly understood, it helps us to see how and why we have a "joy unspeakable" and a "living hope." It should not be avoided or ignored, but rather embraced and proclaimed. This is a message that the readers of this epistle desperately needed to hear; it is also the message our contemporary world needs.

13. For a defense of understanding these terms as a reference to the actual sociopolitical situation of Peter's readers, see Elliott, *Home for the Homeless*.

The Dispersion

Believers are not just any kind of foreigners. They are called foreigners of "the dispersion" (1 Pet 1:1). This is a technical term, found in Jewish literature, which refers to the post-exilic Israelite population living outside of their homeland from the time of the Babylonian exile in the sixth century BC. The term evokes a sense of cultural displacement and social rejection. Not only were the Jews away from home but also, and more importantly, they were not considered as accepted members within their immediate social context. As "the dispersion," they were homeless and friendless.

The readers of Peter's epistle—whether Jewish or Gentile Christians—would have been well aware of this term. In fact, Jewish Christians in the church may have felt a level of rejection even within the growing multi-ethnic community. Gentile believers may have harbored some residual anti-Semitism that was prevalent throughout the ancient Roman empire toward their fellow Jewish brethren in the church. Even Peter himself was guilty of this sin (Gal 2:14). This may explain the strong call that Peter makes to "love one another earnestly from a pure heart" (1 Pet 1:22; cf. 4:8–11). Regardless of any preexisting racial prejudices, it seems that Peter was now identifying Gentile Christians as part of this new "dispersion."

In addition, Peter no longer uses the term in a technical, sociopolitical sense. It now takes on a new theological meaning that applies to both Jewish and Gentile converts alike. Both ethnic groups now compose this newly formed "dispersion" because both are elect and thus "newborn infants" (1 Pet 2:2). As Edmund Clowney states so clearly: "They are the Diaspora, because they are the people of God, scattered in the world."[14] Whatever hostility the Jewish diaspora faced in the past, this new diaspora (of Jewish and Gentile believers) will face an even more intense hostility, due to their new spiritual identity as the "born again" followers of Christ.

Foreigners and Aliens in a Hostile World

As mentioned above, the term "foreigner" occurs with "resident alien" in 1 Peter 2:11. In that passage, Peter specifically states that in light of

14. Clowney, *Message of 1 Peter*, 37.

their new status ("foreigners" and "aliens") they are "to abstain from the passions of the flesh." The effect of these two parallel titles creates a social and theological distance between the believer and his surrounding secular society.

Peter's epistle is saturated with this image of intentional alienation from the world. In 1 Pet 1:17, believers are called not to conform to the values and lifestyles of those around them, but rather to conduct themselves in the fear of the Lord throughout the time of their "exile." Here, the word "exile" is a reference to their entire earthly life. Peter also says that the ways of the world are marred with "all malice and all deceit and hypocrisy and envy and all slander," which they are to put away (1 Pet 2:1) because such values are "futile" (1 Pet 1:18). Those who are part of the fallen world attempt to find pleasure in "sensuality, passions, drunkenness, orgies, drinking parties, and lawless idolatry" (1 Pet 4:3), and these values cannot be shared by the "foreigners" who have been washed clean by the "precious blood of Christ" (1 Pet 1:19; cf. 2:22–25). Instead, they are to reflect the righteous attributes of their Savior (1 Pet 4:7–11). They are even called to "not repay evil for evil or reviling for reviling," for that is the way of the world, "but on the contrary, bless, for to this you were called" (1 Pet 3:9). This is the example Jesus leaves for the believer (1 Pet 2:21).

Thus, Peter uses these sociopolitical terms to help the church understand who they are in light of the death and resurrection of Christ. In Christ, we are now spiritual "foreigners" and "resident aliens" who are journeying through this world until we reach our final homeland, the eternal kingdom of God. Therefore, Peter says, we must not conform to the immoral practices of the world. Such a lifestyle of holiness, so different from that of the world, however, comes with painful consequences. Peter says: "With respect to this, they are surprised when you do not join them in the same flood of debauchery, and they malign you" (1 Pet 4:4). As a result of its counter-cultural lifestyle, the Christian community lives in diametrical opposition to their surroundings. The Christ-centered value system of the church is neither understood nor appreciated by the secular community around it. In fact, the world feels so threatened by this that it maligns Christians.

The early apostles in the book of Acts illustrate this truth. The book begins with the ascension of Jesus and the subsequent outpouring of the

Spirit of God at Pentecost (Acts 2).[15] As you continue to read through Acts, it becomes clear that the more these disciples resemble Jesus, the more they encounter persecution from Jewish and Gentile groups (Acts 4:13). Using the images discussed thus far in 1 Peter, the apostles in the book of Acts received a "new birth" that transformed them into heavenly "foreigners" and "resident aliens" that caused them to suffer and endure tremendous hardship. Perhaps Peter had this reality in mind when he wrote his epistle since he not only saw the hardship of these early Christian leaders firsthand but also experienced it personally and is now writing to encourage those who are experiencing a similar kind of trial.

Our final destination

Although the terms "foreigner," "resident alien," and "dispersion" primarily describe the transitory life of believers on earth and the animosity that is associated with it, they also instill a sense of hope that comes by knowing the final destination of the believer's sojourning. Peter uses these images to demonstrate his eagerness for his readers to see that they are not to consider this fallen world as their permanent place of residence. Rather, their home is the eternal kingdom, where their imperishable and undefiled inheritance awaits them (1 Pet 1:4). Their brief time on earth (1 Pet 1:6; 5:10) is therefore nothing more than a temporary stopover until they are brought to their final destination on the day of Christ's visitation (1 Pet 2:12). They are spiritual immigrants, traveling through this earthly land until they reach their true heavenly homeland—and what a homeland it will be! As this was true for Peter's original readers, so is it true for us.

4) The Suffering of Spiritual Warfare

Although Peter acknowledges that Christian suffering is a direct result of our spiritual identity in Christ—and thus the hallmark trait of the believers' life on earth—there is a deeper reason for its existence. Its ultimate origin is found in Genesis 3, a record of the original sin of Adam and the fall of humanity. Because of Adam's disobedience, God placed enmity

15. Although the book has traditionally been viewed as a record of the Acts of the *Apostles*, it is better to understand it as the Acts of the *Holy Spirit*, who used frail human agents as his instruments through which Jesus "built his church" (Matt 16:13–19).

between the seed (descendants) of the woman and the seed of the serpent (Gen 3:15). This enmity is a curse upon the serpent for deceiving Adam and Eve into violating their covenantal agreement with God.[16] As a result of the serpent's defiance against the Lord and his image bearers, God comes as a judge to execute against the serpent the penalty of the covenant. Thus, God says that there will be eternal enmity between the seed of the serpent and those of the woman.

War of the Serpent

The Hebrew word that is translated as "enmity" communicates a sense of malicious intent. Numbers 35:21–22 describes two different situations in which an individual is struck down dead. One is done "with enmity" (Num 35:21) which results in a death sentence; the other is done "without enmity" (Num 35:22) and requires some discernment in order to determine the appropriate response. The difference between the two scenarios is the presence or absence of "enmity," a conscious intent to cause harm, within the accused.

According to Genesis 3:15, this hostility is what characterizes the friction between these two genealogical lines. The serpent and his "seed" (those who are against the Lord and in league with Satan) will have malicious intentions to harm those in the line of the woman. All of the conflict, tension, and hatred recorded in Scripture is a manifestation of this conflict. This will continue until the final destruction of the "serpent" by the one outstanding "seed of the woman," Jesus Christ (Rom 16:20). Jesus first defeated the serpent in the wilderness temptations (Matt 4:1–11), then again in his death and resurrection. His final victory will be at his return, when Satan will be thrown into the "lake of fire" for all eternity (Rev 20:10).

War Against the Church

Revelation 12 shows that the hatred the serpent harbors is not limited to Jesus the Messiah alone but extends to those who are identified with him

---

16. Although the word "covenant" does not occur in Genesis 1–3, all the literary components that make up a covenant are present. Also, Hosea 6:7 is helpful here, since this passage comments on the original arrangement between God and Adam and calls it a "covenant."

as well. In this chapter, John sees in heaven a glorious, radiant woman who is about to give birth to a child "who is to rule all the nations with a rod of iron" (Rev 12:5). In front of this woman, there is also a great red dragon of immense size with a malicious, cruel, and destructive objective—to devour the child as soon as he is born. However, the dragon fails. The child is born and is immediately "caught up to God and to his throne" (Rev 12:5) where he is safe and protected. The connection between this chapter, Genesis 3:15, and the meaning of each image is self-evident: the glorious woman represents the church, the dragon is Satan, and the child is Christ.

Frustrated by his failure, the dragon now redirects his fiery fury. He first attempts to destroy the woman (Rev 12:6), then the archangel Michael (Rev 12:7–9). He fails in both attempts. This leads to the third (doomed to failure) attempt of the dragon, the most noteworthy for the purpose of our discussion. Once on the earth, the dragon has another opportunity to assault the woman, but she receives two wings of an eagle and flies to the wilderness, to a place God prepares for her (Rev 12:13–16). The dragon proceeds to shift his attention "to make war on the rest of her offspring" (Rev 12:17). The image of the "offspring" of this blessed, glorious woman is interpreted as "those who keep the commandments of God and hold to the testimony of Jesus." This is the church—we are this "offspring." During the period between the first and second comings of Christ, Satan is waging war against us.

These visions may seem confusing, but they are in fact messages of blessed comfort and rest. Because Satan is unable to defeat the Christ-child, the champion of the church, he turns against the church herself and "the rest of her offspring," meaning the individual elect believers. The Lord, however, is the one who protects her during this period of her history where she awaits the return of her eternal bridegroom.

The draconic Satan will attack her ruthlessly and relentlessly with all evil and cruelty—with "enmity." He will place all manners of philosophical and scientific deceits, false dogmas, and misguided teachings in the way of the church, all of which will have the appearance of godliness. Satan does all this in an attempt to lead the church astray. This aggression will be real and painful, yet the Lord provides sustenance and nourishment from his Word in the midst of this satanic onslaught. This will continue until the Lord returns with his heavenly hosts for one final battle of Armageddon, where Satan will finally be condemned for all eternity and the elect in Christ, his church, will be glorified to reign with him in the

New Jerusalem in the New Heavens and New Earth (Rev 21–22).[17] What a day that will be!

Since Revelation 12 clearly alludes to Genesis 3:15, this description of an unwavering conflict between Christ, the "offspring of the woman," and the dragon is characteristic not only of the history of the church but also the entire history of salvation—from the time of the garden to the days of the New Testament. The clash between Abel and Cain (Gen 4) is the initial manifestation of this heavenly warfare. The genealogies found in the book of Genesis are intended to show the continued progression of those two genealogical lines of descent. The confrontation between Moses and the Egyptian pharaoh in the book of Exodus is, in actuality, *the* conflict between Christ and Satan. So also are David versus Goliath, the prophet(s) of Israel versus the prophets of Baal, and Israel versus the nations.

If You Are Not For Me, You Are Against Me

Why do believers face trials? It is because the Lord placed this "enmity" between the wicked descendants of the serpent and the blessed line of the woman. It may be difficult to appreciate such tension as a blessing, but it truly is when we consider the alternative. If there is no "enmity" between Christians and the satanic forces, *it is because we are allies with Satan*—fighting the war with the evil one against the Lord himself. There is no enmity because we are on the same side with the same agenda.

The New Testament Scriptures make this point abundantly clear. In Luke, the disciples of Jesus encounter a man who casts out demons in the name of Christ, yet he is not one of the Twelve (Luke 9:50). Although they attempt to prevent him from doing such work, Jesus commends it and tells the Twelve that, "He who is not against you is for you." Jesus says the same in Mark, "He who is not against us is for us" (Mark 9:40). Matthew 12 teaches this again, through a different account. There, Jesus is accused of casting out demons in the name of the prince of demons, Beelzebub. Jesus responds by labeling such an accusation as foolish. If he were truly casting out demons with the authority of Satan, this would mean that the kingdom of Satan is divided and fighting against itself. What is the logic of that? According to Jesus, he casts out demons because he carries the

---

17. For a biblical description of this, see Revelation 16:14–16; 19:11–21; 20:7–9; cf. Ezekiel 38–39; Zechariah 14:1–10.

authority and power of the Kingdom of God and, "He who is not with me is against me; and he who does not gather with me scatters" (Matt 12:30). There is no neutral ground. Everyone is on one side or the other.

Suffering Comes from Our Union with Christ

Does the description of the suffering Christian sound familiar? It should, because it not only describes the life of a believer in Jesus Christ, it also describes Jesus Christ himself. As we look to him and meditate upon who he is and what he has done to save us from our sins, it becomes increasingly clearer that to read about his life is also to read about our own. Much of the suffering that we endure is similar to that which Jesus faced. There is a correlation between the life of Christ and the life of a believer.

This bond between Jesus and those who believe in him is what theologians call the doctrine of our *union with Christ*. This union with Christ is the foundation of Peter's words of encouragement. It is also critical for understanding the theology of the apostle Paul and the New Testament as a whole. This doctrine will be fleshed out in the next chapter, but for now, it is sufficient to see that several of the suffering images mentioned above apply as much to Jesus as it does to the believer. In fact, we can say that *because* it first describes Jesus, so it also describes us.

"New Birth" in Christ

The "birth" of which Peter speaks in 1:3 is given a major qualifier. It is a birth that is "through the resurrection of Jesus Christ from the dead." Peter is saying something very profound to his readers.

When Peter ponders Jesus's death and resurrection, he also sees our own death and resurrection due to this union that we have with Christ. We were once dead in sin—we could do nothing but sin against the Lord (Eph 2:1). Every decision that we made was sinful and a violation of the law of God. But in Christ's death on the cross, our sinful nature also was put to death (see Gal 2:20). Moreover, we do not stay dead. That same union with Christ raises us from the dead in Jesus's resurrection. This transition from the death of our sinful nature to being resurrected into a new person is what Peter calls being "born again." Therefore, when we are "caused to be born again" (1:3), we are made a new person who is now holy and pure before God, no longer dead in sin. Because this birth is defined by our union with Jesus's resurrection, I like to call it a *resurrection-birth.*

Jesus taught the same thing when he said that in order to enter into the kingdom of God, we need to be "born again." That phrase can also mean "born from above," meaning a *spiritual* birth, a heavenly birth. This means that when we are born again in Christ (John 3:3) our old sinful nature has died and we are now "a new creation" in Jesus Christ, where "the old has passed away; behold, the new has come" (2 Cor 5:17).

In our union with the resurrected Christ, we have been given this *resurrection-birth* and thus a new identity as children of God (John 1:12). It is no wonder, then, that we suffer in this world. Sinful humanity had no problem bringing pain and misery to Jesus. It most definitely will not hesitate to do the same to those who are united to him. Consider the following passages from the gospel of John that illustrate the tension that comes from our union with Christ:

> If the world hates you, know that it has hated me before it hated you. If you were of the world, the world would love you as its own; but because you are not of the world, but I chose you out of the world, therefore the world hates you. (John 15:18–19)

> I have given them your word, and the world has hated them because they are not of the world, just as I am not of the world. . . They are not of the world, just as I am not of the world. (John 17:14, 16)

Notice how John reflects upon the source of Christian persecution and hardship. The fallen world detests the disciples of Christ because their values reflect those of Christ whom the world hated and ultimately crucified.

This "new birth" is truly a blessing, but it comes at a price. That price is hostility with the world; the world has the same hatred for us as it had for our Savior. As Jesus taught: "The world has hated them because they are not of the world" (John 17:14). Yet we are encouraged to remember that the world only hates us because it first hated Jesus: "It has hated me before it hated you" (John 15:18). His suffering now becomes our suffering. Since much of the suffering characteristic of the Christian life stems from our new birth, it is not surprising that this suffering reveals a genuine faith which directs our attention to the only person who can be our help.

Spiritual "Foreigners" and "Aliens" in Christ

Because of our new birth in Christ, we are spiritual "foreigners" and "resident aliens" in an unholy land where our Christian virtues directly oppose those of the world around us. We thus live in conflict within our immediate social contexts.

The life and ministry of Christ may be understood in much the same way. He was the *true* foreigner and resident alien in his incarnation. Philippians 2:5–11 recounts the incredible journey of Christ who leaves his glorious throne to be a "foreigner" in this world. As an "alien" He suffers as a servant, "even death on a cross."

In these days of extreme racial tension when ethnic minorities are considered strange and even unwanted, the term "immigrant" or "minority" may capture Peter's point better. Minorities have been the target of violent acts of hatred for no fault of their own, and attempts to try to live at peace with their surroundings have been met with even greater abhorrence.

One could say that Jesus was the true spiritual "immigrant," his minority status determined not by his ethnicity but by his spiritual place of origin. He was not only rejected by the Gentiles, who would have marginalized any Jew of their day, but also by his own people (John 1:11). He brought a message of life and hope to a world that wanted nothing to do with it. Instead of acknowledging their sinful rebellion and resting in the promise of the forgiveness of their sins, the people of this world hated Jesus, arrested him for crimes he did not commit, subjected him to a kangaroo court, and inflicted him with unimaginable pain that climaxed at his death on the cross.

Since Christ suffered, so we are also called to suffer. This is why we should not be surprised at the suffering we experience.

Our Christ-like Spiritual Armor

Our God is a God of peace . . . except where Satan is concerned. Ever since the garden, the evil one has deceitfully attempted to undermine the will of God and to wage war against his beloved children. No one has more hatred for the church than "the dragon, that ancient serpent, who is the devil and Satan" (Rev 20:2). In order for there to be peace and an end to the conflict, Satan himself must be brought to an end. Only in the victory of Christ and the final defeat of Satan will there be an everlasting peace. This is why Paul says that the "God of peace will soon crush Satan under your feet" (Rom 16:20).

Why do believers face conflict and hardship? It is because we are at peace with God but in spiritual warfare with Satan. Satan has not yet met his final end, and until he does, he will continue to relentlessly assault the church of his sworn enemy. Therefore, to experience the hardship that comes from this spiritual warfare—where Christians are called to combat "not against flesh and blood, but against the rulers, against the powers, against the world forces of this darkness, against the spiritual forces of wickedness in the heavenly places" (Eph 6:12)—is indeed a blessing, because the Lord has chosen us to be his warriors to fight for his cause.

According to Paul, Christ not only redeems us by his great works but he also gives us the means to successfully defeat our adversary. God gives us "the full armor of God so that you may be able to stand firm against the schemes of the devil" (Eph 6:11) and "so that you may be able to resist in the evil day" (Eph 6:13).

The components of our spiritual armory consist of the "belt of truth," the "breastplate of righteousness," the "shield of faith," the "helmet of salvation," and the "sword of Spirit," which is the Word of God (Eph 6:14–19). This is not the first time that Scripture has described this procession of warfare accoutrements. This description in Ephesians reflects less upon the Roman centurion than upon the military regalia of Yahweh as the divine warrior found in Isaiah:

> He put on righteousness as a breastplate, and a helmet of salvation on his head; he put on garments of vengeance for clothing, and wrapped himself in zeal as a cloak. (Isa 59:17)

Isaiah 11 is another well-known passage that gives the image of the coming Davidic messiah. Verse 5 provides a brief description of this messianic figure in his military accessories: "Righteousness shall be the belt of his waist, and faithfulness the belt of his loins." As a warrior, this messianic "shoot from the stump of Jesse" (Isa 11:1) goes and exacts divine retribution against his enemies while wearing righteousness and faithfulness as his belts.

The same will be for those who are in Christ. By alluding to Isaiah 59 (and possibly Isaiah 11), Paul teaches that the union of the Christian believer with the Lord provides not only the basis upon which they receive "all the spiritual blessings in Christ" (Eph 1:3) but also the source of the believer's victory in the spiritual warfare against Satan and his demonic followers. The heavenly soldier of Ephesians 6:14–19 is a depiction of the believer because it is first a depiction of our messiah. Victory is ours because victory was his! He indeed came and "crushed Satan under his feet" (Rom 16:20; cf. Gen 3:15) by proving his powers over sin and death. However, our blessed Savior, our divine warrior, is only able to secure such a victory by first taking upon himself the devastating defeat that should have been ours, and then by imputing to us his triumphal righteousness. Christ as the divine warrior declares his victory in his death and resurrection. Those in Christ also share in that victory.

Peter is aware of the reality of this spiritual warfare which Paul describes. In 1 Peter 4:1, believers are called to "arm [themselves]" with the same way of thinking as that of Jesus, who was willing to give up his life. Peter does not teach believers anything different from Paul in Ephesians 6:14–19 since both admit that the source of the Christian's armament is the Lord. He also does not teach anything different from the Lord Jesus, who teaches his disciples the cost of following him: "If anyone would come after me, let him deny himself and take up his cross daily and follow me" (Luke 9:23).

Peter also acknowledges that the adversary of Christians is indeed Satan, the prince of demons. He even mentions that devilish adversary explicitly in 1 Peter, where he calls believers to "be sober-minded; be watchful. Your adversary the devil prowls around like a roaring lion, seeking someone to devour" (1 Pet 5:8). Our adversary is powerful and we would be wise to remember that. He will strike our heel, although he ultimately will have his head crushed (Gen 3:15).

We are spiritual warriors engaged in spiritual warfare because Christ is the true divine warrior who fights against Satan, the draconic beast, the "ancient serpent" (Rev 20:2). As Christ is the victorious warrior, so we share in that victory—we also are victorious warriors.

Suffering, Then Glory

We are given a *resurrection-birth* in Jesus's resurrection. We journey through this life as Christ did. We also fight the same spiritual war as Jesus, against the same spiritual enemies. For these reasons, it is natural for us to conclude that we will also suffer, just as Jesus suffered. Following Jesus and remaining his faithful disciples will not bring us health, wealth, and prosperity, but rather trials, persecution, and suffering. From the moment of Jesus's birth, his life was filled with suffering—wanderings and temptations in the wilderness, rejection by his people, threats upon his life, slander of his name, and ultimately a humiliating death although innocent of any crimes.

Of course, we know that he did not stay in the grave but was raised from the dead in a powerful and victorious resurrection. So we also do not remain in a state of suffering; we will transition into a life of glory in Christ. That pattern of suffering to glory is also the pattern of the believer in Christ.

What was shocking for Peter's readers—and perhaps for us today—is that the source of our suffering as well as our glory is the same: Jesus Christ. Peter encourages us not to be surprised by our fiery trials because of our union with Christ. This union is the reason that we should not be surprised by our suffering; it is also the reason that we can rejoice in it.

3

The Surprising Source of Joy

The Biblical Foundation for Christ-Centered Suffering, Part 2[1]

> *But rejoice insofar as you share Christ's sufferings, that you may*
> *also rejoice and be glad when his glory is revealed.*

1 Peter 4:13

MAY 6, 2005 WAS one of the most encouraging days of my life. This was
the day when I became an ordained minister of the gospel. Although
I had served the church in a pastoral capacity for many years prior, finally receiving the blessing of ordination confirmed my call to ministry.
It was a great night for me and my family.

One moment in particular has stayed with me all these years—the
pastoral charge given to me by my dear friend, Pastor Dick Ellis. The text
that he preached from was from 2 Corinthians 1:24, where Paul says,
"Not that we lord it over your faith, but *we work with you for your joy*,
for you stand firm in your faith."[2] I can still envision Dick, thundering
away with that challenging charge, "Work for the joy of God's people!"
For a budding Christian leader, these were inspiring words that I took
seriously, praying that the Lord would give me a heart for his people, to
love them so that I could accomplish this noble but overwhelming task.

---

1. This chapter originally appeared in *Reformed Faith & Practice* and is reprinted
with permission. See Lee, "Surprising Source of Joy."

2. Emphasis added.

It was not very long after that when my church community was hit by a barrage of crises. One member was diagnosed with a brain tumor, others strove to fix their broken marriages, and still others faced cancer and death. All these issues occurred within the first several months of my pastoral work. I recall many evenings thinking about that charge—"work for the joy of God's people"—and wondering, "How in the world am I supposed to accomplish this now? How can I instill joy in these people going through such heartache?" How indeed, especially in light of the fact that the majority of these people were faithfully serving the Lord in our church! How was I to tell them that they were called to endure these extreme times of pain?

In God's divine providence, the first series of sermons I preached for that community was based upon 1 Peter. I am not certain whether that series had any significant impact on them, but I do know this—it had a significant impact on me. Much of what I have to share in this chapter comes from those precious moments of study. I may have been the pastor, but I was the one ministered to. The Lord took me back to school in those days and taught me much through his divine, inerrant, and infallible Word.

A Shocking Command

Perhaps nothing is more shocking (and yet comforting) than the word of encouragement that is given here, in 1 Peter 4:13—to rejoice while suffering. In the previous verse, we saw that Peter urged his readers not to be surprised by the fiery ordeal that they encounter as believers in Christ. Their "resurrection-birth" has created them anew as spiritual "foreigners" and "resident aliens," bringing them into the frontlines of a raging spiritual warfare, where their adversaries are not flesh-and-blood beings like themselves but rather demonic forces, whose allegiance is to the prince of demons, Satan himself. These descriptions apply—first and foremost—to our Savior Jesus Christ. Then, as an effect of their union with him, they also apply to his original readers, and finally, to us today. Peter immediately follows by giving a rather odd and unexpected command: instead of being taken aback by the fiery trials that result from this new identity, because of (not in spite of) the horrible suffering that his readers are enduring, he calls them to "rejoice" (1 Pet 4:13).

This does not seem to make any rational sense. In fact, it sounds impossible. His readers had faced all sorts of hardship because of their faith in Christ. They had been mocked and slandered by the secular world around them, and possibly even by their own families (see 1 Pet 3:1–7). Some, perhaps, may have even been harmed to the point of shedding their own blood. They had suffered great loss and had endured much heartache. I would have expected Peter to encourage them to "persevere," or "trust in the Lord," or even to "not fall to temptation." Instead, he tells them to *rejoice*. Not to wallow in self-pity, not to doubt the sovereignty of God, not even to complain, grumble, or challenge what the Lord is doing (alas, Job!). None of that. But rather, *rejoice*. Let me say it again: *rejoice!*

What is even more shocking is that the "joy" that he has in mind is the joy that he mentioned earlier in his epistle, a "joy that is inexpressible and filled with glory" (1 Pet 1:8). That was definitely not a joy that I had, but desperately longed for. At the same time, it seemed impossible to attain this while enduring sorrow and pain. How could I rejoice with a "joy unspeakable" when all I saw was the futility of living a faithful life? I strove to obey, and the only result seemed to be ridicule and slander from my surrounding community. What about my family members who were literally dying before my eyes? What could possibly give me this joy when I experienced nothing but agony? What about our fellow Christian brethren, in persecuted areas of the world, who were risking their lives for the sake of the Gospel? Could they have this joy?

The incredible word of hope that we are given is a bold and resounding *yes*! Yes, you can have that joy, and you can have it *right now*. Although his words come to his readers in the form of a command, they also describe a blessing from the Lord that they can possess. Yes, that is correct—you are called to *rejoice* and, at the same time, the Lord will give you this extraordinary joy as a precious gift. Our "yes" and "amen," however, is true only in Christ.

"Rejoice Insofar as You Share Christ's Sufferings"

All this sounds great, but how can such joy be attained? Let us begin by examining the instruction Peter gives carefully:

> Rejoice insofar as you share Christ's sufferings. (1 Pet 4:13)

Peter says more than this, but first we need to meditate on this opening phrase. He begins by bringing together two concepts that we do not naturally connect with each other: joy and suffering. Specifically, he mentions *our* joy and *Jesus's* suffering. This is a significant pairing that we must never forget. For Peter, the two are inseparable. There are three factors to keep in mind in order to understand how Peter correlates joy and suffering.

1) Not suffering from sin

The first comes from the use of the adverb "insofar as," which is the Greek particle *katho*. He says that we are to rejoice "insofar as" (*katho*) we share in the sufferings of Christ. The significance of this small Greek particle is critical to a proper understanding of this passage because it helps to specify the nature of the suffering in view and provides safeguards to avoid misunderstandings. The suffering that Peter addresses here is not the kind that results from sinful behavior, but that which comes as a result of living a life of faithfulness to God.

Peter states clearly the type of suffering that he does not have in mind when he says, "But let none of you suffer as a murderer or a thief or an evildoer or as a meddler" (1 Peter 4:15). This is similar to what he taught earlier, "For what credit is it if, when you sin and are beaten for it, you endure?" (1 Peter 2:20). This rhetorical question makes the point clear: there is no credit or glory for you if you suffer negative consequences as a result of your sin. Without equivocation, he states, "For it is better to suffer for doing good, if that should be God's will, than for doing evil" (1 Peter 3:17). In the cases where sin has been committed, the individual suffers justly, enduring the consequences of his own violation of the law of God. For example, if you steal, you will suffer imprisonment. If you commit adultery, you will suffer a miserable marriage. If you are arrogant and selfish, you will suffer loneliness, as you will have no friends.

The Scriptures make it clear that the response required for this kind of suffering is not joy but rather confession of the sin, repentance of it, and growth in holiness.

I admit that I am oversimplifying a complex matter in the Christian life: overcoming the powers of sin. Although this is not a book on repentance and restoration, I would be remiss not to mention the forgiveness of our sins that comes from the "great mercy" of God (1 Pet 1:3). This is a message that we need to hear repeatedly because we repeatedly "fall short of the glory of God" (Rom 3:23). Not a day goes by that we do not sin against the Lord in some manner, whether outwardly, in our behavior, or internally, in our motives and the private thoughts of our hearts.

Romans 3:10–18 is a somber yet powerful passage that reminds me of my fallen and sinful nature, that without Christ there is no hope of overcoming the penalty of sin—death (Rom 6:23). We should be condemned for all eternity, because among all humanity:

> None is righteous, no, not one; no one understands; no one seeks for God. All have turned aside; together they have become worthless; no one does good, not even one. Their throat is an open grave; they use their tongues to deceive. The venom of asps is under their lips. Their mouth is full of curses and bitterness. Their feet are swift to shed blood; in their paths are ruin and misery, and the way of peace they have not known. There is no fear of God before their eyes. (Rom 3:10–18)

Peter, like Paul, is able to offer genuine good news since he understands that the sufferings of Christ, the "righteous one," on the cross was on our behalf, "the unrighteous," as our substitute "to bring us to God" (1 Pet 3:18). In so doing, Christ not only pays for the penalty of sin but also takes the guilt of our sins upon himself. A proper understanding of the "sufferings of Christ" leads us to an appropriate, humble response: we must confess and renounce our sins, ask God for forgiveness, attempt restitution where possible, and rest in the promised forgiveness of Christ. Though repentance is dealt with only briefly here, it is far from peripheral to the life of a believer. Repentance is a spiritual discipline absolutely worthy of further contemplation, and I encourage you to do so.[3]

Regarding suffering, however, the point that Peter makes is this: do not suffer due to your own sins. It only brings misery, and there is nothing praiseworthy in this since you are suffering the consequences of your actions (see 1 Pet 4:15). Yet even in such circumstances, the gospel has the power to change the pain from sin into joy. This comes when we realize that Christ paid the penalty for our sins and that in him there is no longer any condemnation for those who turn to him by faith (Rom 8:1). Sinners, therefore, can rejoice once they have repented, but the suffering that comes from that sin is not a source of joy in itself.

---

3. For some helpful treatments on the subject of repentance as a spiritual discipline, see Watson, *Doctrine of Repentance*; Miller, *Repentance*; and Ferguson, *Grace of Repentance*.

2) Christ's sufferings

The second significant feature to observe is also derived from that same "insofar as" particle (*katho*) that we noted earlier. Whereas the previous point emphasizes the kind of suffering *not* in view (i.e., suffering as a result of sin), this second point brings out the positive description of the kind of suffering that Peter does envision: the sufferings of Christ. This is what Peter says is the source of our extraordinary joy: "rejoice *insofar* as you share *Christ's sufferings*." In other words, you can rejoice *because* you share Christ's sufferings.

The phrase "Christ's sufferings" refers to the suffering that Jesus himself endured. What kind of suffering was this? Certainly, it was righteous suffering. He was perfectly obedient to the will of God the Father, both in his motives as well as in his public life. There was no blemish or hint of sin within him. He embodied a perfect love for God and for his people (Matt 22:36–40). In spite of this, he was rejected by his fellow Jews, scorned, and ridiculed for proclaiming the good news of the gospel. He was betrayed by his close companions and followers, even though they swore that they would never abandon him. He was arrested illegally, accused of crimes he did not commit, and sentenced to death. When he was weak and exhausted on the cross, no one showed remorse or granted any mercy. Instead, he was all the more mocked and disdained. Yet throughout all this, he never sinned, never turned against the will of his Father. He was faithful and obedient. If anyone *ever* exemplified a righteous sufferer, it was Jesus.

His suffering is frequently juxtaposed with the "glory that is going to be revealed" (1 Pet 5:1). In fact, Peter describes the life of Jesus in exactly this way—"the sufferings of Christ and the subsequent glories"—in 1 Peter 1:11. He says that this two-fold summary of the life of Christ (suffering then glory) is the message of salvation that was preached by the Old Testament prophets. In 1 Peter 1:10–12, a series of profound terms capture the essence of the prophetic message: "salvation," "grace," "good news," and "things into which angels long to look." The phrase "the sufferings of Christ and the subsequent glories" is in the same procession of redemptive images. For Peter, the gospel message of the suffering and glory of Christ is the fulfillment of Old Testament Scripture.

This is precisely the same summation of the Old Testament that Jesus himself provides. Luke 24:13–32 records two disciples leaving the city of Jerusalem on the day of Jesus's resurrection. They were disillusioned and confused because Jesus had not restored the golden era of the people of God with the highly-anticipated son of David enthroned as the high king of Israel. Instead, he suffered a criminal's death—death on the cross. On the road, they encounter the resurrected Christ, who rebukes them for being "slow of heart to believe everything that the prophets have spoken" (Luke 24:26). He then interprets for them the whole of the Old Testament Scriptures, and shows that it was necessary for the Messiah to first "suffer these things and enter into his glory." Later, in Luke 24:35–47, Peter himself learns directly from Jesus that his suffering and glory is the fulfillment of all of the Scriptures. Therefore, it seems best to understand "Christ's sufferings" in 1 Peter 4:13 as referring to the *righteous* suffering that Jesus himself endured, which is in part a fulfillment of the Old Testament. His suffering, however, is related to the suffering of Christians.

3) Sharing in Christ's sufferings

The third factor is the verb "you share" in 1 Peter 4:13. You can rejoice only "insofar as *you share* Christ's sufferings." The phrase "you share" is the Greek verb *koinōneite* that can be translated "*you fellowship* with Christ in his sufferings." The use of this verb suggests that there is a close relationship between the believer and Jesus. Calling this a "fellowship" suggests a relationship much more intimate than a mere friendship. It is an unbreakable union. Paul uses the same word to describe the close *fellowship* (ESV "participation") that believers have with Christ in the Lord's Supper (1 Cor 10:16).[4] Given that it is Jesus's suffering that we share in, it is *unjust, righteous* suffering that binds Jesus and believers together.

As long as the suffering that believers experience is due to their faithful obedience in Christ and not a result of their sinful rebellion, they *fellowship with Christ* and they do so *in his sufferings*. According to Peter, Christian suffering is reminiscent of the sufferings of Christ. Therefore, to suffer "as a Christian" (1 Pet 4:16) is to suffer "unjustly" (1 Pet 2:19), "when you do good and suffer for it" (1 Pet 2:20), "for righteousness' sake" (1 Pet 3:14), or "for the name of Christ" (1 Pet 4:14).

---

4. For further details on the fellowship/union believers have with Christ in the Lord's Supper, see Griffith, *Spreading the Feast*, 113–44.

Fellowship with the Sufferings of Christ

Each of the motifs described above—1) suffering not due to sin, 2) but for righteousness, 3) which makes suffering a form of Christ-centered fellowship—describes not only the suffering endured by Jesus, but also the suffering of believers who are in union with the suffering of Christ.

Sharing in his sufferings can be easily misunderstood. The following are what "fellowship with Christ's sufferings" does *not* mean.

First, it does not mean that Jesus is presently in a continual state of suffering. His suffering was limited to his earthly life, while he was in "human form" and he "humbled himself by becoming obedient to the point of death, even death on a cross" (Phil 2:8). We rejoice that Jesus arose from the grave, ascended into heaven, is seated at the right hand of the Father, and we await his return—where he will claim his saints who have shared in his sufferings. Jesus suffered for a time, but is now in glory, and we who share in his sufferings will also share in his glory.

Second, to "fellowship with Christ's sufferings" does not mean that Christians are spiritual masochists who rejoice in suffering *per se*. Though we are called to rejoice in our suffering, we are not called to intentionally seek it out, desire it, or even pray for it. Peter assumes that suffering is unavoidable. When Peter says we are called to suffer for Christ's sake (1 Pet 2:21), he is describing what lies in store for believers, not what we are required to do; the command is to "rejoice," not to "suffer." Given that, he encourages us by saying that fellowship with Christ's sufferings will not crush us. In fact, we can find joy in the midst of it.

Third, to "fellowship with Christ's sufferings" does not mean that our suffering atones for our sins or the sins of others. Peter states clearly that atonement is accomplished by the sufferings of Christ "once for sins" (1 Pet 3:18). As such, our suffering has no atoning value; Christ has already paid the ultimate and entire price.

Fourth, to "fellowship with Christ's sufferings" does not mean that our suffering is at the same level of intensity as that of Jesus. Jesus bore upon himself the sins of his elect and endured the wrath of God as our substitute. Whatever suffering we share, it will never be suffering to that extent. Ours is similar, but not identical to his.

Finally, we are not to mimic Christ's sufferings literally. Suffering in union with Christ does not mean that we must follow the pattern of Christ's sufferings in an overly-precise way. For example, since Jesus was hung on a cross, we might falsely conclude that we must also be hung on a cross. Or since Jesus was given a crown of thorns, so we also must receive our own crown. Instead, Peter focuses on a similarity that is *analogical* and *theological* in nature rather than *identical* and *moral*. This means that all suffering endured for the sake of Christ is *qualitatively* similar to those endured by Jesus—suffering due to righteousness and obedience.

When we consider all the points above, the astounding lesson that we learn is this: we can have this joy *not in spite* of our Christ-centered sufferings but *because* of our Christ-centered sufferings!

Lifetime of suffering

Nowhere in his epistle does Peter suggest that the "fiery ordeal" that his readers face will come to an end during their lifetime. He does say that their sufferings will be for a "little while" (1 Pet 1:6; 5:10), but this is a period of time that only terminates at "the revelation of Christ" (1 Pet 1:7). For Peter, the "little while" is to be understood with the background of the two-fold pattern of suffering and glory where the "glory" is revealed at the termination of the "little while." In other words, for Peter, this "little while" is the entirety of the period between the first and second advents of our Lord.

Paul says the same thing in Romans 8. The "sufferings of this present time" (Rom 8:18) comes to an end at the return of Christ, which is the time of the "revealing of the sons of God" (Rom 8:19) and the "redemption of our bodies" (Rom 8:23). Paul sees the time between the initial coming of Christ and his return as a time when "creation [is] subjected to futility, not willingly" (Rom 8:20), where creation maintains a "bondage to corruption" (Rom 8:21), and when "the whole creation has been groaning together in the pains of childbirth" (Rom 8:22). The effects of the fall are broad, encompassing "not only creation, but we ourselves" (Rom 8:23). This means that the entirety of a Christian's earthly life is part of the "little while" in 1 Peter. Peter would even describe the life of the church, which coincides with the "little while" period, as a lifetime of suffering.

We offer a false hope if we comfort believers by telling them that the "little while" of suffering refers to a quantitative time period—a few weeks, months, years, or a season of life. During my time in pastoral ministry, it never ceased to amaze me how quickly new crises would arise within the church after old ones were resolved. Even in the individual

lives of believers, there is rarely a time of respite from trials and hardships. We fight for spiritual sanity while we live in a fallen world because
the nature of a fallen world is unstable. Everything appears to be in chaos.
To quote a famous man of wisdom, "everything is meaningless" (Eccl 1:1)
when life is viewed from "under the sun" (Eccl 1:3).[5] For Peter, our entire
earthly life as "foreigners" (1 Pet 1:1) and "resident aliens" (1 Pet 2:11) is
the "little while"—a time defined by suffering.

Word of comfort

Peter comforts his readers by promising a future inheritance that is "im-
perishable, undefiled, and unfading, kept in heaven for you (1 Pet 1:4).
However, this will not be revealed until "the revelation of Jesus Christ" (1
Pet 1:7), when our suffering will be transformed into glory.

This future glory is neither the only way that Peter encourages his
readers nor even the primary way. The comfort that Peter offers is not
merely the promise of change in our current, harsh circumstances. Rather, he helps us to see and understand the true nature of our hardship—it
is *fellowship with Christ in his sufferings*, and thus it is a blessing.

Until the return of our Lord, what we need is not only a change in
our painful circumstances but also a change in our perception of them.
Peter provides a historical-redemptive context to this reality or, more accurately, a Christ-centered context. This is what makes the words in 1
Peter 4:13 so amazing. In the midst of this "little while," which is characterized by Christ-like suffering, we can have joy. It is true that there is a
greater joy to be revealed at the return of Christ, but we don't need to wait
for that time to know true joy. This does not have to be a time of sorrow
or doubt. We can have a "joy unspeakable" now.

---

5. The phrase "under the sun" is pervasive in the book of Ecclesiastes; see Eccl 1:3,
9, 14; 2:11, 17–20; 3:16; 4:1, 3, 7, 15; 5:13, 18; 6:1, 12; 8:9, 15, 17; 9:3, 6, 9, 11, 13; 10:5.
A comparable phrase, although not as common, is "under heaven." See Eccl 1:13; 2:3;
3:1. These phrases describe the parameters in which everything is "meaningless"; only
that which is "under the sun" or "under heaven" is meaningless. A glimpse of hope,
however, can be discerned by the nature of life "*above* the sun," a phrase clearly implied
by "*under* the sun." If life "under the sun" is all-meaninglessness, then the presumption
in the book of Ecclesiastes is that life "above the sun" must be diametrically opposite:
all-meaningful. The book of Ecclesiastes does not provide descriptions of such a life,
but that was not its intent.

Who Are Those Who Fellowship with Christ in His Sufferings?

Many understand the phrase "fellowship with Christ's sufferings" too narrowly, as referring only to the harsh persecution characteristic of areas hostile to the gospel. You may know of such churches and believers. They risk their lives for things that are a regular, daily practice for others, such as going to church, attending a weekday bible study, carrying and reading a bible (even owning a bible), and sharing the gospel. These believers put themselves in harm's way for what would be considered the basics of the Christian life and suffer greatly because of it. Such believers most definitely "share Christ's sufferings."

Many foreign missionaries share testimonies of persecution. Some have even given their lives for the sake of the gospel. As heartbreaking as this persecution is, it characterizes the ministry of the church in many areas of the known world, the tragedy of which cannot be overstated. The history of the church testifies to the "enmity" (Gen 3:15) that the church has endured for her groundbreaking penetration into areas that are hostile to the gospel. This is becoming more common—even in the United States, where the church has historically lived in relative comfort, free of societal aggression against Christianity. With the pervasiveness of secularism and the ever-growing deterioration of Christian values in our communities, days absent of persecution are becoming more and more a distant memory, and suffering to the point of shedding blood an increasing reality.

According to 1 Peter, however, to *fellowship with Christ in his sufferings* is broader than this kind of suffering. Any believer who endures trials due to their commitment for the Lord suffers righteously and thus shares in his sufferings. The kind of suffering found in the persecuted church around the world is definitely in Peter's mind. But he also thinks of those who endure through the wear and tear of daily Christian living. To illustrate this, Peter considers examples from the privacy of our homes and basic social relationships. For example, he encourages godly spouses who suffer under ungodly ones (1 Pet 3:1–6) and believers whom he says must submit to civil authorities hostile to their faith (1 Pet 2:13–15; cf. Dan 1–6).

To these, we can include numerous other examples that Peter does not mention. What about young single Christians? I have met many who desire to marry, yet struggle to meet a godly partner. The notion of marrying outside of the Christian faith is tempting, but they stay committed to the biblical teaching that they are to marry in the Lord. They obey the Lord, but do so at a price. They struggle with emotional depression and loneliness.

What about the young college student who is barraged with insults about his faith? Many Christian beliefs are not well received in our society—the exclusivity of salvation in Christ, views against homosexuality as a morally unacceptable way of life, certain doctrines (e.g., predestination, total depravity), and others. As a result, many Christians are vilified in social circles and their friendship is not wanted.

What about the married spouse whose partner commits adultery, in spite of her faithfulness and commitment to the marriage? Or the godly parents who tragically lose a child? Or the Christian who shares the gospel with his non-believing friend, only to be ridiculed for holding such archaic beliefs? What about Christians who live with unbelief in their own family?

In each case, believers suffer due to no fault of their own (1 Pet 2:18, 20–21). In some situations, suffering results even when we are obedient to the will of God.

We live in a world inundated with sin, and the damaging and painful effects of sin are all around us—illness, death, and persecution. We certainly see it in the brutality that marks the persecuted church, but we also see it on a daily basis around us. Suffering for the sake of Christ is defined not by its outward manifestation, but by the heartfelt reaction of the believer. Dan McCartney defines this Christ-like suffering well when he says:

> What makes an occasion of suffering a suffering "for the sake of Christ"? Is it the motivation of the person or agent causing the affliction? No, it is the attitude or conscience of the person who is suffering. Thus any affliction can be suffering for Christ, when we endure it for Christ's sake.[6]

Richard Gaffin says similarly, "Where existence in creation under the curse on sin and in the mortal body is not simply borne, be it stoically or in whatever other sinfully self-centered, rebellious way, but borne for Christ and lived in his service, there, comprehensively, is 'the fellowship of his sufferings.'"[7]

6. McCartney, *Why does it have to hurt?*, 70.

7. Gaffin, "Usefulness of the Cross," 237.

The suffering Servant according to Peter

Perhaps nothing illustrates the thrust of Peter's main message in 1 Peter 4:13 better than his appropriation of the well-known passage of the song of the suffering Servant (Isa 52:13–53:12) in 1 Peter 2:22–25. This passage occurs in the larger context of Peter addressing societal relationships, where he encourages believers to submit to their earthly authorities. According to Peter, they are called to do good even if their leaders treat them unjustly. They will suffer even though it is undeserved. In the face of such mistreatment, they must not retaliate, rebel, or complain, but must submit instead.

The task of submitting to those who treat us unjustly is difficult on its own merits. This becomes even more difficult when we consider that the example of the unjust sufferer Peter calls for us to emulate is the lofty model of Christ himself. Peter uses selections from the song of the suffering Servant in Isaiah to illustrate Christ as the model of the unjust sufferer:

> For to this you have been called, because Christ also suffered for you, leaving you an example, so that you might follow in his steps. He committed no sin, neither was deceit found in his mouth. When he was reviled, he did not revile in return; when he suffered, he did not threaten, but continued entrusting himself to him who judges justly. He himself bore our sins in his body on the tree, that we might die to sin and live to righteousness. By his wounds you have been healed. For you were straying like sheep, but have now returned to the Shepherd and Overseer of your souls. (1 Pet 2:21–25)

Surprisingly rare use of the song of the suffering Servant

As powerfully as this passage in Isaiah's prophecy portrays the sufferings of Christ, commentator Karen Jobes makes a surprising observation. She says that there are only six places in the New Testament that quote from this prophecy directly: Matthew 8:17; Luke 22:37; John 12:38; Acts 8:32–33; Romans 10:16; 15:21; and our passage 1 Peter 2:21–25.[8] Of these six,

8. Jobes, *1 Peter*, 192–93. In Matthew 8:17, it is Jesus's miracles of healing (and not his atoning sacrifice) that are said to be a fulfillment of Isaiah 53:4: "He took up our infirmities and carried our diseases." In Luke 22:37, Jesus quotes from Isaiah—"He was numbered with the transgressors" (Isa 53:12)—as the explanation for why his disciples

only two are used in reference to Jesus's suffering: Acts 8:32–33, which narrates Philip's encounter with the Ethiopian eunuch who happened to be reading from Isaiah 53, and this passage, 1 Peter 2:21–25.

Given this exegetical data, in addition to the manner in which Peter uses the image from Isaiah 53, it seems that the suffering of Christ is particularly important to Peter. Perhaps he sees his direct culpability in Jesus's suffering in light of his own, three-fold denial of Christ.[9] For Peter, this makes the unjust nature of Christ's passions that much worse. Not only was Jesus unjustly imprisoned and executed, but Peter was also one who abandoned and betrayed him in his moment of need, despite his previous adamancy that he would never do so. A proper understanding of Peter's relationship with Jesus, therefore, highlights how Peter sees the truly *unjust* nature of his suffering. For Peter, the epitome of the righteous sufferer is Jesus.

Believers as the suffering Servant

While it is obvious that Peter identifies Jesus as the suffering Servant of Isaiah 53, a careful analysis of his use of this prophetic passage demonstrates that he is also saying something more, profoundly more. Peter uses the passage very carefully, in a precise and technical manner. Exploring it in greater depth will prove to be immensely fruitful.

In 1 Peter 2:21, Peter says that Christians have been called to endure unjust suffering as exemplified by Christ. For this reason, we are to follow "in his steps." Astonishingly, if we are called to follow Christ, then the portrait of Christ as the suffering Servant becomes a portrait of the believer as well. In fact, Peter seems to have removed all features from the source-text of Isaiah that applies exclusively to Christ. *The effect of this allows the song of the suffering servant to be applied to the believer as well!*

In 1 Peter 2:22, he quotes from Isaiah 53:9: "He committed no sin, neither was deceit found in his mouth." Here, Peter tells the reader that Christ did not suffer due to sin but rather because he followed the will of God. Then, in 1 Peter 2:23, he gives a brief commentary of the previous verse with an extended application: in the midst of his sufferings, Jesus

---

are to sell their cloaks to buy swords. In John 12:38, the unbelief of the Jews is seen as fulfillment of Isaiah 53:1: "Lord, who has believed our message?" Finally, Romans 10:16 quotes Isaiah 52:7 and 53:1, whereas Romans 15:21 quotes Isaiah 52:15, both of which see Paul's ministry to the Gentiles as fulfilling prophetic prophecy.

9. Matthew 26:69–75; Mark 14:66–72; Luke 22:54–56; John 18:13–27.

did not strike back at his oppressors but rather entrusted himself to God. Thus, in his application of Isaiah 53:9 in 1 Peter 2:22–23, Peter portrays a morally upright servant who does not strike back against his oppressors. This is the ethical model of how we are to respond to our enemies during our own unjust suffering.

In 1 Peter 2:24, Peter quotes from two different places in the song from Isaiah. Specifically, he takes from the first half of Isaiah 53:12 ("He himself bore our sins") and from the last part of Isaiah 53:5 ("and with his stripes we are healed"), then places them together to create a new poetic line. In addition to his citation of Isaiah 53:12, he adds two additional phrases—"in his body" and "on the tree"—which are clearly references to the crucifixion. Since the unjust accusations against Jesus ultimately led him to a cross, it is possible that his followers may face the same fate. Whether a literal or figurative cross, readers are struck by the way that Peter connects the suffering of Christ to the suffering of believers. This is the sober reality that his readers need to know.

Isaiah 53:12, however, continues with the following phrase: "And makes intercession for the transgressors." Peter does not include this in his citation. I cannot help but think that the reason he did not include this is because Christ alone is the true intercessor for the unrighteous. As similar as our suffering is to Jesus, no one can effectually intercede for sinners but the one and only suffering Servant (1 Tim 2:5). It is true that the earlier phrase "he bore our sins" can only be applied to Christ as the one who atones for sins. But the addition of the two prepositional phrases ("in his body" and "on the tree") suggests that it may be an *actual physical* cross that Peter has in mind, and not the *atoning work* of the cross.[10] During ancient Roman times, it was possible for believers to suffer crucifixion on an actual physical cross as a result of their Christian confession, but their suffering would not atone for sins. The inclusion of the two descriptive phrases seems to refer to the physical cross as a means of a potential penal sanction believers might face, but the absence of the second half of Isaiah 53:12 suggests that Peter denies any atoning power in this potential crucifixion.

Peter also quotes from Isaiah 53:5: "And with his stripes we are healed." As before, what is missing is just as important as what is present.

10. As 1 Peter 3:18 shows, Peter does not reject the atonement: "For Christ also suffered once for sins, the righteous for the unrighteous, that he might bring us to God." He seems to maneuver around it in 1 Peter 2:22–25 so that the identity of the servant of Isaiah 53 can be applied to the believer in Christ.

The full text of Isaiah 53:5 says: "But he was wounded for our transgressions; he was crushed for our iniquities; upon him was the chastisement that brought us peace, and with his stripes we are healed." Peter only quotes the final phrase, leaving out the rich descriptions of Christ as the sacrificial substitute for our sins that also brings us peace. Again, why does Peter exclude the earlier portions of this text? The answer seems clear: only the sufferings of Christ have atoning value—ours do not. To make sure there is no misunderstanding, Peter only quotes what is needed for us to appreciate the sufferings of Christ as an example of what lies in store for believers.

Finally, in 1 Peter 2:25, Peter quotes from Isaiah 53:6: "For you were straying like sheep." Just like the other quotations, Peter mentions only a small portion of that passage. The full text of Isaiah 53:6 says: "All we like sheep have gone astray; we have turned everyone to his own way; and the Lord has laid on him the iniquity of us all." As straying sheep, we indeed "turned to our own way." Peter says, however, that because of the work of Christ, we have now "returned to the Shepherd and Overseer of [our] souls." What Peter fails to mention is the final description of our iniquity being laid upon the suffering Servant in Isaiah 53:6. Why? I suggest it is for the same reasons as those mentioned above. Only Christ can redemptively take on our iniquities. Such a description could not be applied to anyone else with the same atoning results. As great as Abraham, Moses, and David were, they could not atone for the sins of others, much less themselves. We too cannot atone for our own sins or that of anyone else. Our righteous suffering, regardless of how much it resembles that of Jesus, does not and cannot atone for sins.

In his use of Isaiah 53, throughout 1 Peter 2:22–25, Peter takes tremendous care by using specific portions of that prophesy for a specific purpose. By interweaving these selections, he crafts a glorious literary mosaic with a carefully designed message. The addition of the two prepositional phrases in 1 Peter 2:24 and the consistent removal of the atonement idioms (with the exception of "He bore our sins") creates a certain level of ambiguity as to whom Peter describes. Is it Christ, or is it the believer, since the description in 1 Peter 2:22–25 can fit either?

Peter excludes phrases that specifically refer to Jesus's work as a vicarious sacrifice in Isaiah's prophecy. There is no doubt that for Peter, the identity of the suffering Servant of Isaiah 53 is Jesus. His use and application of the prophetic text, however, leads to an additional layer of identification. Christ indeed is *the* suffering Servant of Isaiah 53, but

Peter seems to allude to more. Amazingly, he also seems to suggest that Christian believers are also to be understood as the suffering servant as a collective because of our union with *the* suffering Servant, Jesus Christ.[11]

The "Example" of Christ

This is to what we are called (1 Pet 2:21). Christ suffers as a result of his faithful obedience as the suffering Servant of Isaiah 53. Likewise, we also are called to suffer as a result of our faithful obedience to Christ-like discipleship. The "example" that Peter speaks of is a moral one, of which Jesus is the model. First Peter 2:22–23 clearly teaches this, but it says more than that. If Jesus were merely a moral standard to which we are called to measure up, then we would all fail, as no one can conform to such standards of perfection. If this were the case, then the call in 1 Peter 2:21 would not be a call of hope but rather a word of condemnation.

After observing how Peter carefully uses Isaiah's prophetic text, we can see further that the "example" that he mentions is not only a moral one, but also a historical-redemptive one. The life of Jesus as the suffering Servant is an "example" of what our lives will be like as well as what our lives should be like. His life was marred with unjust suffering, so we also will "share Christ's sufferings" by experiencing the same kind of suffering prior to any knowledge of glory at his return. This is the reality of our union with Christ.

Union with the Suffering of Christ

Throughout the first two chapters, I have referred to the fellowship that believers have with the sufferings of Christ as our "union with Christ." The importance of the doctrine of our union with Christ cannot be over-emphasized—in 1 Peter as well as the theology of the New Testament. It is not merely one doctrine among many, but the one concept that embraces the entirety of the redemptive work of God that extends from the eternal plan of salvation "before the foundation of the world" (Eph 1:4) to our eventual glorification (Rom 8:30). This union with Christ underlies every aspect of our redemption.

Although the actual phrase "union with Christ" does not occur in the Scripture, this mystical and Spirit-empowered bond between the

---

11. Karen Jobes reaches the same conclusion. See Jobes, *1 Peter*, 199–200.

Lord and his elect is a living reality, best expressed by the commonly used phrase "in Christ." This phrase is frequently used by Paul throughout his writings. One only need to count the numerous times it occurs in Ephesians 1:3–14 (over ten times!) to be impressed by the conscious effort that Paul makes to state the importance of our union "in Christ."

Union with Christ in Salvation

For Peter, this understanding of our union with Christ is the foundation of our salvation. Although the formulaic phrase "in Christ" is not as present in 1 Peter as it is in the writings of Paul, union with Christ is nonetheless the basis for every aspect of the doctrines of grace in this epistle.

In the previous chapter, we saw that it is through our union with the *resurrected* Christ that we receive the blessing of "resurrection-birth" (1 Pet 1:3). Prior to this, we were "dead in our trespasses and sins" (Eph 2:1). But now, because of our new-birth in Christ, we are "ransomed from the futile ways of our forefathers" (1 Pet 1:18), redeemed by "the precious blood of Christ" (1 Pet 1:19), and possess an inheritance that is "imperishable, undefiled, and unfading" (1 Pet 1:4). It is because of our union with Christ that we have a "salvation ready to be revealed in the last time" (1 Pet 1:5).[12]

The accomplished blessings that Christ merited in the cross and resurrection are no longer distant from us. It is very near us and, in fact, within us (Deut 30:14; cf. Rom 10:8) in the person of the Holy Spirit, who unites the believer to Christ. As John Calvin stated so succinctly and profoundly: "We must understand that as long as Christ remains outside of us, and we are separated from him, all that he has suffered and done for the salvation of the human race remains useless and of no value for us."[13]

---

12. It is significant to note how Peter seems to be influenced by the historical reality of the resurrection of Christ in his union theology (1 Pet 1:3); it is evident in his doctrine of the new-birth ("resurrection-birth" is the term that I used earlier), the Christian life ("living hope"), our inheritance as sons ("imperishable"), and the finality of the salvation blessings in the final day of glory. In *Resurrection and Redemption*, Richard Gaffin makes the case that Paul articulates the resurrection as the focal point in our union with Christ. A similar case can be made for the doctrine of union with Christ in 1 Peter.

13. Calvin, *Institutes*, 537.

Union with Christ in the Christian Life

It is remarkable that for Peter, the source of our salvation is also the source of our suffering. If we have a new life in Christ, what will our life before glory be like? According to Peter, life for believers and the ministry of the church will be like the life and ministry of Christ.

How does Peter describe the earthly life and ministry of Jesus? Suffering, then glory. I stated earlier that the suffering of Christ is part of how Peter understands the fulfillment of the Old Testament Scriptures (1 Pet 1:11). He also says that Jesus was "rejected by men" (1 Pet 2:4, 7) and that he was considered "a stone of stumbling and a rock of offense" (1 Pet 2:8). In 1 Peter 2:22–25, selected phrases are ascribed to Christ that describe the epitome of all righteous sufferers in the Old Testament Scriptures, the suffering Servant of Isaiah 53. Peter says that Christ "suffered once for all, the Righteous for the unrighteous" (1 Pet 3:18) and that he "suffered in the flesh" (1 Pet 4:1). Peter's readers never witnessed the actual sufferings of Christ (1 Pet 1:8); they could only have it preached to them. Unlike his readers, who lacked firsthand knowledge, Peter confesses that he was "a witness of the sufferings of Christ" (1 Pet 5:1), and Jesus is the centerpiece of his confession.

Since Jesus's life was marked by that movement from suffering to glory, a similar movement will characterize the life of those who are united to him by faith. In describing the suffering that Jesus endured on earth, John Calvin points out that not only was Jesus executed on a cross but also that "his whole life was nothing but a sort of perpetual cross."[14] This is most likely the reason why Jesus described the life of a disciple as "taking up his cross daily."[15]

Knowing the Suffering of Christ

Peter describes Jesus as the Son of God who came to his people only to be rejected by them, to be brutally and ruthlessly maligned. He was then beaten, battered, and bruised. He was sentenced to hang on a cross, and he endured penal sanctions for crimes he never committed. He came to save his people from their sins, to be their redeeming king, because he had a "great mercy" (1 Pet 1:3) for them.

---

14. Calvin, *Institutes*, 702.

15. Matthew 10:38; 16:24; Mark 8:34; Luke 9:23; 14:27.

His people, however, did not extend to him the prerogatives and blessings that he rightfully deserved. They accused him falsely of wrong-doings, humiliated him as he took his final walk to the "Place of a Skull," and sentenced him to an ignominious death. [16] And as he hung on the cross, the emblem of curse and condemnation (Gal 3:10), so frail and vulnerable, no compassion was extended to him—rather, he was ridiculed and persecuted all the more.

Even if Jesus had been guilty of violating the law of God, we would still wonder if this penalty fit the severity of the crime and have a modicum of sympathy for the extent of his suffering. What makes the sufferings of Christ so astounding (and gracious) is that he endured all this even though he was completely innocent. According to Peter, the witness, this was the life of Christ; it was harsh, brutal, and unjust.

As believers, we rejoice in our union with Christ as the foundation for our salvation. Our union with Christ is also the foundation for the Christian life. Peter tells us this new life is lived with a "living hope." This life of "living hope," however, is characterized by Christ-like suffering. By experiencing his sufferings, the very sufferings themselves become a blessing since they allow us to "conform to the image of the Son." [17] Growing in increasing conformity to the Son—and thus growing in a greater knowledge of him—is the highest goal for any Christian. What greater desire is there for a disciple of Christ but to grow in his likeness? This is why we rejoice in the doctrine of our union with Christ, both in life and in our salvation.

How much do we want to know Jesus?

Let me pose this question: how much do you *really* want to know Jesus? When we contemplate our growth into the image of Christ, we find deep comfort in our union with Christ, for in that image, we receive the rich blessings of redemption, which were accomplished by the Son and applied to us as believers. We rejoice to know that in Christ we are "elect," "sanctified," and "born again" (1 Pet 1:1–3). In Christ, we are given an imperishable, undefiled, and unfading inheritance; we are given a great salvation that is safeguarded for us and ready to be revealed in the last times (1 Pet 1:4–5). Notice the positive nature of the blessings associated

---

16. Matthew 27:33; Mark 15:22; John 19:17; cf. Luke 23:33.
17. Romans 8:29; cf. Ephesians 4:24; Colossians 3:10.

with this approach. Who would not want this? We all want to be effectually called, born again, justified, adopted as his children, sanctified, and transformed to everlasting glory (Rom 8:29).

What we do *not* want, what we lack the strength of heart and the intestinal fortitude to desire, is the *historical redemptive* reality in our union with Christ. From this approach, our union with Christ means that we "share Christ's sufferings" in addition to sharing his glory. There is no doubt that we do share and will share in the fullness of his glory. That will be a great and magnificent day! I look forward to it and I'm sure you do as well. But the *suffering* and *glory* are a package that cannot be separated because they come from the same divine source. Jesus knew both. To have one without the other amounts to an incomplete knowledge of Jesus because that was not the life that he lived. Let me I say this again: *that was not the life that he lived!*

His life was marred with rejection, ridicule, and persecution, even though he was faithful and true to his call and to the people of God. We are called to fellowship with Christ in his sufferings so that we may know the true Jesus, the whole Jesus, and the real Jesus. And because we know Jesus, we can indeed rejoice. If you take away this Christ-like suffering from the Christian life, ostensibly, you also take away any chance of knowing this "joy unspeakable" because we no longer can say that we know the source of that joy, the suffering of Jesus Christ. According to Peter, Christian joy is not found in the positive circumstances of life, in the abundance of material goods, or in the success of our professional, academic, or private lives. It is found in a pure and genuine knowledge of our blessed Savior.

As Paul states so powerfully as he contemplates the loss of all things for the sake of Christ: "I want to know him and the power of his resurrection, and *share in his sufferings*" (Phil 3:10). What an amazing statement of faith! What an amazing source of joy! We, too, can find it where we would never expect—in the midst of Christ's sufferings. To know Christ's suffering is to know Christ. To know Christ is the heart's desire of the Christian disciple. To know Christ is to know a "joy unspeakable."

A personal illustration

Let me provide an example from my own life. The Lord has been truly good to me and has blessed me in more ways than I can count. I have been happily married for many years to a wonderful and godly wife who is a daily reminder to me of the grace of God. The Lord has blessed us with six wonderful children who are steadily and faithfully growing in their love for the Lord. I graduated from seminary with a Master of Divinity degree and continued in my education, earning my second masters and my doctorate in Semitic languages and literature. I am now a professor of Old Testament at a prestigious reformed seminary in Washington DC, where I teach and train future leaders of God's church. During my entire education, I was fortunate to have studied under godly and knowledge-able instructors who have made a lasting impact upon my theological, spiritual, and academic growth. In addition to all this, I am an ordained Presbyterian minister and have served as a pastor for several decades. In 2004, the Lord opened up an opportunity for me to start a new church, which provided me with one of the greatest pastoral experiences I have known.

These are some of my accomplishments, and they are helpful to keep in mind if you want to know me. However, this synopsis does not tell of all the heartaches, the trials, and the pain that I have suffered throughout in my life—many of which are too painful to even mention here. These are still very much a part of who I am. As much as I would like to forget them, I cannot. Let me tell you a valuable lesson that I have learned over the years: I have had more failures than successes and more defeats than victories. This is not unique to my experience, and I have little doubt that this describes many of you as well.

If all you knew of me were those things that you can find on my *curriculum vitae*, then you really do not know who I am. That is only part of me—and truthfully, not even the most interesting parts. Unless you know the dark underbelly of my life, you will never know the real me. It is filled with sorrow; it is murky and at times very surprising. Yet it is still part of who I am. There are only a few who know this darker side of my life, and thus there are only a few who can say they truly know me.

Christ-like suffering is a blessing

Knowing me may not mean too much for most, but to know Christ is a different matter. We do not really know Christ until we know of his sufferings.

Regardless of how much Peter may redeem the virtue and value of Christ-like suffering, turning that suffering into a source of joy, it cannot compare with the joy that will be found in the last days. Peter himself acknowledges this when he says that you are to "rejoice insofar as we share Christ's sufferings," so that "you may also rejoice and be glad when his glory is revealed" (1 Peter 4:13). That final clause is better captured in the NASB, where it states: "You may rejoice with exultation." The NIV states similarly: "You may be *overjoyed* when his glory is revealed." [18] See also the KJV, where it says: "Ye may be glad also with *exceeding* joy." [19] These various English translations accurately describe that there is indeed joy when we experience Christ-like suffering, but it pales in comparison to the joy we will know when we experience "his glory."

All of this is true, and that day will be marvelous. In the meantime, we who fellowship with Christ in his sufferings do not need to wait in a state of misery and despair until that day when we share in his glory. We tend to see suffering as something negative that should be avoided at all cost. According to Peter, sharing in the sufferings of Christ is not a negative experience, while sharing in his glory is a positive one. Sharing Christ's sufferings is not to be considered bad, while sharing Christ's glory is considered good. For Peter, sharing Christ's sufferings is *good*, but sharing Christ's glory is *better*. There is a relative degree of blessing in both, not a contrasting and dramatic antithesis.

This is similar to the way that Paul describes death in Philippians 1:21–23. He begins with the famous line, "For to me to live is Christ and to die is gain" (Phil 1:21). The following two verses provide commentary. "To live is Christ," suggests that Paul's earthly life is filled with "fruitful labor" (Phil 1:22), productive and meaningful ministry to the people of God, specifically to the Philippians, for whom he realizes that he must remain "in the flesh on their account" (Phil 1:24). Although he does not state it here explicitly, it seems clear that Paul derived much joy from his gospel work.

Yet Paul also acknowledges that he is "hard pressed" (Phil 1:23) between two choices. Shockingly, his options are living or dying. For most people, this is not a hard decision to make. Most would quickly and easily choose life over death in a heartbeat. Most people would see life (even life in ministry) as good and death as bad. Paul, however, was not like most

18. Emphasis added.
19. Emphasis added.

people. He, like Peter, was driven by a different set of values. For Paul, the choice was not between a negative option (death) versus a positive one (life). The choice was between a *good* blessing (life) and a *better* blessing (death). What is surprising and radical is the fact that Paul calls death not only a good option, but an option better than life. He even says it is "far better" than life! Why is death *far better*? For Paul, this is true because only in death will he "depart and be with Christ" (Phil 1:23).

What determines and defines the nature of true joy for faithful followers of Christ *is Christ*. It is not health, wealth, or anything else. We constantly look for joy in the wrong places, so we must reiterate this again and again. For Paul, life in the rigors and heartaches of gospel ministry is a precious good, but to "share his sufferings" (Phil 3:10) is by far better.

This was also the case for Peter. Peter's desire, above all else, was to know Jesus in his fullness. If that meant that he must know the agonies of Christ in his sufferings, then so be it. His instruction reflects a profound humility and deep spiritual wisdom. It is clearly counter to our natural instincts regarding pain and suffering.

Of course, Peter would not wish pointless suffering upon any believer. For that reason, he provides a new insight into our pain. To *fellowship with Christ in his sufferings* is most definitely not pointless. Sharing in the sufferings of *the* unjust Sufferer defines our pain, gives it purpose, provides it with meaning, gives us godly instruction, and transforms our perception of it.

The reality is that we will face hardship (remember, "don't be surprised" in 1 Pet 4:12). When we do, it need not be a crisis that utterly destroys us. By the extraordinary grace of God, our Christ-like sufferings can be an invitation from our Lord to grow into a more intimate knowledge of him. When we endure unjust suffering, it truly is a blessing because it is a time of intense and meaningful fellowship with Christ *in his sufferings*. It is true that to share in his glories is a greater blessing, but don't be fooled into thinking that being rejected and ridiculed for the sake of Christ is a state of misery to be pitied. According to Peter, to share in the sufferings of Christ is a blessing as well. Truly, I do not know a greater source of joy in a fallen world than this.

Preach, Teach, Share the Suffering of Christ

All Christian leaders desire for God's people to have joy in life. They passionately pray for it, work towards it, and humbly offer it through the ministry of the Word. However, they are not always pragmatic about how this joy should be gained; they do not teach ways to gain joy that can be found in a secular world or within a sinful lifestyle separated from Christ. As many can testify, truly meaningful joy cannot be found in these places because joy does not exist there. The truest and richest experience of any substantial joy cannot be found in a place, a situation, or a concept. It is not gained by a large income, promotion in professional status, a great vacation, or even a happy and healthy family. It cannot be bought or bartered. It is found exclusively in a person, in *the Person*. It only comes by knowing the Lord of suffering and glory. It comes by knowing Jesus Christ.

According to Peter, it is not a generic knowledge of Christ that brings this blissful delight; even demons have this knowledge (Jas 2:19). Ironically, the apostle teaches us that this heavenly joy can come only by sharing in the unjust sufferings of Christ as well as his magnificent glories. His unjust sufferings and a "joy unspeakable" are conjoined as a collective whole that cannot be separated. The flipside, then, is also true: the inability to share in this Christ-like suffering may bring temporary respite, but ultimately leads to eternal wrath and condemnation.

Necessity of sharing the Suffering of Christ

We live in a fallen world, where the people of God are verbally and even physically abused by the world around them. Imagine the comfort that can be given if they see that they do not suffer alone. Not only do they share in the sufferings of other believers, but they share in the sufferings of their Savior. Jesus is no longer a God who is distant. He is "near you" (Deut 30:11–14; cf. Rom 10:3–5). Indeed, he is Immanuel, "God is with us" (Isa 7:14; Matt 1:23). More than that, he "sympathizes with our weakness" (Heb 4:15), and now we can say that we have "fellowship" with his suffering. This is what Peter says in our theme passage, 1 Peter 4:12–13.

Imagine if such a message were withheld from believers. The tragic reality is that it may indeed be absent in the church today, and the opportunity to provide profound comfort to many is lost. Christian suffering is rarely seen as a form of fellowship with Christ. It is more commonly

explained as a necessary but unfortunate experience that we must tolerate until we gain the glory of Christ. As true as this may be, this view
does not portray Christ-centered suffering the way that Peter sees it—as
a source of joy. We hear about Jesus's sufferings that he endured throughout his life and then distance ourselves from it. After all, we instinctively
avoid anything that pains us. The suffering of Christ—so powerfully and
eloquently portrayed in the Easter season—remains separate from the
sufferings of his people. Believers do not fellowship with Christ in his
sufferings because that invitation is not made by God's church, either in
Sunday school classrooms or the pulpit.

Practicality of sharing the Suffering of Christ

Consider the preaching of the Word. Regardless of one's philosophy of
ministry, all church leaders would agree that preaching is one of, if not
the central ministry of the church. What are pastors to preach? In the
words of Paul, it is "him we proclaim" (Col 1:28). Nothing more and *definitely* nothing less. Peter acknowledged that the central message of the
Old Testament is the *sufferings* and the glory *of Christ* (1 Pet 1:10–11; cf.
Luke 24:26–27). Therefore, it seems more than reasonable to conclude
that to preach from the Holy Scriptures is the same as to preach Christ in
his sufferings as well as his glories.

What is heard from the pulpits in the churches of America? The messages will vary. Many churches provide instructional preaching that helps
us with the daily challenges of life, such as how to live as loving spouses
or parents, ways to manage anger and finances, strategic initiatives on
renewing our cultures, etc. These are worthwhile and commendable messages to communicate from the pulpit of God's church, *as long as they first
and foremost hold to the primary message of preaching Jesus Christ.* In fact,
it is only when we understand that we are "resurrected-born" believers
in Christ (1 Pet 1:3) who are now dead to sin that we can truly love our
spouses and raise our children in a godly way. It is only when we see ourselves as spiritual "foreigners" and "resident aliens" in Christ that we can
combat the values of our secular world and live as citizens of the kingdom
of God (Phil 3:20). Indeed, it is only when we remember that in Christ we
are called to a war that is against "rulers, against the authorities, against
the cosmic powers over this present darkness, against the spiritual forces

of evil in the heavenly places" (Eph 6:12) that we can overcome the evil one and his devilish schemes that can lead us astray.

There are social concerns in the United States that weigh heavily upon us: racial tensions, immigration concerns, marital issues, teen crises, violence in the public arena, and sexual promiscuity, just to name a few. I sympathize with churches that desire to address these important matters head on from the pulpit and through ministry programs. I fear, however, that this is done at the expense of preserving the central place of Christ in both the preached message and in the life of the church. The result is to reduce this wonderful message of the gospel of a suffering Savior to nothing more than a moral and/or social imperative.

This leads me to ponder many questions. In the name of being relevant to such needs, I wonder if the church is capable of addressing the issue concerning the suffering of God's people. Has the church succumbed to preaching a message that does not address the heart of the matter, which is offering hope to those whom Jesus loved so dearly that he shed his own blood? Have we reduced the message of Christ to nothing more than clichés, religious catch phrases, and moral platitudes, and forgotten the profound, theological foundation of our hope in times of tremendous suffering and pain? Are we merely encouraging people to "try harder" when they are struggling without clear direction as to what they are to "try harder" doing? Are we so focused on the future glory that awaits us that we cannot offer hope in the here-and-now?

Why would the world oppose a moral message from the church? Is this not the same message that you can also get from any non-Christian organization? It is very possible that the reason the church in the United States does not face hardship for the sake of Christ is because we have come to reflect so much of the values of the secular world around us so that we are perceived more as an ally than a threat. Has the church embraced a preached word that can be aired on any daytime talk show and be accepted with little resistance? Many "sermons" in the church remind me of the comment made by the great American reformed theologian, B. B. Warfield, in his critique of the moralistic preaching of the revivalist Charles Finney from the Second Great Awakening in the nineteenth century: "It is quite clear that what Finney gives us is less a theology than a system of morals. God might be eliminated from it entirely without essentially changing its character."[20] I cannot think of a more condemning comment to make towards a preacher of the gospel than this.

Was this the way the early Christian leaders preached Christ? No! They boldly and courageously preached Christ crucified and resurrected; they did not reduce him to a mere moral standard that they needed to obtain in their own strength. As a result, they were imprisoned countless times (Acts 4–5, 16), beaten (Acts 5:40), and even stoned (Acts 7:59; 14:5).

Stay the course

The task before modern preachers today is the same as the task of the ancient ones: preach Christ. Preach him, because salvation is found in no one else, "For there is no other name under heaven given among men by which we must be saved" (Acts 4:12). It is against the spirit of the religious consciousness in our contemporary society to preach a message that exalts only one worldview as the one and only truth, as opposed to a worldview that is one of many truths. Only the Christian gospel of Christ has the "power unto salvation" (Rom 1:16; cf. John 14:6); all other religious instructions lead to wrath and condemnation.

Stay the course and preach Christ, because by embracing by faith a suffering Messiah, God's people have access to a rich and full knowledge of their Savior. Those who consider suffering futile can now find hope. However, all this can come only if the Christian church remains faithful to her commission and proclaims the Savior who suffered for them and will raise them to eternal glory. To not preach the sufferings of Christ is to not be true to the central message of the Scripture. The most practical message that we can give for those living in a fallen world is the gospel of Jesus Christ.

We must keep in mind that many of the social concerns of our day are manifestations of sinful humanity. The solution to these matters is not found in a message that merely provides strategic ways to control it. Sin cannot be controlled by positive thinking, social reforms, political agendas, judicial legislations, or sheer will power. Our society is filled with sin because it is filled with sinners. Their sinful nature must be transformed. That transformation only comes when we acknowledge our fallen nature and thus our need for a Savior who gave his life as a substitute for us. We

20. Warfield, *Perfectionism*, 193.

do a gross disservice to those who come into the church overwhelmed with the destruction of sin and its resulting guilt by withholding the life-saving power of a Christ-centered message. They do not need to be told that they can have their best life now, nor do they need to be given three steps on how to overcome sin—as if overcoming sin can be achieved in such a simplistic manner. This might be what people *want* to hear, but what they *need* is something radically different. They need Christ. Many in America (and other parts of the world) do not want to be told that they are sinners who face eternal condemnation. They scrutinize and ridicule churches that hold to such "negative" and archaic views. That is the price we pay for committing to a biblical vision of reality. We do not preach Christ because this is a *comfortable* message. We preach Christ because this is a *comforting* message.

In recent days, there has been a growing surge of interest in the church to focus on the centrality of Christ and his gospel as the core of the preached word as well as the Christian life. I rejoice in this and thank the Lord for raising godly leaders who have committed to such a glorious message. I continue to press this issue in the hope that not only pastors but also Christians in the pews will offer godly counsel to each other with the same Christ-like saturation. What a glorious thing that would be. I pray for it. I pray for it indeed.

Joy Unspeakable in Life's Worst Scenarios

Imagine someone who suffers indescribable pain—mourning of loved ones, betrayal by close friends, rejection from family members. All this due to no fault of their own. Imagine now this person with a supernatural joy, a "joy unspeakable." That is what 1 Peter 4:12–13 offers.

What follows in the next several chapters is a brief portrait of some of the great heroes of the faith who suffered excruciating pain in situations similar to ones that many face today. Chapter 4 will take us to the book of Psalms, which records many laments that so characterize our fallen world. These psalms of lament capture much of the heartache that we endure in our world today, but they also lead to wondrous joy and praise that is found in the Lord of the Psalms. Chapter 5 will introduce us to Job. If anyone in the Holy Scriptures exemplifies a life of unjust suffering, it is Job. He knew the fallen nature of our world well, but it brought him to a joy unspeakable in Christ. Chapter 6 will describe an incident in the life of the patriarch Abraham when he was asked to do the unimaginable, to sacrifice his only son Isaac. Of course, we know that his son was spared, but through that incident he experienced an agonizing sorrow that only mourning parents can know. Chapter 7 will take us to the prophet Hosea, a faithful husband who suffered the agony that came from an unfaithful spouse. That is something many in our society have come to know. According to Hosea, the Lord was no stranger to this pain as well. Chapter 8 will conclude our brief journey by taking us to the ministry of the prophets. They shared a profound and powerful message to a people they loved only to be alienated and rejected by them—like so many pastors and Christians today, like Christ himself.

The fiery trials that Christians endure for the sake of Christ can be a source of Christian joy. Again, not in spite of our suffering, but because of them. How? Because when we suffer for the sake of Christ, we share in the sufferings of Christ. And to know his sufferings is to know him wholly—in his sufferings and glory. Nothing is more valuable than this. To know Jesus is to have a "joy unspeakable."

4
_____

Joy in Singing Songs of Lament

Let me remember my song in the night; let me meditate in my heart.

Psalm 77:6

I MET ROGER AND Julie many years ago at a time in their lives when things were going very well for them. They were faithfully serving in their local church and happily married with a wonderful daughter, Anna. Having a child brought them so much joy that they desired for more. In His divine providence, however, the Lord did not see fit to provide another child. They endured painful years of failed attempts, hours in prayer, and tragically, many miscarriages. Sadly, many have shared in the pains of such barrenness and loss.

One incident in particular remains vivid in my mind. Another couple in the church was blessed with twins, but quickly faced a monstrous choice. Due to complications in the womb, they were told that only one child could survive, and they needed to decide which. They discovered a medical procedure that could preserve the life of both unborn infants, but at huge risk to them as well as the mother. Facing an impossible decision, by faith they chose to take the risk. The church community was informed of this and spent countless hours in prayer on their behalf. By God's mercy, both infants and the mother were saved, and the entire church rejoiced with them.

Roger and Julie did so also, but not without grief. Several weeks earlier, Julie had received word that she was pregnant with their second child, which brought tremendous relief and joy for both of them. However, after having carried this infant for several months, Julie lost the child, in spite of every medical procedure taken in an attempt to save this life. I'll never forget the night when Roger prayed, "Why, O God, did you save their child, but did not save mine?" We prayed together in tears. I had no answer.

Roger and Julie are not the only ones to know sorrow. I have known it as well. My father was one of the greatest men I have ever known. For me, no one exemplified hard-work, dedication, loyalty, and sacrifice more than he did. He also epitomized what it meant to be generous. Anyone in monetary need who knew him came to him, and he was always more than willing to help out. I often felt that many took advantage of his generosity by asking him for money to start new business ventures. It was frustrating, but he gave anyway. Whenever our family went out to a restaurant for a meal and met another family that we knew, my father always took the initiative to pay for their meal. That was the kind of man he was, and I loved him dearly.

On January 8, 2013, my father suffered a heart attack. He died that day and went to be with the Lord. That was one of the most difficult times of my life. I felt his absence immediately. Even though he lived thousands of miles away, my father called me regularly. He checked to make sure that my wife and children were doing well, and that I wasn't in financial need (he was convinced that, as a pastor, I was always living just above the poverty line). He was always filled with proverbial wisdom and anecdotes of life experiences. Those chats are now over. When he died, I felt alone.

After several years, you would expect the pain of his death to have abated. It is better, but my heart remains heavy. Small things trigger memories of my father and I am easily reminded of him. When I watch a young dad walking his child to school or a father and son playing baseball at the park, I immediately think of him. I can't even watch a greeting card commercial without being reminded of him. At every one of my children's graduation or school events, I have the same thought—"If only my father were here; he would be so proud of these kids." Since his death, Father's Day has never been the same, and I face it with mixed emotions. During such moments, I find myself fighting off uncontrollable tears.

I have yet to overcome this sense of loss. I loved my father, love him still, and not a single day has gone by that I have not thought of him.

Psalms of Lament

Sorrow. Confusion. Abandonment. Loneliness. Life in our fallen world is commonly marked by these powerful and painful experiences. Roger and Julie know this. I know this, and I have little doubt that you may know people like them as well. Perhaps you are such a person—one who knows all too well that our lives are filled with tragedies that bring about these desolate feelings. This is a universal truth that requires no proof, upon which all peoples, nations, and religions agree.

There is a collection of ancient poems that capture the cry of the human heart: the book of Psalms. For millennia, the one hundred and fifty poems that compose this biblical book have been loved by God's people because they minister to the whole person, to both our intellect as well as our hearts. It is a book that I turn to regularly.

The psalms are filled with rich theology and profound images of the Lord, which remind us that a sovereign God is the one who is working for our good. They also capture the wide range of emotions that we experience throughout the course of our lives. Perhaps no other book in the Holy Scriptures better exemplifies what it means to have a "heart for God and a mind for truth"[1] than the psalms. John Calvin referred to the Psalms as a "mirror" of the soul:

> There is not an emotion of which anyone can be conscious that is not here represented as in a mirror. Or rather, the Holy Spirit has here drawn to the life all the griefs, sorrows, fears, doubts, hopes, cares, perplexities, in short, all the distracting emotions with which the minds of men are wont to be agitated.[2]

Since the days of the great German scholar Hermann Gunkel, the classification of each psalm into genres has become standard in studies of the psalms.[3] Within the biblical psalter you find hymns of praise, songs of thanksgiving, and even instruction in wisdom. In this chapter, we will focus on *psalms of lament*.

Although there are psalms that celebrate the times when God brings blessings to his people, there are also psalms that record their sorrows, as

1. This is the vision statement for Reformed Theological Seminary.
2. Calvin, *Commentary on the Book of Psalms*, xxxvi–xxxvii.
3. Gunkel, *Introduction to the Psalms*. Gunkel identifies six major types (hymns, royal psalms, enthronement psalms, communal complaints, individual complaints, and individual thanksgiving psalms) as well as a number of smaller genres and mixed types.

they struggle through the difficulties of life. These psalms of lament are more than the cries of an ancient people enduring times of destruction and darkness. In many ways, they capture the same kinds of experiences that we know well today.

Comfort from Laments

The psalms of lament are filled with vivid images that remind us that our days are not always filled with blessings and pleasure, but instead are more often filled with confusion and anguish. Yet they offer great comfort. First, they remind us that we are not alone. We are not created to be on our own, no matter what we may think or say. Suffering in isolation is a lonely experience that intensifies our pain. These laments, however, tell us that we are never alone. Not only do we have a merciful God who hears the cries of his people, our God is a "Father of mercies and God of all comfort, who comforts us in all our affliction, *so that we may be able to comfort those who are in any affliction, with the comfort with which we ourselves are comforted by God*" (2 Cor 1:3–4).[4] There are actually communal laments, intended to minister to an entire community of believers who struggled with similar issues we struggle with today. These poems allow believers to "weep with those who weep" (Rom 12:15) and to ponder upon their pain within a God-centered context.

Second, these laments remind us that there is nothing unusual or sinful in experiencing sorrow. There is a mindset in the Christian church that says we should not be struggling with pain or distress. Those who do so are viewed as spiritual deviants, ridiculed for their lack of faith in the Lord. The rationale is that if one truly believes in Jesus, they should only know happiness and joy, whatever their circumstances. These laments correct this faulty line of reasoning and show that to struggle with pain, doubt, or sorrow is not antithetical to a Christian life. The laments permit believers to suffer without the fear of being condemned.

Third, these laments provide a voice for our pain. We sometimes experience anguish that is too deep to describe. When asked, "How are you doing?" we do not know how to respond. We often answer with a mechanical, "I'm okay," which usually conceals our true emotional struggle. Frequently, the intensity of our pain is excruciating, to the extent that it leaves us in a state of emotional and spiritual "groaning" (Rom 8:23). We

---

4. Emphasis added.

want to share our pain, we *need* to share our pain, but we are unable to speak of our pain. We are encouraged to pray to the Lord, but our senses are immobilized during those agonizing times. For the mute sufferer, these psalms of lament provide what they desperately need—a voice to express their agony. For the broken and destitute, these laments give them a lyrical setting to verbalize their pain. Sufferers are finally given a voice, and it is directed to the one and only person who is their help.

Fourth, these psalms allow us to continue in worship while we suffer. Because of their liturgical use, the laments are not merely cathartic expressions of misery. They do not vent just for the sake of relieving pent up, negative emotional energy. They are a collection of elegant and heartfelt *prayers* that have been scripted for the sufferer; they reflect a real state of misery and allow us to pray directly to the Lord, to communicate to him the tragic matters of our lives, and to appeal to him for deliverance. We are free to enter into a place of worship and to bring our sorrows with us through the laments. A pleasant demeanor is not a prerequisite for proper worship. These laments allow us to bring our brokenness to the Lord in prayer as an act of worship while still in our sorrows, and to remind us of his mercy and grace towards us. Without them we do not have the means to bring our heartbreaking cries to the Lord.

Knowing the impact of a fallen world upon his people, the Lord provides these psalms to minister to us during our times of peril.

An Ironic Book of "Praises"

Given the enormous amount of comfort that these lament psalms have to offer, it is tragic that they are not more widely celebrated within the church. They are not commonly incorporated in the liturgy of worship, and even more rarely preached. Psalm 22 will get its due recognition during the passion season, but that is about it. The psalms are most commonly used as a call to worship, to begin the formal public worship of God. Given this very limited use, the average church attendee may inaccurately think that psalms of praise compose the majority of the biblical Psalter. Jewish tradition even entitles the book of Psalms as "the Book of Praises." In actuality, there are more psalms of lament than any other kind of poem in the biblical psalter. If the title of the Psalter is intended to reflect the majority of the type of poems found within it, then "the Book of Praises" is an ironic title; it should be called "the Book of Laments and Sorrows" instead.

We try to avoid pain

There are reasons why the laments are not as popular as their uplifting counterparts—they remind us of what we desperately try to avoid. The psalms of praise are wonderful in that they teach us a simple yet important fact that we should never forget—our blessings are from the Lord, so he is worthy of all our praise. In light of all that we suffer in a sin-infested world, we must intentionally and aggressively maintain a hope that can only be found in the sovereign Lord. Psalms of praise help us do that.

Walter Brueggemann comments that while it is admirable that the church fights to sustain hope in a fallen world, this is not the reason why these "sad songs" are overlooked. In a most compelling statement, he says:

> It is a curious fact that the church has by and large continued to sing songs of orientation [psalms of praise] in a world increasingly experienced as disorientated. . . . It is my judgment that this action of the church is less an evangelical defiance guarded by faith, and much more a frightened, dumb denial and deception that does not want to acknowledge or experience the disorientation of life. The reason for such relentless affirmation of orientation seems to come not from faith, but from the wishful optimism of our culture. Such a denial and cover-up, which I take it to be, is an odd inclination for passionate Bible users, given the large number of psalms that are songs of lament.[5]

No one desires to be in pain; no one wants to be reminded of their sufferings. Even Jesus requested that the "cup" of the cross pass before him, if that were at all possible.[6] For this reason, Brueggemann's comments are not merely an insightful observation on the structure of the psalms, but also a helpful reflection of the human psyche. By primarily using psalms of praise, we give the impression that this is the way life should be and thus encourage people to avoid and/or deny the horrors found in everyday life.

5. Brueggemann, *Message of the Psalms*, 51–52. What I have been referring to as "hymns" and "psalms of praise" Brueggemann calls "psalms of orientations." Also, "psalms of lament" he calls "psalms of disorientation."

6. Matthew 26:39; Mark 14:36; Luke 22:42.

The bulk of our lives are not filled with marvelous events that lift up our souls. The stark reality is that there are often times of discouragement and suffering, and we constantly struggle with dissonance and incoherence. Perhaps this is why there are so many psalms of lament—they capture an emotional state that all people know well, regardless of who they are, where they are, or even *when* they are. Though these psalms were written millennia ago, they still capture the misery of life in our contemporary world. These experiences of pain are not ones that we wish to remember, and we attempt to avoid them by avoiding these laments.

Consider the contemporary praise songs that are popular in the worship of the modern church. I cannot think of one that captures the brokenness that is such a hallmark trait of our lives. Many classic hymns found in traditional hymnals frequently express the depth of Christian theology and the blessed life as disciples of Christ, but rarely do they lead God's people to meditate on their sorrows, a state that is undoubtedly prevalent in the hearts of people as they enter into any given public worship setting.

As he mourned the death of his adult son, Nicolas Wolterstorff states:

> I tried music. But why is this music all so affirmative? Has it always been like that? . . . I have to turn it off. There's too little brokenness in it. Is there no music that speaks of our terrible brokenness? . . . Is there no music that fits our brokenness? The music that speaks about our brokenness is not itself broken. Is there no broken music?[7]

By being ignored, these psalms of lament have been functionally "de-canonized," and their identity as "God-breathed" as well as their usefulness (2 Tim 3:16–17) are largely disregarded.[8] In essence, the abandonment of the psalms of lament is not an act of faith and trust, but rather one of unbelief. We cannot comprehend that the Lord would bring trials upon his people and we attempt to "wish away" this theological and emotional discord by ignoring anything that reminds us of them. More explicitly, we simply do not trust that the Lord is greater than our pains. Suffering often blinds us so that we forget theological truths and

---

7. Wolterstorff, *Lament for a Son*, 52.

8. This notion of a practical "de-canonization" of particular portions of the Word of God is taken from class lectures of Dr. Tremper Longman in his courses on the Old Testament poetical books.

the reality that Jesus is the Lord of blessings *and* sorrows. He knew both and calls us to know them as well (1 Pet 3:9).

While the desire to avoid dark times is understandable, the inclusion of such psalms is intended to remind us of what we want to forget, and to help us face what we do not want to confront. The psalmists who recorded their laments did not do so with a complaining heart, like Israel in the wilderness. Rather, they made desperate and prayerful cries to the Lord, appealing to his sovereign mercy and strength. Only by embracing our personal heartaches and lifting them to the Lord can we begin to understand them, possibly appreciate them, and ultimately give thanks for them. Thus, to embrace and sing these laments is a bold act of faith and trust in the Lord because he is indeed greater than even the most intense and excruciatingly painful experiences (Jer 32:17, 27).

Movement from Lament to Praise

While the psalms of lament are the most common type of psalm, the book of Psalms is not exclusively a collection of dark and depressing poems. There are psalms of praise that celebrate the blessings that we graciously receive from the Lord. There are also psalms of thanksgiving where we thank the Lord for his provision of victory and deliverance through our dark times. These praises remind us that there is a hope that can be found in the midst of our tragedies. In spite of what we may see, think, or feel, the Lord has not abandoned us and works for our good. Thus, as dominant as these laments are within the psalter, the overall message of the psalms is one of high exaltation of the Lord. This movement from lament to praise can be observed within individual psalms as well as in the overall organization of the book of Psalms.

Movement within the psalm of lament

There are two parts in the general structure of a psalm of lament. First, there is a "plea" section, where the psalmist describes his dire circumstances and makes an intimate, heartfelt petition before the Lord. It is clear that the psalmist is in desperate need of help that no mere man can provide. He requires supernatural intervention, so he makes an impassioned plea for the Lord to engage in his life. The nature of this plea varies, depending on the circumstances that the psalmist is facing. There are times when he is burdened with guilt and thus confesses sins that he has held within himself (e.g., Ps 32; 51). At other times, he cries out for the Lord to defend his cause against his enemies (e.g., Ps 27). Regardless of the situation, the psalmist knows that the resolution to his suffering is beyond his abilities. He needs the Lord, and thus urges God to act.

However, the psalm does not remain a sorrow-filled cry. In the second half of the lament, there is a sudden, striking transition, where the tone and heart of the psalmist takes a radical turn to "praise." Here, a huge burden has been lifted from the psalmist, and his dark and desperate laments have now become an uplifting and glorious exaltation to the Lord. Sorrow may be how these days begin, but that is not how they end. It is not clear what has brought about this transformation—perhaps a change in his circumstance, a resolution to his crisis, the defeat of his enemies, etc.[9] It is enough that the psalmist is given a venue to unload his thoughts in honest pleas and heartfelt prayer directed to the Almighty God, who sincerely and willingly hears them.

Movement within the book of Psalms

This movement from plea to praise can also be seen in the overall organization of the book of Psalms. Many scholars have observed that the majority of the psalms of lament are found in the earlier part of the psalter. After the introductory Psalms 1 and 2, the majority of psalms in the first half of the psalter are psalms of lament. For example, consider the following:

- How many are my foes! Many are rising against me; many are saying of my soul, there is no salvation for him in God. (Ps 3:1–2)

- Answer me when I call, O God of my righteousness! You have given me relief when I was in distress. Be gracious to me and hear my prayer! (Ps 4:1)

- Give ear to my words, O LORD; consider my groaning. Give attention to the sound of my cry, my King and my God, for to you do I pray. (Ps 5:1–2)

9. See Futato, *Transformed by Praise*, 18–20, for a few other explanations of this transition.

- Be gracious to me, O LORD, for I am languishing; heal me, O LORD, for my bones are troubled. My soul also is greatly troubled. But you, O LORD—how long? (Ps 6:2–3)

- O LORD my God, in you do I take refuge; save me from all my pursuers and deliver me, lest like a lion they tear my soul apart, rending it in pieces, with none to deliver. (Ps 7:1–2)

As forebodingly as the book of Psalms begins, it most definitely does not end this way. As there is a radical transition within any given psalm of lament, there is also a similar transition as we move further along the psalter. The book ends with the highest concentration of praise in the entirety of Scripture with the "Hallelujah" Psalms, 146–150. Each of these psalms begin (and often end) with the exalted line "Hallelujah," which means, "Praise Yahweh."[10] The crescendo of praise climaxes with the apex of praise in Psalm 150, where each poetic line begins with that phrase "Hallelujah"—Praise Yahweh.

The people of God who had been in mourning and lament for so long have been introduced to the Lord and his messiah (Ps 2:7) throughout the psalms. As we grow in our understanding of the universal reign of the Lord over all of creation, our thoughts focus upon him, and so we are led away from our troubles.

What brings about this transition is not necessarily a change in our situation or even a resolution to our conflict, but an adjustment in our perception. When we look upon our plight, we are naturally burdened with doubt, loneliness, and sorrow. When we look towards our God most high, however, we realize that he is greater than any of the hardships that have troubled us. As the psalms close, we are called to praise the Lord along with "everything that has breath" (Ps 150:6), as all of creation joins together to sing a majestic anthem of praise.

Thus, the book of Psalms is appropriately named "the Book of Praises" by the Jewish rabbinic tradition. The *quantity* of laments cannot outweigh the *quality* of praise when such praise is directed towards our living and loving God. As the people of God, our lives will not ultimately culminate in lament, but eternal praise of our great God and Savior Jesus Christ.

---

10. Psalm 145 is entitled "A Song of Praise," which is a translation of one Hebrew word *tehillâ*. This is the only psalm in the biblical psalter that is given this title of "Praise."

Prophetic Psalms

I have described how the psalms of lament and the book of Psalms as a whole transition from lament to praise. Although the ancient poets may have suffered through an initial time of sorrow, they eventually turned their gaze upward to the Lord "who [is] enthroned in the heavens" (Ps 123:1). As they do so, their life experiences, marked only by suffering earlier, end on a note of celebrative adoration of God.

There is, however, a deeper and more meaningful message in the laments than merely knowing that "the sufferings of this present time are not worth comparing with the glory that is to be revealed to us" (Rom 8:18).

David the Prophet

Current studies in the psalms have shown that they were received by the New Testament writers as yet-to-be fulfilled prophesies.[11] In other words, they were not merely ancient poems that described the cries and praises of people from long ago. They foretold of a coming messianic son of David, who would sing these songs in a way special and unique to him.[12]

For this reason, David was seen by the New Testament writers not only as the primary author of the psalms, but as a prophet (Acts 2:29–30), or one who possessed a prophetic function.[13] There are texts within the Old Testament that already suggest this prophetic role for David. For example, 2 Samuel records the final words of David, calling them "the oracle of David, the son of Jesse, the oracle of the man who was raised on high" (2 Sam 23:1). The word translated as "oracle" (Hebrew word *ne'um*) is strongly associated with prophetic revelation, occurring countless times in prophetic texts.[14] Nehemiah 12:24, 36 also refers to David as

11. In the centuries prior to the days of the Jesus (i.e., Second Temple Judaism), many Jewish writings also show an identical understanding of the prophetic nature of the psalms and of David. The most famous support for this is a line from a copy of the psalms found among the Dead Sea scrolls, which states: "All these [David] spoke through prophecy, which was given to him by the Most High God" (11QPs^a 27.2–11).

12. Psalm 2:2, 7; 110:1; cf. 2 Samuel 7:14; 1 Chronicles 17:13.

13. For verses that describe David as a prophet, see Acts 1:16; 2:25, 34; 4:25; Romans 4:6; 11:9.

14. The prophetic word *ne' um* also occurs in Psalm 110:1.

"a man of God," which is a title frequently used for prophets.[15] The New Testament writers, therefore, are taking this clue from the Old Testament and applying it to the best-known of the Davidic materials—the book of Psalms.

Psalm 110 best illustrates this prophetic function of David. According to the gospel writers, in Psalm 110:1, David refers to his future royal descendant as "lord" instead of the expected title of "son" because he recognized that this future "lord" of David is superior to him.[16] The gospels make it very clear that this future Davidic messiah is Jesus Christ. It is uncertain if David consciously had the doctrine of the incarnation in mind, but this does not deter from the reality that David knew the hope of Israel rested upon the coming of an ideal "lord"—one who shared a striking similarity to the divine Lord himself.

Lessons from Luke 24

The transition from lament to praise becomes even more significant when we realize that not only Psalm 110 but also the entirety of the biblical psalms can be seen as anticipating the coming of Jesus. In Luke 24, two disciples who had followed Christ are now leaving the city of Jerusalem to the small town of Emmaus. On their journey, they encounter a man who is, surprisingly, unaware of the past week's events concerning their teacher, Jesus of Nazareth. They share how they had believed him to be the coming messiah who would restore Israel to her former days of glory. Instead, he was executed and hung on a cross, suffering a shameful and humiliating death before the known civilized world. Thus, they are on the road, presumably heading home, discouraged and disillusioned with following what seemed to be a self-declared, presumptuous king. Unbeknownst to them, the man whom the men encounter is the resurrected Christ, the true messianic fulfillment of the Scriptures. Jesus rebukes these two men for being "foolish" and "slow of heart to believe all that the prophets had spoken" (Luke 24:25). Jesus reveals to them that the Christ had to "*suffer* these things and then enter into his *glory*" because he fulfills "Moses and all the prophets," meaning "all the Scriptures."[17]

---

15. Deuteronomy 33:1; Judges 13:6, 8; 1 Samuel 2:27; 9:6; 1 Kings 13:1–31; 17:18; 2 Kings 1:12; 2 Chronicles 25:7, 9.

16. Matthew 22:42–45; Mark 12:36–37; Luke 20:42–44.

17. Emphasis added.

Jesus even "interpreted to them in all the Scriptures the things concerning himself" (Luke 24:26–27). Later that same day, Jesus has a second
meeting—this time with his disciples—where he gives to them the same
teachings: everything written in the Law and the Prophets and Psalms
(i.e., all the Scriptures) are fulfilled in the suffering and glory of Christ
(Luke 24:36–53), to which they are eye-witnesses.

The magnitude of Luke 24 for biblical interpretation cannot be overstated. Though much can be said, for our purposes we will focus on three
points:

1. *The message of the Scriptures*: In the encounters on the road with the
   two men and later with his disciples, Jesus refers to "all the Scriptures." Whereas in his meeting on the road to Emmaus he used the
   reference to "Moses and all the prophets," with his other disciples,
   he used a fuller reference to the Law of Moses and the Prophets and
   Psalms.[18] In either case, these are references to the entirety of the
   Old Testament canon, not merely parts of it.[19]

2. *The message of the Scriptures is ultimately about Jesus*: There is a
   unity to the message of the Scriptures that is found in the person
   and work of Jesus Christ. This "Christo-centric" interpretation is
   not optional nor should this be seen as an academic exercise. For
   the well being of his people, God intends us to understand that the
   final message of the Scriptures is realized in Jesus Christ. Notice the
   response of the two men when they realize the true meaning of the
   Scriptures: they say rhetorically, "Did not our hearts burn within us
   while he talked to us on the road, while he opened to us the Scriptures?" (Luke 24:32).

18. It should be pointed out that the English translations of Luke 24:44 include a
definite article prior to "Psalms," reading "the Law of Moses and the Prophets and *the*
Psalms," whereas in the Greek text, such an article is absent. In other words, Jesus did
not envision a three-fold Old Testament canon, but rather two (Moses and the Proph-
ets/Psalms). This suggests that the Psalms were seen as an extension of Old Testament
prophecy, confirming our earlier suggestion that there was a prophetic understanding
at the time when the psalter was received by the New Testament writers.

19. The Rabbinic Old Testament canon is organized into three sections—the Law,
the Prophets, and the Writings. At the time of Jesus's meeting with the disciples, the
textual evidence in the New Testament generally supports a two-fold division of the
Law and the Prophets (see Matt 5:17; 7:12; 11:13 [in reverse order]; 22:40; Luke 16:16;
John 1:45; 13:15; Acts 13:15; 24:14; 28:23; Rom 3:21). It would seem that the rise of
this third section was a much later development in the formation of the Old Testament
canon. For more information on this topic, see McDonald, *Biblical Canon*.

3. *Jesus in his suffering and then his glory*: The text states in two places that the Scripture-based message of Christ is specifically concerning his "suffering" and his "glory" (Luke 24:26, 46). This transition from "suffering" to "glory" is reminiscent of the redemptive flow in the book of Psalms. Amazingly, this is also how Jesus summarizes his own life. He even specifically mentions the book of Psalms in Luke 24:44. It is as if the book of Psalms is a poetic summary of the ministerial career of its subject, the true messianic Son of David.

Luke 24 is not the only time in the New Testament when we are told that Christ is the fulfillment of the Scriptures. Peter says much the same in 1 Peter 1:10–11:

> Concerning this salvation, the prophets who prophesied about the grace that was to be yours searched and inquired carefully, inquiring what person or time the Spirit of Christ in them was indicating when he predicted the sufferings of Christ and the subsequent glories. (1 Pet 1:10–11)

This is also the message in many other passages:

> Do not think that I have come to abolish the Law or the Prophets; I have not come to abolish them but to fulfill them. For truly, I say to you, until heaven and earth pass away, not an iota, not a dot, will pass from the Law until all is accomplished. (Matt 5:17–18)

> If you believed Moses, you would believe me; for he wrote of me. (John 5:46)

> When they had appointed a day for [Paul], they came to him at his lodging in greater numbers. From morning till evening he expounded to them, testifying to the kingdom of God and trying to convince them about Jesus both from the Law of Moses and from the Prophets. (Acts 28:23)

> But now the righteousness of God has been manifested apart from the law, although the Law and the Prophets bear witness to it—the righteousness of God through faith in Jesus Christ for all who believe. (Rom 3:21–22)

The True Singer(s) of the Psalms

Getting back to the book of Psalms, what this Christocentric approach tells us is that the ancient poets were not merely describing the suffering and triumphs of a group of ancient Israelites, the nation of Israel, or even David himself. It is true that David wrote many of these psalms for his own heartfelt purpose, and that they were used by the people of Israel as their hymnbook in their temple worship; the psalms of lament were their cries of sorrow during desperate and dark times. However, given the significance of Luke 24 and other similar passages, our understanding of the message of the Psalms *cannot* stop there.

Through Luke 24, we can see that the cries of pain found within these psalms are not merely those of the psalmist but also anticipatory of the sufferings of Christ. Think again of Psalm 22:1, "My God, my God, why have you forsaken me?" These are the words of David during an unspecified time of despair in his life when the presence of God seemed disturbingly absent. Since these are the words that Jesus uttered as he hung on the cross, atoning for the sins of his people, it becomes clear that Psalm 22—*like all the other psalms of lament*—do not merely describe the sufferings of David but also, more properly, describe the sufferings of Christ. The *true* singer of the psalms of lament is Jesus Christ, the *true* Son of David, and these are *his* cries.

Yet we cannot stop there either. Because of our living union with Christ, not only do these laments describe the agonies of Jesus, but they also describe the agony of his people.

Thus, there is a three-fold understanding of the identity of the voice in these psalms. First, they are the words of the ancient poets during critical times in their lives. Second, they are the words of Christ as he suffered for the sake of his people. Third, these are also the words of those who are in Christ as they participate and "share in the sufferings of Christ" (1 Pet 4:13).

Fellowship with Christ in the Psalms

Consider this three-fold understanding as we sample a few lines from several psalms of lament.

The betrayal of a friend

David was certainly justified in uttering the words of Psalm 55:12–14:

> It is not an enemy who taunts me, then I could bear it; it is not an
> adversary who deals insolently with me, then I could hide from
> him. But it is you, a man, my equal, my companion, my familiar
> friend. We used to take sweet counsel together; within God's
> house we walked in the throng.

The historical books describe a time when David was betrayed by
those closest to him. Think of his dealings with King Saul. David was
favored and beloved by the king. He was brought into his royal court and
treated as a son. However, once Saul turned against the Lord and failed to
submit to his divine kingship, the Lord chose David as the new sovereign,
a "man after his heart" (1 Sam 13:14). Saul did not accept David as this
newly appointed monarch and turned against him, attempting to take
his life on numerous occasions. Saul, a onetime father-figure and royal
shepherd, now turned against his sheep and hunted him down.

Did David commit a sin that brought about this jealousy and danger? Had David been disrespectful to the king or offended him to such a
degree that justified his peril? Was David in need of rebuke regarding his
relationship with the king? Certainly not. The only reason for the wrath
of Saul was David's dedication to the Lord; he was a man after God's own
heart. The result of David's faithfulness, however, was not blessings of
riches, fame, or glory. He was hunted by one whom he loved so dearly.
Sadly, this was not the only time that David faced betrayal. Think of Absalom, Joab, or Adonijah. Any of these situations (or possibly all of them)
could have inspired the agonizing words of Psalm 55.

The betrayal that David experienced is a shadowy reflection of that
of the true David, Jesus Christ. Consider Judas Iscariot. He was one of the
original twelve disciples of Christ; he was a close companion, a trusted
friend. Many would have been envious of his position as one of the twelve:
to live with the incarnate God-Man, to hear his teachings, and to witness
the wondrous miracles—feeding of massive crowds, healings, and even
the dead returning to life. Judas saw all of this and more. Yet it was this
trusted friend who schemed Jesus's arrest. It was this beloved companion
who took advantage of the grace of Jesus and used it for his own greed. It
was this "familiar friend" (Ps 55:14) who shattered the heart of Christ for
something as mundane and meaningless as money.

Moreover, Judas was not the only one guilty of this. Jesus had eleven other disciples who seemed dedicated and committed to his cause—particularly Peter. When Jesus pronounced his coming execution, Peter and the others swore that they would not abandon him when he was most vulnerable and in need; they swore that they would remain with him to the point of death.[20] Sadly, we know how this ended. Jesus was arrested, tried, and ultimately executed; he was alone and humiliated without any support from his disciples. They were well meaning, but when it mattered the most, they sought their own safety at the expense of their dear Master-Teacher.

We cannot stop with the twelve disciples. After all, are we any different? John 1:11 tells us that "He came to his own, and his own people did not receive him." Jesus was not only abandoned by his closest followers, but even by the people for whom he gave his life. The message of the Christian gospel is built upon the foundational truth that we are unable to save ourselves. Even after our regeneration into a new creation (2 Cor 5:17), we still struggle with sin. After his conversion, Paul is appalled by the sinful tendency that he sees within himself to continue in the sin that he does not desire to do (Rom 7:15). It is truly amazing to realize that Jesus gave his life on the cross knowing that we would still sin against him after our conversion! Did Jesus know betrayal, abandonment, and desertion? Indeed, he did.

Have you known these negative experiences as well? Have you been betrayed by a family member or a close friend? As the psalmist says, we expect malice and hate from our enemies. That is why they are our enemies. When we are forced to interact with them, we are cautious and on guard. We never take their words at face value and even take extra precautions not to expose ourselves to them. We are selective about what thoughts we reveal to them and do not reveal our true intentions.

With a friend, all this changes. We leave ourselves open, free, and exposed. We share with them our most intimate and cherished thoughts, dreams, and passions, and they do the same with us. After all, "a friend loves at all times, and a brother is born for adversity" (Prov 17:17), and "a man of many companions may come to ruin, but there is a friend who sticks closer than a brother" (Prov 18:24).

Now imagine that this "friend" turns against you. He violates you in a way that is unfathomable. The specific way in which this happens

---

20. Matthew 26:33, 35; Mark 14:29, 31; Luke 22:33.

is not as significant as the fact that your faith has been abused, leaving you humiliated and emotionally/physically devastated. If the damage were limited to something physical as a broken bone, time would heal it. Violation of trust is something that lingers and rarely heals no matter how much time passes. All this because of a so-called friend.

If you know such pain and sorrow, you are not alone. You are invited to join in communion with *one* who knew the ultimate betrayal. You are called to know the agonizing pain of Jesus Christ himself. You are called to know Christ when he was at the lowest point of his life, when his closest friends abandoned him.

Divine abandonment

Moments of betrayal were not the only time of sorrow for David. He knew the excruciating pain of losing a child, the deafening silence of loneliness, the torment of enemies, and even defeat in battle. Perhaps it was one of these times that caused him to write the well-known cry of dereliction in Psalm 22:

> My God, my God, why have you forsaken me? Why are you so far from saving me, from the words of my groaning? O my God, I cry by day, but you do not answer, and by night, but I find no rest. (Ps 22:1)

Or in Psalm 10:

> Why, O LORD, do you stand afar off? Why do you hide yourself in times of trouble? (Ps 10:1)

Or even Psalm 13, which is particularly troubling:

> How long, O LORD? Will you forget me forever? How long will you hide your face from me? How long must I take counsel in my soul and have sorrow in my heart all the day? How long shall my enemy be exalted over me? (Ps 13:1–2)

Notice the source of David's lament. Not only is he troubled by his enemy (Ps 13:2), not only is he dissatisfied with his own self-counsel (Ps 13:2a), but he also recognizes that the true origin of his troubles is the Lord himself (Ps 13:1a). The Lord is the one who has "forgotten" him, and David says that this feeling of abandonment has been going on "forever." Bad enough as it is that the Lord has *passively* forgotten him, what is worse is that he says the Lord is *actively* "hiding" his face from him (Ps 13:1b)! David has nowhere else to turn but to seek counsel from within himself and to struggle with watching his enemies victorious at his expense.

Jesus clearly knew what it meant to be abandoned by his own heavenly father. As he hung on the cross, burdened with the sins of his people, we know that he was "stricken, smitten by God, and afflicted" (Isa 53:4). On the cross, Jesus was the object of the divine wrath of his father, not the recipient of his divine favor. Although the gospels record Jesus uttering the words of Psalm 22 only, we do not need to be so limited in our understanding of the laments as to conclude that this is the only psalm that records the lament of Christ. Every lament in the book of Psalms are properly and ultimately the lament of Jesus. Therefore, the abandonment of David in Psalms 10 and 13 above is also anticipatory of Christ on the cross.

For those who believe in the sovereignty of God, these specific laments are truly difficult. We may not be surprised by the betrayal of our friends since they are sinners; we may even expect it. But we are traumatized when we consider that it is the almighty God himself who has left us in our most desperate times of need. During these times of abandonment, our doctrine of divine sovereignty becomes harder to comprehend. After all, if he is in complete control, then not only does God have the power to pull us out of our crisis, he has the authority to design our lives in a way to avoid it before it ever happened. The distinction that God "allows" trials to occur as opposed to "decree" them gives little comfort, since neither view resolves our experiential conundrum—we suffer, and that suffering could have been prevented by God.

Although we know in our theology that this sense of divine abandonment is not a genuine reality, the experience of it is real nonetheless. Since Christ cried out the words of Psalm 22:1 and presumably could have chosen to use any of the psalms, these words do not only belong to the psalmist. They are not only Jesus's words either. In Christ, they are also ours, and we now have the opportunity to share in a similar experience with Christ in our union with him.

Ceaseless weeping

The psalmist knew pain that brought on times of endless tears, as we find in Psalm 42:

My tears have been my food day and night. (Psalm 42:3)

The image here is of a man in the midst of a troubling time. The cause of his lament is not mentioned, but it is clear that his circumstance is a source of pain for him, so much so that it causes him to weep without ceasing. That is what this line describes—day and night, tears that fall from the eyelids along the perimeter of his face and down his cheeks until they work their path into his mouth. The suffering that the psalmist endures has killed any sense of hunger or thirst. He is numb to his internal desires, and his only source of sustenance is his ceaseless tears.

Jesus also knew mourning that brought tears that would not cease. He wept at the death of his friend Lazarus (John 11:35). He wept for the rebellious heart of the city of Jerusalem and longed to see her repentance (Luke 19:41). He wept knowing that a time would come when he would be separated from his heavenly father and receive his divine wrath for the sake of his elect (Heb 5:7; cf. Luke 22:41–44). Jesus wept, and he did so often.

Perhaps you also have known such times—a memory or thought so intense that whenever it comes to your mind, you are led to tears. I know such pain. This psalm has been one that has given me much comfort over the years. The death of my father was (and remains) particularly difficult for me. Although I find great comfort in knowing that he is with the Lord in glory, I seem unable to overcome this overwhelming sense of loss.[21] Since the day he went to be with the Lord, not a single day has passed that I do not think of this dear man. He was no saint. Like all of us, he had flaws that were irritating. Yet he was significant to me and taught me much about the values of life. As I think of him each day, I weep; I am heartbroken and fight to maintain a sense of hope.

I have found tremendous joy and comfort in reading Psalm 42 because it reminds me that there is nothing wrong with mourning the death of loved ones, even those who now rest with Jesus. The psalmist knew this, but more importantly, so did Jesus. He also knew such tears, and I fellowship with him by weeping with him who wept and continues to weep.

---

21. Chapter 6 will focus on this in greater detail, from the perspective of the parental loss of a child.

Songs about Christ, to Christ, with Christ

Betrayal, abandonment, and sorrow-filled tears that never cease—these are a few themes taken from a few laments. These psalms are filled with vivid images that remind us that our earthly days are going to be filled with suffering such as these. If you are struggling with the guilt of your sins, then there are definitely psalms for you, psalms that lead to repentance and joy in the forgiveness of your sins.[22] And if you are suffering for no particular wrong that you have committed, though you have remained faithful in the Lord, then there is still a great source of joy and hope for you in the psalms of lament.

The laments not only provide a description of the pains of God's people; they describe the sufferings of our messiah, Jesus Christ. Not only has he redeemed us from the *penalty* of sin and death, he has redeemed us also from the *pains* of sin and death. By subjecting himself to the sufferings of our fallen world, he has properly defined the expectations of a life of discipleship. Accordingly, this life will be filled with Christ-like sufferings. As we share in that suffering, we can say that we know the heart and mind of our Savior that much more. I cannot think of a greater joy than to say that we know Jesus. Joy is no longer measured by success or failure, wealth or poverty, fame or ill repute, or health or sickness. It is gained by knowing the Lord of suffering by sharing in his suffering. It is gained by knowing the Lord of joy.

Jesus is the true singer of the psalms, even the psalms of lament. However, our union with Christ not only identifies Jesus as the true singer of the psalms, but we, his chosen people, can now sing these psalms of lament as well. We do not merely sing *about* Jesus, nor do we merely sing *to* Jesus. By the grace of God, we sing *with* Jesus. In our heavenly union with Christ, his songs become our songs. In Christ, we have joined a glorious choir with Jesus as our choirmaster, in which we sing psalms that reflect and meditate upon the sorrows that we endure during times of darkness. Because it is Christ who knows such agony better than any of us and suffered in a way that no one else has, because our suffering brings us into a closer bond with the experiences of Christ, through these laments we can say that we "fellowship with Christ in his sufferings" (1 Pet 4:13).

If you were to meet Roger and Julie today, you would never have suspected that they knew such pain so many years ago. They are a family

---

22. Psalms 32; 38; 51; 130.

at peace and content with the blessings of the Lord. Little Anna is growing in her love for the Lord, maturing into a beautiful, godly young lady. Ask them about that time of trials and you might be surprised at what they say. The loss is real and the pain does not ever go away. Yet, they are thankful—not in spite of what they endured, but because of it. In an extraordinary way, their testimony is filled not with self-pity or agonizing pain; rather, they speak of the glory and mercy of their loving and gracious God and they want others to know how amazing he is. They have followed the path of their Savior and gone from lament to praise.

As for myself, I am going through a similar journey. I rejoice to know my father is with Christ in glory, and I struggle to know how to refer to him—what tense do I use? As a Christian, I know that "whoever believes in [Jesus], though he die, yet shall he live" (John 11:25). In a very real way, the gospel tells me that I can speak of my father in the present tense, "he *is* alive, he *is* in peace, he *is* resting with Jesus." At the same time, I speak of him in the past tense: "he *was* in pain but no longer, he *knew* agony but no longer, he *was* frail and weak but no longer." I praise God that, in Christ, we can speak about our deceased loved ones in this way.

I have also found comfort from the psalms. I have thought of Psalm 116 often since the death of my father, especially verse 15, "Precious in the sight of the LORD is the death of his saints." I rejoice that he rests in glory with the Lord, but it would have meant so much to me had he lived to see the publication of this book. His death was profoundly precious to me, and I truly and unreservedly rejoice to know that his death was also precious to the Lord. In this sense, I weep as Jesus once wept (John 11:35). If it happens that I mourn his passing for the remainder of my earthly life, then I am thankful. Not only is glory waiting at the end of this sorrow, but I mourn with him who mourned the death of my beloved father even more than I do.

Suffering is all around us. It is part of the nature of a world affected by sin. Grieving loved ones is one form of this. Our Savior will soon bring a new heavens and new earth where there is no longer any death and suffering. Until then, he has provided a special blessing, the Lord's songs of lament. Our sufferings are his invitation to join him in singing these songs: "At night, his song is with me" (Ps 42:8). I thank God that he has given to us a "song in the night" (Ps 77:6; Job 35:10). The psalms of lament are for people who suffer as he did—they are for us. The loss is real and the pain does not ever seem to go away. Yet we can be thankful, not in spite of what we endure, but because of it.

In an extraordinary way, our testimony can be filled with neither self-pity nor meaningful agony. Rather, we can speak of the glory and mercy of our loving and gracious God and even want others to know how amazing he is as well. We have followed the path of our savior and gone from lament to praise. In that sense, we also have come to a deep and intimate knowledge of Jesus and can rejoice in that.

5

Joy in the Perfect Storm of Job

Naked I came from my mother's womb, and naked shall I return. The LORD gave, and the LORD has taken away; blessed be the name of the LORD.

Job 1:21

LET ME BEGIN BY stating the obvious: the book of Job is disturbing. Not only are the linguistic issues in Job among the most difficult within the Hebrew Bible,[1] it also deals with one of the most perplexing theological and philosophical questions that has burdened mankind for ages— "Why do we suffer?" To this question, Nicolas Wolterstorff says:

> To the 'why' of suffering we get no firm answer. Of course some suffering is easily seen to be the result of our sin: war, assault, poverty amidst plenty, the hurtful word. And maybe some is chastisement. But not all. The meaning of the remainder is not told us. It eludes us. Our net of meaning is too small. *There's more to our suffering than our guilt.*[2]

It is easy to think that all suffering is a result of our sins. A quick read through the book of Job, however, immediately rids us of that simplistic conclusion. If there were a book of the Bible that obliterates any

1. Emphasis added. There are more *hapax legomena* (words which occur only once in the Bible) and rare words in the book of Job than any other biblical book. This makes translation of it very challenging.

2. Wolterstorff, *Lament for a Son*, 74.

notion that suffering is a direct consequence of sin only, it is the book of Job. It confirms the shocking truth that it is possible (even probable) that we will suffer even though we are obedient and faithful to the Lord. Remember that Peter says such suffering is honorable.[3]

This is not what we would expect. In our limited way of thinking, we often believe that suffering is for the immoral and faithless, that it only happens to bad people. If we suffer a tragedy of some kind, it is because we did something wrong. That makes sense—it seems fair and we can understand it—painful, but reasonable. Once we admit that suffering can still result despite our faith and obedience to the will of God, we become unsettled, to say the least. It seems to make no sense. This conflict cultivates one of the driving themes within the book of Job. The inability to find a resolution to it frustrates all of the characters involved.

The quest for this answer—to know why the innocent and faithful in the Lord suffer—may be the foreground of the book. The real issue, however, is one of wisdom. Who is truly wise? The discussion on suffering provides the context for this larger and more important question. In a roundabout debate (Job 4–27), Job's three friends (and Job himself) offer their unsophisticated words of wisdom to explain why we suffer. Elihu, a curious character who comes late into the discussion, throws his thoughts in as well (Job 32–37). At the end of their deliberations, we find that no one has a satisfactory answer. It takes the Lord to finally step in and silence the speakers, showing them that they are all more foolish than wise (Job 38–42).[4] By the end of the book, we are left with

3. 1 Peter 2:20; 3:14, 17; 4:14–16.

4. To humble Job in particular, the Lord appeals to his acts of creation and challenges him to explain their mysteries—if he is able (Job 38–42). Job could not. I find it curious that the Lord would appeal to creation to illustrate how little Job knows when so many in the church today seem so dogmatically confident that their view of creation (i.e., interpretation of Gen 1) is the only correct one. There exists such fervor over this issue that it continues to divide the church and break bonds of Christian fellowship. For whatever reason, many believe that only a literal, twenty-four-day interpretation of Genesis 1 is biblically acceptable, in spite of solid exegetical and theological evidence to suggest otherwise. If indeed Job is a book of wisdom, perhaps the lesson we can learn is this: it would be wise for us to explain creation with more care and sensitivity than holding onto opinions with a militancy that quickly condemns opposing views as unorthodox. The Lord refers to creation to humble Job because no one can fathom all its complexities and wonders. So how can we be so bold as to condemn the views of other godly interpreters who are just as committed to the authority of Scripture when they offer alternative views? As the Lord said, "Where were you when I laid the foundation of the earth? Tell me, if you have understanding" (Job 38:4). There are certain principles that cannot be (and should not be) compromised (e.g., creation ex nihilo,

no clear answer. Job is never informed about the heavenly dialogue that took place between God and an "accuser,"[5] and provided less information than his readers!

We do, however, learn a more important truth: it is wise to trust in the Lord, who comes as a Job-like sufferer—in Jesus—in order to turn our suffering into an amazing source of joy.

Whenever we think of the epitome of the righteous sufferer in the Old Testament, immediately, we think of Job. Unsurprisingly, when I shared with people that I was writing on this theme of the righteous sufferer, without fail, everyone presumed that there would be a section dedicated to Job. The fame of Job is so well established that even those outside of the church know of him and the heartbreaking events that nearly ruined his life. For obvious reasons, those who endure similar tragedies can identify with him.

What we see in Job, however, is not merely an account of a man whose misfortunes provided instruction for ancient Israel but rather the expectation that there will come a greater Job along with a community of Job-like sufferers.

In Defense of Righteous Suffering

The book of Job can feel like an odd fit in the Old Testament canon. Much of the Scriptures tells of the sins of the people of God and the hardships that they face because of it. The sinfulness of humanity is made clear as early as in the days of Cain and Abel, where Abel, though innocent of any wrongdoing, was killed by his brother. Sin progressed into the days of Noah, where "the wickedness of man was great in the earth," and "every intention of the thoughts of his heart was only evil continually" (Gen 6:5). God makes it clear that the wickedness of humanity is the reason for the destructive floodwaters.

As soon as the earth was repopulated by Noah and his sons, humanity sinned against the Lord again, building a tower to the heavens so that they could "make a name" for themselves (Gen 11:4). Even the patriarchs

---

historical Adam and Eve, historical fall from grace, rejection of macro-evolution on the origins of humanity, etc.), yet within these parameters, there should be a gracious spirit concerning other factors (e.g., age of the earth, order of the creation days, etc.) that are examined more on exegetical-theological grounds than tradition.

5. More will be said regarding this figure below.

Abraham, Isaac, and Jacob demonstrated lack of trust; manipulation and deception rooted in sin brought about dreadful consequences.

An examination of the nation of Israel also exemplifies this sinful tendency. As soon as the Israelites received the blessed law of the Lord at Mount Sinai, they immediately rejected their redeeming God and worshiped false images; this led to devastating results (Exod 32–34). Their rebellion and lack of faith led them to wander an additional forty years in the wilderness instead of receiving the land of Canaan without delay (Num 13:1–33; Deut 2:14–15).

The book of Deuteronomy outlines a series of covenant curses (Deut 28) that would afflict ancient Israel if they violated the Lord's commands. Their history is a testament to their ineptitude, their violation of the covenant, and the realization of those covenant curses. Although there was one generation—led by Joshua—that trusted the Lord, the next generation after them abandoned Him and worshipped the false gods of the Canaanites (Judg 2:8–11).

Eventually, Israel asked for a king "like all the nations" (1 Sam 8:5, 20), thus rejecting the Lord as their true sovereign (1 Sam 8:7; 10:19; 12:12). This led to the oppressive reign of Saul. David and Solomon followed and established a brief time of monarchical solidarity, but their sins (particularly Solomon's) led to even greater misery and eventually the division of the kingdom. Thereafter, both the northern and the southern kingdoms fell into idolatry and moral collapse. This led to the ultimate form of suffering—the exile.

Simply put, Israel sinned, and therefore, Israel suffered.

How does Job fit in all this?

The majority of the historical books of the Old Testament chronicle the failures of God's people who suffer miserably because they failed to obey God's laws. Among this canon is the book of Job, which portrays a man who endured unimaginable pain. Unlike Israel, however, his suffering was unmerited. Job did not overtly violate the law of God, yet suffered nonetheless.

In many ways, Job can be seen as the Old Testament defense for the legitimacy of righteous suffering. Many find such a concept difficult to grasp because of the Scripture's clear and unmistakable assertion of the sinfulness of humanity. Paul says that "all have sinned and fall short of the glory of God" (Rom 3:23). This is not limited to any particular ethnicity; sin is without prejudice, and thus "Jews and Gentiles alike are all under sin" (Rom 3:9).

The book of Job does not contradict the doctrine of the total depravity of man. The "wages of sin is death" (Rom 6:23), and the message of the gospel has remained the same, from the days of Adam to our day—*salvation is by grace alone, through faith alone, in Christ alone, as revealed in the Holy Scriptures alone, for the glory of God alone!* Job, like all sinful men, was in need of such salvation and received it by the sovereign mercy of God. There is no other foundation other than the gospel that allows the Lord to declare Job as righteous, as he does in Job 1:8: "Have you considered my servant Job, that there is none like him on the earth, a blameless and upright man, who fears God and turns away from evil?" Those who embrace Christ by faith also share in this free gift of eternal life. Therefore, there is "now no condemnation for those who are in Christ Jesus" (Rom 8:1).

We live, however, in a fallen world that is polluted with sin. Even though the *penalty* of sin has been defeated by Christ, the *power* of sin remains, and by faith in Christ, we fight to overcome it each day of our lives. Job reminds us that suffering is a regular experience in a fallen world. Where there are sinners, there are also those who have been sinned against. There are those who sinfully hurt others and there are those who have been sinfully hurt. It is true that pain and suffering are a result of our sins, but to attribute all suffering as a direct consequence of *one's own* sin is wrong. This is one of the words of wisdom from the book of Job: it is possible to be a *righteous* sufferer.

Argument of the three friends

Consider the dialogues found between Job and his friends in chapters 3–37.[6] The rationale of Job's friends is as follows: if you sin, then you

6. The book of Job can be subdivided into three parts that compose a single historical drama. Thus, we can see these three subdivisions as acts of a play. Act 1 (chapters 1–2) introduces us to the protagonist Job as a righteous sufferer. Act 2 (chapters 3–37) begins with a long cry of Job, where he mourns the day of his birth (Job 3). This is followed by his dialogue with his three friends: Eliphaz the Temanite, Bildad the Shuhite, and Zophar the Naamathite (Job 4–27). After each friend gives his explanation of why Job is suffering, Job gives a lengthy response. There are three cycles of this give-and-take. Curiously, Zophar does not take his third opportunity to speak to Job. Chapters 28–31 is a beautiful and moving poem by Job that praises the value of wisdom. This

will suffer; if you are suffering, it is because you sinned.[7] Their word of counsel to Job is that since his sin is the cause of his suffering, he needs to acknowledge this sin, confess it, repent, and the Lord will restore him.[8]

There is much truth to their counsel—if Job had indeed sinned. Therein lies the weakness in their argument. Job is not suffering because of any sin he committed (Job 31), and this makes his friends' analysis of his struggles naïve and unsophisticated. Of course, there are nuances and subtleties to their argument which cannot be addressed here. Ultimately, these men were rebuked by the Lord for making such simplistic and false conclusions that gave Job more pain than resolution (Job 42:7–9).

Argument of Job

What is surprising is that Job agrees with the line of reasoning of his three friends. The issue for Job was that he did not sin, yet he suffered intensely nonetheless. Therefore, Job concludes that God is unjust and demands an audience with him so that he can state his case.[9] Neither Job nor any of his friends are wise enough to explain the cause of his suffering. Where Job's friends falsely see all suffering as a direct result of one's own sins, Job falsely sees the Lord as unjust for causing suffering upon him in his innocence. In this way, Job utilizes the same type of syllogistic logic that his friends practiced in reverse—Job did not sin; therefore, he should not suffer.

Lessons from the book of Job

There are incredible, necessary words of wisdom that can be found in this book. Without them, I fear that much of the Christian counseling in our day would easily sound like Job's three friends, where people in agony are told to repent of a sin that they never committed. Counseling then becomes an endless and futile search for an unacknowledged immorality

---

is followed by the speech of the enigmatic Elihu, who repeats many of the arguments made by the previous group of three (Job 32–37). In the finale, Act 3 (chapters 38–42), we finally hear from the Lord himself in his whirlwind speeches.

7. Eliphaz in Job 4:6–11; 5:2–7; 15:20–35; Bildad in Job 8:3–4, 11–21; 18:5–21; Zophar in Job 11:11; 20:5–29.

8. Job 5:8–16; 5:23–27; 8:5–7; 11:13–20; 22:22–30.

9. Job 7:1–10; 9:11–14; 10:6–7; 12:1–25; 13:14–15; 19:4–22; 21:22–26.

that leaves both the counselor and the counselee in a continuous state of frustration.

We need wisdom in order to effectively minister to those who are suffering righteously. This begins by acknowledging that righteous suffering is a spiritual reality that many experience. The book of Job makes an indispensable contribution to the ministry of Christian counseling by providing godly insights into the nature of righteous suffering and the potential dangers of assessing it incorrectly. Here are a few thoughts to consider as we begin our discussions on this book of wisdom.

1. *Righteous suffering is a reality.* It is possible to suffer for righteousness' sake (1 Pet 3:14). We should not be surprised by this type of suffering (1 Pet 4:12), as this is more common than we think. A correct assessment makes all the difference in times of crises. The book of Job illustrates the frustration that results when suffering is misdiagnosed as a result of sin. The opposite is just as damaging—to attribute righteous suffering to one who is in fact guilty of sin. It takes tremendous wisdom, dialogue, humility, and courage to distinguish between the two, but this distinction needs to be made.

2. *Righteous suffering can lead to sin.* When we suffer righteously, we must not see it as an injustice of God like Job did, but trust in the Lord and his sovereign wisdom. Job's suffering could have led him to experience a profound blessing, or it could have led him to wallow in self-pity and make false accusations against the Lord for treating him unfairly. Job chose the latter. In his misery, he *judged* the Lord rather than *trusting* in him. Job's faulty reasoning misleads him to a false understanding of God. Although he initially reacts to his afflictions by blessing the Lord and trusting him, he is unable to sustain this because he does not accept the reality that the innocent can suffer righteously. This, in turn, led to his sin, his arrogance before the Creator.[10] More than a resolution to his pain and an answer

---

10. In light of his innocence, Job 42:6 is truly perplexing: "Therefore I [Job] despise myself, and repent in dust and ashes." If Job was truly innocent in his suffering, then why does he repent? Job 42:10 adds to the puzzlement. After Job repents in verse 6, it says in verse 10 that: "The Lord restored the fortunes of Job." From these two passages, it seems that his friends were correct in their assessment of Job, yet the Lord rebukes them: "You have not spoken of me what is right" (Job 42:7). In order to solve this difficulty, we need to see that Job's initial suffering was due to his faithfulness—he was a righteous sufferer (Job 1:1, 8; 2:3). However, throughout his interaction with his friends, we see that Job's spiritual stamina begins to deteriorate when he arrogantly

to his question about his plight, Job needed a proper doctrine of God, which is what the Lord provides in his whirlwind speeches (Job 38–42).

3. *We are to discern our circumstances—especially our sufferings—based upon Scripture.* It is dangerous to think that we can gain an understanding of God by our experiences alone. All of the characters in the book of Job based their theology and their counsel upon their own logic and ability to reason, not upon the revelation of God. These two are not always in harmony with one another, and we must allow Scripture, not our senses, to be our final word of authority on all matters of life and doctrine.

4. *The ultimate answer to righteous suffering is in Christ.* Job was limited in his ability to appreciate his sufferings because Christ had not yet arrived. To what extent he would have discerned that the messiah would be a "suffering servant" is unknown. All righteous suffering—whether they occur in the Old Testament or the New Testament, including those of Job—reflects the true righteous Sufferer. In that regard, Job is a type of Christ.

An Introduction to the Central Character of Job

With these words of wisdom in mind, we now look to the book of Job.[11] It opens by introducing us to the main protagonist:

> There was a man in the land of Uz whose name was Job and that man was blameless and upright, one who feared God and turned away from evil. (Job 1:1)

judges God as unjust in light of his righteous suffering. Thus, Job's temperament in chapters 1–2 is radically different than in chapters 3–37. When he faces the Lord in chapters 38–42, he stands before God guilty of falsely accusing him of injustice. This is the sin of which Job repents, not any secret, unconfessed sin from chapters 1–2.

11. This chapter is not meant to be an exhaustive study or an overview/introduction of the entire book of Job. My thoughts are focused primarily on the first two chapters, especially as they portray Job as a righteous sufferer.

Job as the man of wisdom

From the beginning, we are given significant pieces of information about Job. First, he is portrayed as a man of wisdom. Specifically, we are told four things about his character: 1) he was "blameless"; 2) "upright"; 3) he was "one who feared God"; and 4) he "turned away from evil." Tremper Longman comments that these virtues also describe the wise man in the book of Proverbs.[12] Such a man is "blameless"[13] and "upright."[14] In Proverbs, this moral man is well respected within his community. He is an exemplary model of integrity and honesty with impeccable character.

Proverbs also says that a wise man "fears the Lord." The fear of the Lord is the beginning of "knowledge" (Prov 1:1) and "wisdom" (Prov 9:1; 15:33; cf. Ps 111:10; Mic 6:9). The overarching trait of the wise man is a "fear of the Lord," meaning he has a proper understanding of the Creator-creature distinction and the sovereignty of God. He lives in respect of God's power and authority and in full appreciation of the fact that he is privileged to be in an intimate, covenantal relationship with one who is so holy. Not only does a wise man have a healthy horizontal relationship with humanity ("blameless" and "upright"), he also has a healthy vertical relationship with his creator ("fearing God"). For these reasons, his life strays "away from evil."

These characteristics of the prototypical wise man in Proverbs describe Job so well that even God pronounces, "There is none like him on the earth" (Job 1:8). Given his glowing review, we expect Job to maneuver through the challenges of life with success. As the drama unfolds, however, we find that this is not the case.[15]

Job as a loving father

Second, not only is Job portrayed as the prototypical man of wisdom, but also as a loving father, devoted to the well being of his family (Job 1:2, 4–5). Verse 2 tells us that he had ten children, seven sons, and three

12. Longman, *Job*, 79.

13. Proverbs 2:7, 21; 11:3, 20; 13:6; 19:1; 20:7; 28:6, 10, 18; 29:10.

14. Proverbs 1:3; 2:7, 21; 8:6, 9; 11:3, 6; 12:6; 14:11; 15:8; 16:13; 20:11; 21:2, 8; 23:16; 29:10.

15. By using the word "drama" to describe Job, I do not reject its historicity. A historical text can portray a dramatic narrative character. See Provan et al., *Biblical History of Israel*, 1–107.

daughters.[16] His numerous children show how blessed Job is. The fact that he has seven sons is significant since the number seven is often associated with completeness in the Old Testament.

These children do not argue among themselves. Verse 4 describes their close relationship as they regularly celebrate together in festivals. Any parent with multiple children would be envious to read about the intimacy these siblings had with each other. Although not stated explicitly, the harmony among his children may have been due to the fact that Job raised them well. Job is a godly parent with biblical priorities.

Verse 5 says that after each of these parties, Job would offer sacrifices for them. Job's fear was that in the midst of their celebration, his children might have sinned and "cursed" God.[17] Job is portrayed as a father-priest who offered an atoning sacrifice on their behalf. There may be questions here regarding proper modes of offering sacrifices in a pre-Levitical setting, but what is important is to see that Job is a father deeply concerned for the spiritual well being of his children. More important than their wealth, health, or professional aspirations, Job strove to be sure that his children could stand righteous before the Lord. In that sense, he is in total alignment with the duties given to fathers in the book of Deuteronomy.[18] He does not fall into the social trap that ensnares so many Christian families in our day, where the spiritual development of our children is largely seen as the responsibility of pastors, youth directors, and Sunday school teachers. Parents today are often more interested in the academic, athletic, and even social successes of their children than their growth in the gospel. This was certainly not the case for Job.

It is interesting that when Job is restored after his confrontation with the Lord, he is given double the number of sheep, camels, cattle, and donkeys than before (cf. Job 1:3 and 42:12), but his number of children remain the same (1:4; cf. 42:13). Many commentators have interpreted this to mean that his earlier set of seven sons and three daughters, though they died prematurely, experienced the new life that comes to recipients

16. Job's wife is not mentioned in this introductory opening, but is clearly implied since he has children. She does not come into the narrative until 2:9, as a quarrelsome woman.

17. The Hebrew word that is here translated as "curse" is actually the word for "bless." This appears to be a euphemism to mean "curse." Most likely, the writer of Job seems to not want to connect "curse" with "God."

18. Deuteronomy 6:7, 20–25; 11:2; 31:12–13.

of the grace of God; they shared in the "first resurrection" and would not know the "second death" (Rev 20:6).

If this view were correct, and Job's children are now in glory, this would largely be due to the fact that they had a godly father who had a proper view of what is most important in the upbringing of covenant children, raising them in the fear of the Lord. For ancient Israel, notorious for failing to pass their faith onto their children, this was an important covenantal lesson to learn.[19] This is a lesson that we also need to remember and not forget in our day.

Job as a wealthy man

In addition to being a man of wisdom and a godly father, Job was wealthy. The Bible says that he had a great number of animals—7,000 sheep, 3,000 camels, 500 yoke of oxen, and 500 female donkeys—and many servants (1:4). Given our current monetary system, it may be difficult to appreciate this, but wealth was not always measured by the amount of precious metals or jewels. In the ancient world, the number of animals you owned determined your affluence. Abraham was considered a wealthy man because of all the animals he amassed throughout his life.[20] Job also had many servants, who were the workforce in the ancient world. They were the ones who produced the goods and commodities (e.g., hide, meats, milk, etc.) that Job would have used to trade or barter with in his business dealings.

The wealth of Job should not surprise us since it is a natural result of living wisely.[21] This does not mean that the book of Job (or biblical wisdom literature in general) promotes a "health-and-wealth" gospel. Rather, it teaches that if one can live as a wise steward over their resources and material goods—especially in secular commerce, where riches are the highest goal and thus greed has become a virtue—then success and

19. Judges 2:10; cf. 1 Samuel 2:22; 3:13; 8:5.

20. Genesis 12:16; 13:5–7; 14:21–24; 24:29–31, 35. The historical setting of Job has been generally understood as taking place during the patriarchal era, the time of Abraham, Isaac, and Jacob. This is supported by the way in which Job's wealth is described in 1:3. This should not, however, be mistaken with the date of the book, which was most likely written much later. The reference to the Sabeans and Chaldeans (in verses 15 and 17, respectively) suggests a late date for the writing of the book.

21. Proverbs 3:9–10; 8:18; 11:18; cf. 10:14.

prosperity may be expected, even without succumbing to the temptations of avarice.

Of course, with great wealth comes great responsibility to care for the impoverished (Prov 28:27; 29:7). It also does not compare with the higher value of gaining wisdom (Prov 16:16; 28:6). Job would have known all this (cf. Job 28:13–20; 31:24–28).

At the end of this brief, biographical introduction, we see Job as a wise and wealthy man who is living an idyllic life of bliss with his children nearby. He was truly a blessed man. All this, however, would change— quickly, dramatically, and drastically.

The Perfect Storm

As soon as we are told about the success and happiness of Job, he immediately suffers the single worst day of his life (Job 1:13–20). The day began no differently than any other. There was nothing to warn him of the tragedies that would come upon him. Nothing clued him to the fact that a heavenly dialogue had taken place that would change the course of his life. He probably awoke that morning grateful to the Lord for the blessings that were bestowed upon him. All this would come to an abrupt end, however, and he would lose everything suddenly.

A bad day

Job's losses are narrated to us in four disastrous events. First, his oxen and donkeys were stolen by a tribal group from south Arabia, the Sabeans. These marauding thieves also executed his servants by the edge of the sword (Job 1:13–15). Second, his sheep and more servants were consumed by an act of God: "A fire of God . . . from heaven" (Job 1:16). The third event was yet another raid by another invading foreign power. This time it was the Chaldeans, an Aramaic speaking tribal group, who took his camels and executed the remainder of his servants (1:17). The fourth and final disaster to come upon Job was the worst, the death of his ten "young people" (Job 1:19). They were in their home, celebrating a special day for his oldest son (most likely his birthday), when a powerful wind came from the wilderness and collapsed the house, killing everyone inside (Job 1:18–19).

The loss of his animal possessions was equivalent to the loss of wealth in the ancient world. The loss of his servants meant that even if he were able to recoup from his animal losses, he had no manpower to produce the material goods needed to do business with others. The death of his ten children delivered an emotional pain that requires no further comment.[22] He was essentially left with no money and no family, helpless and homeless.

Each of these four disasters follow an identical literary pattern. After the initial report in Job 1:13–15, the other three begin with the phrase: "While he was yet speaking." The "he" refers to the lone survivor of the previous disastrous events (Job 1:16, 17, 18). Each cycle also ends with the phrase, "And I alone have escaped to tell you" (Job 1:15, 16, 17, 19), again referring to the same survivors respectively. What this means is that these events are being reported to Job at the same time on the same day, as if these messengers are speaking at the same time. If this was a musical opera, I would envision four tenors/baritones singing the first line, "While he was yet speaking," in unison and the last line, "And I alone have escaped to tell you," with dissonant, overlapping voices in-between. This brings together not just two or three tragic events, but four. Any one of these four would be a hardship that could easily overwhelm anyone and traumatize him for the rest of his life. Job suffered all four on the same day.

Another bad day

For Job, the onslaught did not stop here. One day of suffering was not enough; he had to endure more. His predicament went from bad to worse. The first group of four targeted Job's possessions and relationships, but his physical body had been untouched. On another day (Job 2:1–8), a fifth and final tragedy hit Job, where he suffered physical ailments so intense and extreme that his three friends—who later came to visit him— were unable to recognize him (Job 2:7, 12).

As if this were not bad enough, Job also had to endure the foolish words of his wife, who scolded him for holding onto a ridiculous faith in a cruel God who does nothing but bring trouble. She basically said it would be better for him to end his life (Job 2:9). The pain of hearing

---

22. See chapter 6, "Joy of a Mourning Parent."

such blasphemy from his wife may have been worse than any of the other disasters combined.

Like a powerful tempest that devours everything in its path, so these five events left every aspect of Job's life in utter chaos. A single storm would be discouraging. Two would be destructive. Three devastating. Four an unimaginable act. Five a supernatural event. It was the *perfect storm* and Job was right in the middle of it—alone.

Why?

The Reason for Job's Suffering

Job 1, in addition to introducing us to the main protagonist, also records a heavenly dialogue between the Lord and a member of his divine, angelic counsel. Job 1:6 and 2:1 describe two separate occasions when a host of angelic beings came to present themselves before the Lord. Most likely, they were returning (as messengers commonly did in the ancient world to their king) to report to God the results of their survey of the earth.

The focus of these heavenly scenes turns to the Lord's interaction with one being in particular, someone simply referred to in Hebrew as *haśśāṭān*, which means "the accuser." There has been a great number of discussions on the identity of this figure. For reasons that are obvious from the transliteration, this word is commonly understood to be the personal name "Satan," so many identify this figure as the devil.[23] However, the *ha-* prefix in *haśśāṭān* is the Hebrew definite article, which makes any interpretation of it as a personal name awkward.[24] It would be equivalent to saying, "My name is *the* Peter." This would be what someone, wanting to establish himself as one of a kind without any comparison, would do; it is an extremely lofty assertion with possible delusions of grandeur. The use of the definite article does this. In a regular dialogue, the definite article accompanying a personal name is inappropriate. Of greater importance,

---

23. The Septuagint (the Greek translation of the Old Testament) also seems to interpret this as the personal name of "Satan" by using the word *diabolos*. However, this Greek term does not necessarily mean that this is the devil. The Greek translation of Numbers 22:22 uses the infinitive form of this word (*endiaballō*, "to be an adversary") to translate the same Hebrew word *śāṭān*. This suggests that it is possible for the Greek word *diabolos* to be taken in a more generic sense, "the slanderer, accuser, adversary" and not as a personal name. It is very possible that this being in the book of Job did not have malicious intentions at all. See above for further details.

24. The Septuagint also includes a definite article, *ho diabolos*.

however, is the function that this being serves in the narrative. He is an "accuser," or in this case, "*the* accuser."[25]

The Lord seemed eager to hear the reports of this specific accuser after his return from patrolling his allotted portion of the earth. Precisely what the accuser was looking for is not mentioned, but the Lord's response is telling. In Job 1:8 and 2:3 he asks about Job and wonders if the accuser took notice of his fidelity: "Have you considered my servant Job, that there is none like him on the earth, a blameless and upright man, who fears God and turns away from evil?" It seems he had not. However, the mere fact the Lord specifically mentions the loyalty and faithfulness of Job suggests that this was what these angelic beings were sent to the earth to search for.

The Lord sought out the report of this specific accuser since his tour of the earth included the area where Job lived, and he is enthusiastic to draw the attention of his angelic court to Job. Job caught his eye as an outstanding devotee. The Lord even calls him "my servant," which, in the Old Testament, is a hallowed title that only appears for those who have a special standing before the Lord and serve him in profound ways.[26] If the Lord had been expecting a glowing report from this accuser along the lines of, "There is a man, Job, in the land of Uz. There is no one like him among all men on the earth," he was to be disappointed.

Faithfulness can lead to suffering

There are two significant points in this interaction. First, Job's virtuous character is not in question. The narrator identifies Job as an ideal man with that four-fold description in verse 1, and God himself confirms this in 1:8 and again in 2:3. The accuser does not deny that this is true; he only challenges Job's motive. So everyone—the narrator, God, and even the accuser—acknowledges that Job is an outstanding, faithful man.

25. The use of the definite article here is unusual since this is the first time that this "accuser" is mentioned in the book of Job. The article presumes that this being was mentioned earlier in the narrative. This may be a case where the oral tradition of Job existed long before its inscripturation and canonization. The readers of this text must have been very familiar with this "accuser" because of the oral tradition of Job. Therefore, he is referred to as "*the* accuser" because the readers would have known which accuser this is referring to—the one from the oral stories they were familiar with. A similar use is possible with "the serpent" in Genesis 3:1 and "the bush" in Exodus 3:2, as there was no previous mention of either in their respective narratives.

26. For example, see Moses in Exodus 14:31 and David in 2 Samuel 7:5.

It is this attention to Job that instigates the accuser to share his doubts about the sincerity of Job's faith and desire to challenge it. In other words, had Job been a selfish, greedy tyrant, a father who used the obedience of his children to promote his own vainglory, a deceitful and dishonest business man with ambitions for riches at all cost—had this been Job, then he would not have had to face the catastrophes that he did; none of the heartaches that he suffered would have happened. It is *because* he is such an obedient and faithful follower that he suffers. Since Job is of interest to the Lord, he becomes of interest to the accuser.

Notice how normal Job's life was before everything fell apart. He was not on the mission field, he wasn't preaching the gospel on the street corners, he wasn't evangelizing to those of other religious beliefs. He was an average man, simply living a life of faithful obedience to the Lord and raising his children in the ways of godliness. Many of the trials that we face in our day occur in a similar context, in everyday life. We do not plan for them because they are not expected. When they occur, it is shocking.

As we discussed in an earlier chapter, righteous suffering may easily be mistaken as persecution for taking a stand for the faith. Some believers truly do suffer because they are bold in proclaiming the gospel on street corners, shopping malls, college campuses, and foreign countries.[27] Yet there are others who suffer merely because they chose to obey the Lord and not give in to the sinful demands and pressures of the world. They suffer while trying to live a day to day life of faithful, humble obedience.

It is this final group that can identify with Job. You may know such people. These are the believers who struggle to maintain a peaceful home with sinful children or family members, who strive to love and respect unethical and tyrannical supervisors or coworkers, or who try, at all costs, to live at peace with demanding neighbors. They do not grace the cover of magazines or headline news reports. They are not the subjects of blogs nor do they revel in fortune and glory. They have not published books on Christian living, they do not have thousands of followers on Twitter, and they do not update their videos regularly on YouTube. They are regular, everyday believers who love the Lord and desire to live for him, who face an uphill battle due to the sinfulness around them. These people can identify with Job.

Again, this notion of suffering for obedience and faithfulness is disturbing. It challenges our core concept of God and what we consider as

---

27. See chapter 8, "Joy as a Rejected Messenger," for more details.

justice in the world. After all, if we suffer even when we are faithful, then what is the point of being faithful? This is precisely the question that Job's wife asks as he sits in utter misery: "Do you still hold fast your integrity? Curse God and die" (Job 2:9). Job challenges us to reexamine why we believe and obey the Lord. Is it possible that we turn to God just for our personal gain? Or is he worthy of our obedience because of who he is, because he is God? This leads us to the second significant observation.

The greatest blessing is the Blessor

Second, it is the Lord who brings the accuser's attention to Job, not the accuser to the Lord, and this happens on two different occasions (Job 1:8; 2:3). The accuser is sent off on two excursions of the earth, each time returning with very little to report. No one stands out as noteworthy, not even Job. Clearly, the accuser is not as impressed with Job as the Lord is.

It should be noted that at this point, Job was safe from harm—the accuser was ready to close the books on his file and move on. Had the Lord remained silent, had he brought no further attention to Job, the accuser would have had nothing to challenge, and subsequently would not have sought permission to test Job with those initial four disastrous events. Even after Job proves the genuineness of his faith, still praising God despite those tragedies (Job 2:10), the accuser remains dubious about his motives. This leads to physical torments for Job. It is only because the Lord points out Job as unique that the accuser presents his doubts about him and raises the most obvious critique of such a blessed man—*Job is faithful because of the good things that the Lord has given to him; if God were to remove all these, even bringing him bodily harm, then Job would curse him to his face* (Job 1:9–11; 2:4–5).

The accuser found Job's faithfulness suspicious because it had never been challenged. If it had been, then Job would show himself for who he truly was and his true intentions would be revealed; namely, it would be revealed that Job loved the blessings rather than the Blessor. The accuser believed that Job merely saw the Lord as an instrument to possess what he truly desired—health, wealth, and a good family. This, by definition, is idolatry, where the Lord serves as a means to a greater end, not an end in himself.

Such shallow faith is a possibility for someone so materially blessed, and this accusation should not be dismissed too quickly. There are many who easily and willingly misunderstand Matthew 6:33: "But seek first the kingdom of God and his righteousness, and all these things will be added to you." Some may think, "This is a great deal. If I just *seek first the kingdom*, then I will get all the things that I have ever wanted! Isn't Christianity great?" Psalm 37:4 seems to say the same thing: "Delight yourself in the LORD, and he will give you the desires of your heart." If I just delight myself in the Lord, then he will give me the deepest desires of my heart.

The sin of the rich young ruler in the synoptic gospels reflects this warped system of values. The ruler found superficial obedience to the law rather easy, but when he was faced with the requirement to set his wealth aside for the sake of the gospel, he faced a price he was unwilling to pay and walked away sorrowfully.[28] This is similar to the hundreds who followed Jesus in his early ministry. As he began to make more outstanding claims of his deity, spoke of his atoning death on the cross, and clarified the demands of discipleship, many left him. When he stopped providing free meals, more left as well. His eccentricity was tolerable as long as they received something of value in return.

Given Job's spiritual decline in chapters 3–37, we are forced to ask if the accuser was truly right about him. At the end of Job 2, it seems that Job had endured those fiery trials and remained faithful to the Lord, proving the accuser's assessment wrong. This may have been the immediate result, but what about the long term? Job may have won the initial skirmish, but will he win the long and arduous war?

According to Job 3–37, it seems that the accuser may have been correct all along. Phrases like "blameless," "righteous," "God-fearer," and "turning from evil" may have described Job in chapters 1–2, but not so in chapters 3–37. We would instead use phrases like abusive, arrogant, grumbling, defiant, accusatory, and borderline blasphemous. Yet at the end, after encountering the powerful presence of God, Job learned his place.

Notice that no answer was given to Job to explain his hardship; he was never told about the deal made between the accuser and the Lord. What we realize is that Job did not need to know about this. What he needed was to relearn who his God is. The knowledge of God is what restores Job's spiritual composure and thus restores a proper perspective on life. Again, the fear of the Lord is the beginning of wisdom.

---

28. Matthew 19:16–30; Mark 10:17–31; Luke 18:18–30.

At the end of the drama, Job once again becomes the same virtuous man we saw at the end of Job 2, someone who blesses the Lord whether he gave or took away. After Job 2, the accuser is never heard of again, but his presence is felt subtlety as we read about Job's spiritual disintegration. His accusation in Job 1, which remained a silent constant throughout the entire book, is finally proven to be thoroughly and absolutely wrong by the end. Job now appreciates that knowing the Lord is the highest of all virtues.

In light of the accusation, it is imperative to note that Job came to this theological realization (Job 42:2–6) *before* God restored his wealth and family (Job 42:10). Otherwise, his motive would still be suspect. God is truly worthy of our worship simply for who he is, not merely for what he gives to us.

Today, the book of Job is a reminder and a challenge for us to place God as God in our lives because he is the most precious person in our lives. As important as the discussions on the place of faith in the life of believers may be, it should not detract from the highest of all commands, to "love the Lord your God with all your heart and with all your soul and with all your might."[29] We are to love God because he is God, "for [his] love endures forever" (Ps 136:1). Even if we were to lose all that we own, we remain richly blessed—simply because we still have the Lord. As the psalmist says, "Whom have I in heaven but you? And there is nothing on earth that I desire besides you. My flesh and my heart may fail, but God is the strength of my heart and my portion forever" (Ps 73:25–26). For those who have been so dearly loved by God, there is no greater blessing than to know the Blessor.

Job in Fellowship with Jesus

In each series of challenges, whether the original four of chapter one or the physical afflictions of chapter two, Job unbelievably remained faithful to the Lord. This was no small feat, and it is worthy of our awe. James 5:11 even says the "steadfastness" of Job is exemplary of the type of perseverance believers need to have. During times that would have caused many to wallow in doubt and regret, Job did not. Remarkably, he even blessed God. Job's wife reaction was completely the opposite. Seeing her husband tormented, finding it incomprehensible that he would remain steadfast to

29. Deuteronomy 6:5; cf. Matthew 22:37; 1 Corinthians 13:1–3, 13.

a God who would subject him to such misery, she enticed him to "curse God and die." Yet Job did not curse God, but remained faithful.

At the end of the first day of trials, he gave an incredible testimony: "Naked I came from my mother's womb, and naked shall I return. The LORD gave, and the LORD has taken away; blessed be the name of the LORD" (Job 1:21). To make Job's innocence clear, the narrator even stressed that: "In all this, Job did not sin or charge God with wrong" (Job 1:22).

At the end of the second day, Job testified in a similar way despite the foolish words of counsel from his wife, "You speak as one of the foolish women would speak. Shall we receive good from God, and shall we not receive evil?" Again, the narrator comments that: "In all this Job did not sin with his lips" (Job 2:10). Job found contentment in the Lord simply because he is the Lord. He was able to overcome the horrible circumstances of his life because his eyes looked up to his God in whom he trusted. We know that Job weakened as the drama progressed, and he failed to gain a proper understanding of the true nature of his sufferings, but at this early point in his suffering, he gave thanks to God and found peace in knowing him.

There is a powerful image of Christ in Job's anguish which cannot be missed. This relationship between the two highlights why after the second century AD, it became customary for the church to read the book of Job during the passion week of the Christian calendar.[30] Like Job, Jesus endured untold sufferings when he hung on the cross. Like Job, this was not due to any wrong or sin that he had committed. Like Job, Jesus was completely righteous. Like Job, Jesus's obedience was what brought about his suffering. If there were anyone who was "blameless," "upright," "feared God," and "turned away from evil," it was Jesus Christ.

Did Job realize that his Savior would be one with whom he shared so much in common? His response to his ungodly wife in 2:10 suggests that he may have had an inkling. He says it is foolish to think that God would only give good and not also give evil. He willingly recognizes that it is inevitable for believers, such as himself, to experience both. It would be easy to accept the good as a gift from God and not the bad, but he correctly acknowledges that we cannot accept one without the other.

For Job, since both had the same divine origin, he received both as a gracious gift (cf. Phil 1:29). Not having the fullness of revelation as

30. Delitzsch, *Book of Job*, 261.

we do today, Job may not have known that suffering and glory are the two dominant aspects of the life-experience of the coming Messiah, who would give his life for the salvation of his people. At the very least, he was wise enough to know that God, in his divine providence, permits his precious children to know both.

If he had even the smallest appreciation of whose "steps" he was called "to follow" (1 Pet 2:21), then you can imagine that such "fellowship" would have been a great source of comfort. It would have been a source of joy for him to say that he had such a deep connection to his Savior. In that sense, it is not Jesus who is like Job, but Job who is like Jesus. In fact, Job is merely a picture, a reflection of the one who would come to suffer for all. Although Job experienced a meaningful and joyous restoration at the end of the book (Job 42:10–17), he did not need to wait for that in order to know this supernatural joy. He could have experienced it even in the midst of his sufferings because he believed in the person with whom he was in fellowship.

Job and the Book of Psalms

Earlier, I stated that there is a movement in the book of Psalms from lament to praise, from suffering to glory.[31] There is a similar movement in the book of Job. Job also begins with suffering and agony similar to those found in the lament psalms (see below). However, he does not remain in lament, but ends in restored glory (Job 42:10–17). The fact that this pattern can be discerned in both the biblical psalter as well as the book of Job helps to establish a correlation between these two books.[32]

---

31. See chapter 4, "Joy in Singing Songs of Lament."

32. In the order of the Old Testament canon in the Hebrew Bible, the book of Job immediately follows the book of Psalms. This is followed by the book of Proverbs, then Ruth (Psalms, Job, Proverbs, Ruth). Many scholars have identified Ruth as the embodiment of Lady Wisdom of Proverbs 31:10–31 for two reasons. First, Lady Wisdom and Ruth are the only women in the Old Testament who are called a "woman of valor," ʾēšet-ḥayil (cf. Prov 31:10; Ruth 3:11). For our purposes, the second reason is more interesting: Ruth immediately follows Proverbs in the canonical order, which further confirms the connection between Ruth and Lady Wisdom. If this is the rationale for the order of Proverbs–Ruth, then it is reasonable to consider that the two books prior to them (Psalms–Job) are canonically adjacent for a similar reason. Job is the singer of the psalms. For reasons explained above, Job is also envisioned as the wise man of Proverbs, thus making Proverbs an obvious choice to follow Job.

Because of the progression from lament to praise in both the Psalms and Job, the singer of the book of Psalms can be seen as someone similar to Job. And inasmuch as Job is only a shadowy reflection of the true singer of the Psalms, Jesus Christ, both books (Psalms and Job) allow us to "fellowship with Christ's sufferings." We embrace one as a lyrical expression of the life of Christ in songs and the other as a powerful portrayal in an operatic drama. Both describe our beloved Savior, but they also describe Job as an early, shadowy reflection of the true righteous sufferer.

This connection between the Psalms and Job begs us to reexamine the Psalter and to see if there are psalms that fit the righteous suffering of Job. What we discover is that there are several psalms that seem to have a special connection with him. These "psalms of the righteous sufferer" so accurately reflect his cries that we can almost picture Job as the composer of these "songs in the night" (Job 35:10).

Psalm 26

For example, think of Psalm 26. Verses 1–3 open with an appeal to the Lord to vindicate the psalmist because "I have trusted in the Lord without wavering" (Ps 26:1) and "I walk in your faithfulness" (Ps 26:3). The psalmist, like Job, is innocent of any wrongdoing, yet he is oppressed by his enemies. Verses 4–8 describe how he avoided interacting with "men of falsehood" or with "hypocrites" (Ps 26:4) because he detested "the assembly of evildoers" (Ps 26:5); Job "turns away from evil" (Job 1:8; 2:3). Rather than associating with "the wicked" (Ps 26:5), the psalmist says he found comfort in the "habitation of your house . . . where your glory dwells" (Ps 26:8). For these reasons, in verses 9–10, the psalmist appeals to the Lord not to "sweep my soul away with sinners." He ends in verses 11–12 by restating his innocence.

Psalm 44

We should also consider Psalm 44, which is a startling lament. Although this is the cry of a community, the content of the poem fits very well with the theme of the righteous suffering of Job.

The psalm begins with an opening section where the psalmist reflects on God's favor in the past (Ps 44:1–8). He provided victory for the psalmist's forefathers over their enemies (Ps 44:1–3). This leads the psalmist to remember that God also gave victory to him over his own enemies (Ps 44:4–8).

Yet in verses 9–22, his current situation is one of despair, and he struggles with God's apparent rejection of him in the present. The psalmist's enemies have utterly defeated him; he and his people are disgraced and humiliated before them (Ps 44:9–16). He says he feels rejected by God, which he finds confusing because of his innocence. He is defeated "though we have not forgotten you, and we have not been false to your covenant; our heart has not turned back, nor have our steps departed from your way" (Ps 44:17–18). These are bold claims, but the psalmist goes on further and makes even bolder claims in verses 20–21:

> If we had forgotten the name of our God or spread out our hands to a foreign god, would not God discover this? For he knows the secrets of the heart

The fact that the psalmist, on behalf of his community, is eager for the Lord not only to examine their outward conformity to the demands of the covenant but also to probe the inner motives of their hearts, may appear audacious, but it does show the depth of their innocence. In every aspect, externally in their living and internally in their heart's motive, the psalmist insists that his community was faithful and obedient to the Lord. They did not abandon him to worship false gods as some did; they did not follow the words of the false prophets who cried out false words of "'peace, peace' when there is no peace" (Jer 6:14; 8:11). They loved the Lord their God (Deut 6:5) and followed his laws. Despite that, they find themselves in utter devastation.

The words of Psalm 44 are strikingly similar to the claims that Job made in his dialogue with his three friends, where he relentlessly defended his innocence (Job 4–27). There is no resolution in Psalm 44. In most laments, there is a transition from lament to praise. However, no such transition is found in this psalm. We in fact find the reverse; it begins with praise (Ps 44:1–8) but ends in lament (Ps 44: 9–26).

The final section (Ps 44:23–26) is the only one that shows even the smallest glimpse of hope, where the psalmist cries out to the Lord for a potential restoration. It is not difficult to see the possibility of Job alluding to or reciting portions of this psalm in his cries.

Psalm 73

Psalm 73 is another Job-like psalm. It is a wisdom psalm that asks the same kinds of questions asked in the book of Job. It begins setting up the psalmist's dilemma in verses 1–3. The psalmist reminds the reader that: "Truly God is good to Israel, to those who are pure in heart" (Ps 73:1). This is an important point to establish at the outset, since its premise will be challenged by the psalmist's life experience. He shares how he stumbled in his faith in the Lord because he was "envious of the arrogant" when he "saw the prosperity of the wicked" (Ps 73:2–3). Verses 4–12 goes on to describe the success of the wicked that caused his envy. They are rich and healthy (Ps 73:4–5) although they are arrogant and abuse others (Ps 73:6–8). They are even blasphemous, challenging the sovereignty of God (Ps 73:9–11). Yet in spite of all this, God seems to allow them to prosper and does not strike them down in his wrath (Ps 73:12).

The psalmist is able to tolerate this apparent injustice as long as he is left alone, but verses 13–16 tell us that he experiences the complete opposite. He is stricken and rebuked daily (Ps 73:14). He cannot share his internal doubts with others, since that could cause them to stumble, so he is isolated and alone (Ps 73:15). He wonders if maintaining a "clean heart" and "pure hands" is worth all this trouble or whether or not it is all in vain (Ps 73:13). The more he searches for the answer to this crux, the more elusive it becomes (Ps 73:16).

From verse 17 onward, the tone of Psalm 73 shifts as the psalmist regains his spiritual wisdom and begins to understand the meaning of life. This occurs when "he entered the sanctuary of God" (Ps 73:17). He realizes that the life of the wicked is short and unstable (Ps 73:18–20), and that he was a fool to think otherwise (Ps 73:21–22). Ultimately, things of this earth will "fail" (Ps 73:26). The only thing that lasts is the Lord, who is the "strength of my heart and my portion forever." It is in him that true joy comes (Ps 73:23–28).

Job would not have known these final words of contentment and satisfaction in Psalm 73 until after his direct encounter with God in Job 38–42, but the shared frustrations between the psalmist in verses 3–16 and Job is striking.

One can easily envision Job as the author of the psalms above or, at the very least, as their subject. Among the psalms of confession/repentance of sin (e.g., Ps 32; 38; 51; 130) and general psalms of lament, which capture the heartache of living in a fallen world, there are also a meaningful and prominent collection of Job-like laments, ministered to those individuals and communities in the days of ancient Israel who were enduring similar kinds of sufferings.

Job, the Church, and Christ

The parallels between Job and Jesus are so clear that they hardly need to be mentioned. Throughout the descriptions above, it is impossible not to think of the sufferings of Christ in his innocence. In Christ is the true embodiment of the ultimate righteous sufferer, whose coming was anticipated in Job. Jesus also suffered the single worst day of his life. In fact, this day was the worst day in the history of redemption—the death of the innocent, righteous, and holy God-Man. At the lowest point in his earthly life, Jesus, like Job, was also abandoned by his close friends. Many called for his execution, others mocked him, and his disciples disassociated themselves from him. Jesus was totally alone.

Not only is there similarity between Jesus and Job, but there is also precedence. In the same way that we must be reminded of the gospel each day, so we also need to be reminded that the true righteous sufferer is not Job, nor is it believers; it is Jesus. We must not forget which is the reality and which is the copy. In the eternal decree of God, Jesus was crucified "before the foundation of the world" (Eph 1:4). Jesus and his suffering is the reality. He is the paradigm of all righteous suffering. Job only anticipates this.

When we read about Job and his misery, we may say, "I can completely relate to him." But how does this help us? We may no longer feel alone, but what value is there in identifying with Job? He is a sinner, just like you and me. But to identify with Jesus is altogether different because he is our Redeemer. To know him, even his sufferings, is worth more than all the riches of the world (Phil 3:8):

> It cannot be bought for gold, and silver cannot be weighed as its price. It cannot be valued in the gold of Ophir, in precious onyx or sapphire. Gold and glass cannot equal it, nor can it be exchanged for jewels of fine gold. (Job 28:15–17)

To know our Savior is worth its weight in gold. Nothing is more precious. Without Jesus, we would not have the book of Job, nor would our suffering have any value.

Returning to our theme passage of 1 Peter 4:12–13, we can see that those in Christ, including Job, are called to *fellowship with Christ in his sufferings* (1 Pet 4:13). Because of the reality of the believers' union with Christ, to read about one is to read about the other. In chapters 1–2, Job was "grieved by various trials" (1 Pet 1:6), yet he kept his "conduct among the Gentiles honorable" (1 Pet 2:12). By "doing good," he "put to silence the ignorance of foolish men" (1 Pet 2:12, 15). He "endured sorrows while suffering unjustly" (1 Pet 2:19). He did a "gracious thing before the sight of God" because he did "good and suffered for it" (1 Pet 2:20). He was richly blessed because he suffered "for righteousness' sake" (1 Pet 3:14) and "for doing good" (1 Pet 3:17). Who are we really describing here? It is indeed Job, but more so it is Christ. And, profoundly, in Christ, it is also the church.

The apostle Paul reminds believers that their union is with Christ who suffered pain and agony "without cause."[33] He was one who "knew no sins" (2 Cor 5:21). Astonishingly, in Philippians 3:10–11, Paul expresses his desire to grow in his knowledge of Christ in his death and also his suffering. Not only do we have a high priest who is able to sympathize with our suffering (Heb 4:15), we are also called to sympathize with his. Those who have known unspeakable pain can also know an unspeakable joy in Christ (1 Pet 1:8; 4:13)! To know the Lord as a righteous sufferer gives the believer a full, whole knowledge of Christ who knew both suffering for righteousness and blessed glory, just as Job did.

The book of Job reminds us that suffering can result from faithful obedience to the Lord. When this occurs, we will be tempted to see it as an injustice of God. Job encourages us not to. There is nothing wrong with God or with your faith. Rather, this righteous suffering gives us a glorious opportunity to know our savior, the true righteous sufferer. Job had such an opportunity but squandered it in favor of his own sense of moral and judicial superiority over the Lord himself.

Had Job had the full revelation of Scripture as we do today, would he have made the same error, or would he have valued his suffering for what they truly are—a call to share in the sufferings of his savior? We will never know. The reason why the Lord could not reveal to Job and his friends the true answer to their questions is largely due to the fact that Christ had not yet come. It would take the coming of the true righteous Sufferer to

---

33. Job 2:3; 9:17; cf. Lamentations 3:52.

answer their questions about the reality of righteous suffering. Instead, the answer to their questions was in the form of dim shadows and copies.

What we do know is that we have the fullness of revelation now, and the same call is before us. The question is, "How will we respond?" The wisdom of the world tells us to curse God and die. The wisdom of God tells us that there is joy here in our suffering that is supernatural; its value is "above pearls" and more precious than "pure gold" (Job 28:18–19).

I pray that God's people would know such joy.

I pray that I would know this myself.

6

Joy of a Mourning Father

Blessed are those who mourn, for they shall be comforted.

Matthew 5:4

It was 2:34 AM, early on a Wednesday morning, April 27th, 2005. I received a phone call. This was the call that I feared to receive one day, the call that no pastor ever wants to get. On the other line was my close, personal friend Sam. His daughter, Kaitlyn, had collapsed earlier that day for unknown reasons. He and his wife Cassie rushed her to the hospital. He was calling me from the Pediatric Intensive Care Unit, where Kaitlyn was being treated. After several examinations, none of the physicians knew what was wrong with her, but she was not doing well. She was dying and no one knew why.

I desperately want to tell you that it all turned out well, that Kaitlyn was the recipient of miraculous healing by the Lord and she is now a healthy young teen. Unfortunately, I cannot say that. Later that evening, Kaitlyn went to be with the Lord, and Sam and Cassie joined a community of parents whose only prerequisite to membership is knowing the unbearable pain of losing a child. Kaitlyn was 4 years old. I know others who share in their experience. Mark and Lucy lost their beloved Julia when she was 19 years old; James and JiWon lost their beloved Deborah when she was 11; Sean and Stephanie lost their beloved Jesse when he was only 10 months; and Greg and LaNita lost their unborn child when he or she was 20 weeks—in fact, they lost five unborn children, each time at 20 weeks old![1]

These are just a few members of this group of mourning parents. I'm sure that you can add more names of people you know to the list. Now, they all find it difficult to answer what used to be rather simple questions: "Will your family all be home for Christmas?"; "How many children do you have?"; and "Are you doing ok?"

No matter who dies, death is traumatic. Nothing makes us feel so vulnerable and reminds us more of our own mortality than death. It shakes the foundations of family and friends and causes us to come face to face with the condition of our faith in Christ. As painful as it is to see a loved one pass away, it is even more heartbreaking when that loved one is a child, whether that child is stillborn in the womb, a few hours old, or an adult. Although it is not the will of God "that one of these little ones should perish" (Matt 18:14), it is ironic how frequently this seems to occur. Perhaps no other emotional experience is as numbing and paralyzing. Watching our children suffer is a fate worse than death. As parents, we strive, working furiously, and save for their well being. We can tolerate an extraordinary amount of hardship and discomfort for their sake and feel a great sense of satisfaction in their growth and success. Perhaps this is why it feels so wrong for a child to die before their parents. We accept the inevitable fate that our parents will pass away after a good, long life and we will have to bury them. Not so with our children. We have sacrificed so that they do not have to suffer the heartaches we have. We have dreams that they will be the citizens of a new generation of leaders of our families, the church, and the world. They should bury us, and it feels like death to bury them.

There are many in Scripture who also knew the heartbreaking loss of a child. An outstanding instance of this is the well-known event in the life of the patriarch Abraham[2] in Genesis 22, when he was called by God to do the unthinkable—to sacrifice his "only son" Isaac (Gen 22:2, 12, 16). Of course, it may seem that Abraham should be disqualified from membership within this select group of mourners because, ultimately, he did not lose his son. Isaac was spared at the very last second and a ram

1. In good conscience, I cannot refer to an unborn child, who still is an image bearer of God, with the impersonal pronoun "it."

2. We are introduced to the patriarch as "Abram" in the early portions of Genesis; his name is not changed to "Abraham" until Genesis 17. For the sake of simplicity, I use the more popular reference of "Abraham" throughout this chapter.

was provided as his substitute. I would be remiss not to mention that this ram has obvious theological implications to aid our understanding of the biblical doctrine of the substitutionary atonement of Jesus Christ.

The significance of this passage, however, is not only due to the salvation of Isaac but in furthering our understanding of Abraham. In his role as a father, this chapter points to a future day when another father, the *Heavenly Father*, would be required to also give up his "only begotten son" (John 1:14; 3:16).[3] It is this Father who not only belongs with that select group of mourning parents, but it is *his* sorrow that provides the foundation for why this can be seen not as a loss that will devastate the lives of families but rather, remarkably, as a source of comfort and joy.

I apologize at the outset that the bulk of my comments below have a strong fatherly focus and seems to ignore mothers. This is because Genesis 22 describes a very powerful event in the life of Abraham (a *father*) and Isaac. For whatever reason, the Scriptures do not describe Sarah's thoughts on the command to sacrifice Isaac. Perhaps this was intentional, to isolate the father-son focus which has monumental theological importance (this is the substance of this chapter). This does not mean that mothers cannot gain anything from this chapter. Far from it. My sincerest hope and prayer is that mourning mothers will also take to heart the lesson taught here, in a way that allows mothers to apply the lesson to themselves, and find it just as beneficial as fathers.

Significance of Abraham in the History of Salvation

In order to appreciate the magnitude of what is at stake in Genesis 22, we must consider the role that Abraham has in the history of salvation. The significance of Abraham and the subsequent narratives of his life in the book of Genesis (i.e., Gen 11:27–25:11) cannot be underestimated. It is in these chapters that we find the Lord dealing with him in a profoundly gracious way. According to the New Testament, Abraham himself is portrayed as the paradigm of the man who is justified by faith in Christ.[4] Many key themes that are central in the history of salvation can find

---

3. The Greek word here is *monogenēs*. Compare with Hebrews 11:17, where the same word is used to describe Isaac, thus affirming that Isaac is a type of Christ. See below for more on this matter.

4. Romans 4:3, 11–12; Galatians 3:6; James 2:21–23.

their covenantal origins in God's dealings with Abraham.[5] It is in Genesis 12:1–3 that God calls Abraham from his patriarchal land of Ur of the Chaldeans to his ultimate home in the land of Canaan. As he settles in this new land, God then addresses Abraham with an amazing promise:

> And I will make of you a great nation, and I will bless you and make your name great, so that you will be a blessing. I will bless those who bless you, and him who dishonors you I will curse, and in you all the families of the earth shall be blessed. (Gen 12:2–3)

The specific promise that God makes to Abraham is mentioned in Genesis 12:2: "I will make of you a great nation" (cf. Gen 18:18; 35:11). Embedded within this single promise are several necessary elements. In order for Abraham to become a "great nation" he must first have numerous descendants who will make up its citizenship; second, he needs a homeland for his people to dwell; third, he needs a constitution (or law) so that these people may live under order and not under the chaos of anarchy; and fourth, a king is required to provide godly leadership. For this one promise of nation-formation to be fulfilled, its component parts must be developed. In other words, the promise that God made to Abraham can be understood as both a single promise (nationhood) and multiple promises (descendant, land, law, and king). These four themes are so dominant within the biblical corpus that a case could be made that the fulfilling of these four-fold promises is one and the same with the unfolding of the history of salvation.

The People of Abraham

For our purposes, we will focus on only one of the four: the promise of descendants. When we examine the Abrahamic narratives, we see that God promised that He would bless Abraham with innumerable descendants. God uses three different images to communicate this. In Genesis 13:16, he says Abraham's descendants will be "as the dust of the earth, so that if one can count the dust of the earth, your offspring also can be

---

5. I stress the word "covenantal" since many of these themes (e.g., descendants/seed, land, sacrifice, faith, and nation) are found earlier in Genesis (Gen 1–11). They continue as blessings in the covenant that God makes with Abraham, which is inaugurated in Genesis 12, ratified in Genesis 15, and given a sign (circumcision) in Genesis 17.

counted."[6] In Genesis 15:5, God says his descendants will be "as the stars in the heavens."[7] In Genesis 22:17, God says his descendants will not only be as the stars of the heavens, but also "as the sand is on the seashore."[8] The common denominator of these three images is that the people of Abraham will be so numerous that they cannot be counted.

The rise of the sons of Abraham into the nation of Israel confirms that God is true to his word. By the days of Moses (approximately five hundred years after Abraham), the Israelites had become "fruitful and increased greatly; they multiplied and grew exceedingly strong, so that the land [Egypt] was filled with them" (Exod 1:7). The two censuses in the book of Numbers (chapters 1 and 26) also confirm that the children of Abraham had grown immensely. As they prepared to enter into the land of Canaan to begin the Israelite-Canaanite war, Moses alluded to God's promise to Abraham: "The LORD your God has multiplied you, and behold, you are today as numerous as the stars of heaven" (Deut 1:10).

By the time of Solomon, the Israelites had become "as many as the sand by the sea" (1 Kgs 4:20). In his prayer of dedication at the completion of the temple construction, Solomon acknowledged that the Lord had made him king over a people "as numerous as the dust of the earth" (2 Chr 1:9). These images are commonly used by the prophets to depict the blessed people of God—the true Israel—as a unified composite of the once divided houses of Israel and Judah, plus the inclusion of Gentiles (Hos 1:10–11).

The Old Testament fulfillment of the descendant-promise to Abraham, however, is only a shadowy reflection of the true fulfillment that the Lord had intended all along. The innumerable people that God had in mind are the ones who embrace by faith the true son of Abraham, Jesus Christ. Paul states in Galatians 3:7 that "it is those of faith who are the sons of Abraham." He also says in Galatians 3:29 that "if you are Christ's, then you are Abraham's offspring, heirs according to promise." The identity of the true descendants of Abraham, therefore, is not (nor has ever been) based upon a person's ethnic heritage, but rather faith in Christ, the true "seed" of Abraham (Gal 3:15).

Paul stressed that Abraham was justified prior to his circumcision and then received circumcision only as a seal of the righteousness that he

---

6. See also Genesis 28:14.

7. See also Genesis 22:17; 26:4, 24.

8. See also Genesis 32:12.

received by faith. The reason for this order (justified-circumcised) was to identify Abraham as the father of the uncircumcised Gentiles, insofar as they also embrace Christ by faith (Rom 4:10–12).

From this perspective, we can appreciate the extent of the fulfillment of this descendant-promise with greater depth. The church of Jesus Christ is a direct fulfillment of the promise that God made to Abraham. You and I can call Jesus "my Lord and my God" (John 20:28) because of the promises God made to Abraham. We are the true children of Abraham, heirs of the covenant blessings, proper citizens of the true "great nation" that God had promised him (i.e., the eternal Kingdom of God), and the rightful inhabitants of the true promised land (i.e., the New Heavens and Earth of Isaiah 66 and Revelation 21–22).

The Son of Abraham

We are given a rather significant piece of information at the outset of the Abrahamic narratives. Genesis 11:27–32, the introduction to Abraham, provides some of the themes that are found in the subsequent chapters (e.g., descendants, land). In verse 30 we are told that Sarah, Abraham's wife, was barren and had no children.[9] This poses a critical problem for Abraham in light of the descendant-promise described above. We established that in order for Abraham to become a great nation, he needs to have innumerable descendants; in order for Abraham to have innumerable descendants, he needs to have a family that would extend beyond his life; in order for Abraham's line to extend beyond his life, he must first have a son; in order for Abraham to have a son, his wife must be fertile and able to conceive. Sarah, however, is neither. So right from the start, Abraham faces an obstacle that seemingly prohibits the fulfillment of this promise. The resolution to this dilemma comes down to a single, necessary factor—Abraham needed to have a son. This was the first, indispensable step for Abraham. The covenantal promises that God made to him were dependent upon this.

From this point onward, Abraham eagerly awaits the birth of his son. Tension is built into the narrative as we read about various situations that threaten this birth from happening. Sarah is nearly disqualified to be the mother of this blessed child in the encounter with the Egyptian

---

9. The name of Abraham's wife is initially "Sarai" and is later changed to "Sarah" (Gen 17:15). She will simply be referred to as "Sarah" throughout these discussions.

pharaoh, who comes very close to taking her as his own wife (Gen 12:10–20). Later, a near identical event occurs with the king of Gerar Abimelech (Gen 20:1–18). If Sarah were to become the wife of another man, she could not be the wife of Abraham, and thus could not be the mother of Abraham's child.

As both Abraham and Sarah grow in age, they remain childless. They reach the age where they are both physically incapable of having children (Gen 17:17). Abraham tries to remain faithful and trust the Lord, but he grows increasingly unsure. The Lord had led him through an ancient ritual where he took upon himself a self-maledictory oath, which meant that the Lord would take the death-curse of the covenant upon himself if he failed to uphold his promise (Gen 15:1–6). Since the Lord cannot die, Abraham was initially assured, comforted, and believed in him (Gen 15:6).

Over time, however, Abraham grows more and more doubtful of the Lord's promise. His faith weakens, he grows desperate, and of course "desperate times call for desperate measures." Unable to discern how the Lord will fulfill this promise, he attempts to take matters into his own hands by engaging in an ancient practice of surrogacy, impregnating Hagar, Sarah's Egyptian handmaiden (Gen 16). Although this results in the birth of a son for Abraham, Ishmael (Gen 16:15), we are told that the Lord would fulfill his descendant-promise through the one born of Sarah (Gen 17:15–19).

Whenever we take matters into our own hands—instead of waiting for the Lord to work in our lives—things always get worse. This was certainly the case for Abraham. Tensions arise between Sarah and Hagar that ultimately ended with Hagar and Ishmael being forcibly removed from the household of Abraham. Abraham failed to see that the Lord was the cause of Sarah's barren womb (Gen 20:18). If the Lord had caused this, then only the Lord is able to open her womb. The one to whom Abraham needed to trust is the Lord; no scheme of his would overcome the Lord's divine will.

The Crises of Genesis 22

There was much at stake with the birth of Isaac. Abraham needed it. Truthfully, the Lord also needed it, to be true to his covenantal promise. Finally, by supernatural means, the blessed child is born in Genesis 21.

Isaac is born! Abraham can finally rejoice and celebrate. Not only was the Lord true to His covenanted word, Abraham can now experience the joys of fatherhood with the birth of his son. Isaac's birth also brought resolution to a tension that had been building in intensity throughout nearly ten chapters—from Genesis 12–21. God had promised that this child would come to Abraham, and he finally came. The promise of innumerable descendants was now possible. Everyone could breathe a sigh of relief.

At this point, however, Abraham's life takes an unexpected and shocking turn. The narrative of Genesis 22, which details the divine command to sacrifice Isaac, follows immediately after the narrative of Isaac's birth in chapter 21. In Genesis 21, we just experienced the release of some pent-up frustration with the birth of Isaac. We had enjoyed a moment to celebrate with Abraham and the Lord. In Genesis 22, however, we are thrown right back into a state of tension; we are hurled into both a theological and emotional tizzy from the command to end the life of this child of promise.

Theological Crisis

Theologically, the sacrifice of Isaac would mean that the Lord would have to violate his own covenantal obligations. Since he stressed that the descendant-promise would be realized specifically through Isaac, without Isaac, there would be no way for Abraham to become a great nation. As tragic as it would be for Abraham to remain without an heir, the notion of God as a covenant violator shakes the very foundations of our concept of God. Abraham would have been aware of this.

Also, the theme of descendants ("offspring" or "seed") entails a major motif in the Abrahamic covenant as well as the book of Genesis as a whole. It stems from as far back as Genesis 3:15, which mentions the birth of the "seed of the woman," who would come to crush the head of the wicked serpent. There are several genealogies in the earlier chapters of Genesis, which are designed to show the development of both the line of the woman and the line of the serpent.[10] According to this genealogical development, the blessed seed of the woman would come through Seth (5:1, 3), Noah (6:9), Shem (11:10), and then Abraham. This

10. For the line of the serpent, see Genesis 4:17–24; 10:1–32. For the line of the woman, see Genesis 5:1–32; 11:10–32.

would continue through Isaac. Not only would it be through Isaac that the Lord would make Abraham's descendants innumerable, but it would also be through Isaac that the birth of the "seed of the woman" would come. So the promised seed of Genesis 3:15 would also be a "son of Abraham" (Matt 1:1; Gal 3:16), and through this son, "all the nations shall be blessed" (Gal 3:8; cf. Gen 12:3; 22:18). To sacrifice Isaac, therefore, threatens the coming of this messianic seed.

In his reflections on this crisis, the author of the book of Hebrews suggests that since Abraham knew that the promise would be realized specifically through Isaac (Heb 11:17–19), he must have deduced the reality and power of the resurrection. In fact, according to Hebrews 11:19, Abraham received Isaac back from the grave, "figuratively speaking." Thus, the answer to this particular dilemma is the resurrection. Abraham believed that God would have raised his son back to life—and symbolically, Isaac *was* brought back to life.

Emotional Crisis

The emotional difficulty is more complex and is not addressed in Scripture as directly as the theological issue. It is this emotional struggle that led the Danish philosopher Søren Kierkegaard to describe this passage as "the teleological suspension of the ethical."[11] According to Kierkegaard, this incident placed Abraham into a crisis of faith, where he was called to violate a moral standard that God himself established. Kierkegaard concluded that there was a "suspension" of the "ethical" law during this crisis in order to fulfill the purpose (the "telos") of God's divine will. In simpler terms, "the end justifies the means."

The result of this conflict was that Abraham demonstrated his steadfast trust in the Lord, and Isaac was spared. All ends well. Without this incident, we would not have the picture of Abraham as the exemplary model of a man of faith (Rom 4:11).

Many have found this explanation by Kierkegaard intriguing, but not satisfying. This was best illustrated for me in a dialogue I had with the daughter of a very close pastor-friend. This young woman had a rather disgruntled childhood (as many children of pastors do). This was not due

11. Kierkegaard, *Fear and Trembling*, 68–70. This work, which was published under the pseudonym of Johannes de Silentio, shows that Kierkegaard was particularly intrigued by this specific event in the life of Abraham.

to any neglect on the part of the father but rather her inability to accept the validity of the truths of Scripture. Tragically, she ultimately rejected her Christian upbringing and abandoned her faith in the Lord. It was in this state of unbelief that I briefly conversed with her regarding the challenging events in Genesis 22. For obvious reasons, this passage invites difficult questions about the nature of God, and she was filled with them.

While it is true that it is through this event that we see Abraham as an outstanding man of faith and Isaac is spared, this young woman found it difficult to comprehend that God would even place Abraham in such a compromising position in the first place. Yes, everything worked out and all seems well, but did the Genesis 22 account have to be done in such a *traumatic* way? Why even put Abraham in such a horrifying position? I had no answer for her . . . at the time.

Quick-paced and Slow-motion narrative

The text of Genesis 22 tugs at our emotional heartstrings. The Lord commands Abraham to bring Isaac to Moriah to offer him as a burnt offering. Even if the loss of his son were the only thing Abraham had to experience, that alone would be sufficient to bring him (and the reader) excruciating grief. It is worse. Not only is Isaac to be sacrificed, but it also must be done by the hand of his very own father. Abraham is not permitted to simply hand him off to someone who would do this unimaginable act for him; he must be there, look his son in the eyes, and slaughter him—this son whom he adores—himself.

The narrative in Genesis 22 has moments when the action moves along quickly as well as moments when the action slows down. When you read the chapter, there seem to be times when the action slows to focus the attention on the relationship between Abraham and Isaac as father and son. All other actions are paced quickly so that the focus remains on this father-son motif. In doing this, we cannot escape the dreaded act of sacrifice, towards which the narrative builds. A father is called to sacrifice his son, and we are not given a moment to forget this.

Narrative slow down to describe Isaac

The narrative takes painstaking care to articulate the paternal affection that Abraham has for his son. This is elaborated by four descriptions of Isaac in verse 2, each one aggravating the anguish of this loving father. First, God refers to Isaac as "your son." The word "son" occurs ten times in verses 1–19, emphasizing the familial setting of the text. This alone is enough to make us pause and ponder the necessity of what is about to follow. Does God really expect Abraham to offer up his "son" as a sacrifice?

Not only is he called "son," but secondly, he is "your only" son. We know that this is simply not true. Ishmael was also a son of Abraham. In fact, he was the older son, a status of prominence in the ancient world. However, the descendant-promise was specifically to be fulfilled through Isaac (Gen 21:12). In light of this covenantal promise, Isaac truly was the "only son" of Abraham, since he alone was able to continue Abraham's family line.

Thirdly, God says that this son is the "one whom you love." This description seems superfluous and perhaps even cruel in light of what God requires of Abraham. To sacrifice "your son" who is also "your only" son is gut-wrenching enough, so why add the fact that this son is "one whom you love"? That description does nothing but intensify what this father is about to lose. It does nothing more than to strike a cutting blow upon an already open and sensitive wound.

Finally, this son is specified as "Isaac." Just in case Abraham tries to find a loophole and intentionally misunderstands God's will by offering some other "son" within his household or possibly the "son" of one of his valuable livestock instead, God specifies that it is Isaac whom he is to offer up.

Fast-pace movement to Moriah

Verse 2 is painful because each description slowly hits Abraham (and the reader) with successive and furious force. Verses 3–4, however, are fast paced, as they take us through a series of actions that speed up the tempo of the narrative. Between verses 2 and 3, three days pass, and Abraham has now arrived at the mountain range where this sacrifice would be offered—at Moriah (verse 4). For Abraham, however, these have been a difficult three days. John Calvin captures this well when he says, "God does not require him to put his son immediately to death, but compels him to revolve this execution in his mind during three whole days, that in preparing to sacrifice his son, he may still more severely torture all his own sense."[12]

After attending to the servants who had accompanied them on this trip (verse 5), Abraham takes his son Isaac and goes up the mountain to worship the Lord. A curious image is brought out in verse 6, where Abraham takes the wood to be used for the burnt offering and places it upon Isaac, again specified as "his son." Thus, Isaac carries upon himself the wood that would be used for his own sacrifice.

Slow-down for Father-Son Dialogue

As this father and son duo make their way up the mountain, the son notices something anomalous in verse 7. He says that they have the wood and the fire for the sacrifice, but they are missing the most important element—the lamb. Once again, the drama slows down in verse 7 so that this father-son interchange develops before us gradually, with the heart-wrenching dialogue drawn out line by line.

Isaac calls out to Abraham as "my father." Abraham responds with "Here am I, my son." The explicit references to "my father" and "my son" only highlight the tragedy that is about to befall them both. Abraham's answer to Isaac's question regarding the whereabouts of the lamb is well known: "God will provide for himself the lamb for a burnt offering, my son" (verse 8). Isaac trusts in his father, and verse 8 ends with the picture of the two continuing their journey "together."

Fast-pace setup for the sacrifice

The scene shifts in verse 9. They are now at the location where they had been instructed to go—Mount Moriah. The narrative quickly moves through a series of events: Abraham builds the altar, he arranges the wood for the sacrifice, he binds his son (again, the phrase "his son" adds to the emotional angst), and he places his son upon the altar.

12. Calvin, *Genesis*, 565.

Slow-down act of sacrifice

But in verse 10, the scene slows down dramatically, where the actions of Abraham are given to us step by step, almost second by second. He "sent out" his hand; then, with that same hand, he takes the knife. He is on the verge of thrusting that blade into Isaac, like a sacrificial lamb, and slaughtering *his son, his only son, the one whom he loves, namely Isaac.* The tragedy that the chapter has been building towards is about to be realized, and the drama of that moment is heightened by the depiction of the narrative in slow motion.

As the knife is about to be plunged into the son, at the final second, there is salvation. A voice, the divine Angel of the Lord, interrupts Abraham, halting him just as his hand is about to strike down upon his son (verses 11–12). Yes, Isaac is spared and a ram is given as his substitute (verse 13). To memorialize the event, Abraham names the place "The LORD will provide; as it is said to this day, 'On the mount of the LORD it shall be provided'" (verse 14).

Foreshadow of the Passion (Suffering) of the True Isaac

As I read this chapter, I am struck by the remarkable parallels with the gospel narratives of the passion of Christ. Consider the following:

1. *In both events, there is a divine call for a sacrifice.* As Isaac is to be a sacrifice, so Jesus Christ is also to be the sacrificial lamb at the cross.

2. *In both events, there is a father who endures the loss of his son.* Perhaps the most commonly overlooked parallel between Genesis 22 and the passion narrative is the presence of a father. In both events, there is a father who loses his son. Abraham's loss is figurative (Heb 11:19), while God the Father actually and truly loses his Son.

3. *In both events, the sacrificial son is described as the "only" son.*[13] As mentioned above, Isaac is the "only" son in terms of the covenantal promise to make Abraham into a great nation. Likewise, Jesus is the "only" Son of God who can bring salvation for his sinful people.

4. *In both events, the sons carry the wood that would be used for their sacrifice.* Isaac carries upon himself the wood that would be used for his imminent sacrifice (verse 6). The gospel of John depicts a similar

13. See Genesis 22:2, 12, 16; John 1:14; 3:16, 18; 1 John 4:9.

image of Jesus bearing his own cross as he heads towards Golgotha (John 19:17).[14]

5. *In both events, the sons remain dead for three days.* Jesus is in the tomb for three days; this is of first importance (1 Cor 15:4). Something similar is noted for Isaac. At the moment the divine command is given to sacrifice his son, it was clear that there was no way to avoid the inevitable. Abraham must do the unthinkable. He tried to avoid the will of God in previous events in his life, which led to disastrous results. But this time, Abraham would not falter. He would trust in the Lord and obey. Thus, at the moment when God instructed Abraham to offer up his son, Isaac had died, "figuratively speaking" (Heb 11:19); he would remain so until his "figurative" resurrection, three days later (Gen 22:4).

6. *In both events, the climax is reached in nearly the same locale.* Jesus is crucified and reaches the apex of his suffering on Golgotha,[15] which is nearby the city of Jerusalem. The location is not on a mount per se, but it is on a skull-like mound that gives it some elevation. Likewise, Abraham is called by God to take Isaac to the land of Moriah, specifically on one of its mountains. Moriah is mentioned in only one other place in the Scriptures, 2 Chronicles 3:1. This passage states that the location Solomon chose to construct the temple of God was on "Mount Moriah." We know that the temple mount is associated with Mount Zion, although the precise relationship between Moriah and Zion is not clear. They may be the same mount, with Zion being the new name for the previous Moriah, or they are near each other. In either case, this means that the ancient location of Moriah is possibly within the city-limits of Jerusalem or its outskirts. This suggests that the events of Genesis 22 occurred in the same vicinity where Jesus would be crucified many years later.

14. Although it is not stated explicitly in John, in the synoptic gospels, there is reference to Simon of Cyrene, who carried the cross for Jesus after he had done so for a period of time (Matt 27:32; Mark 15:21; Luke 23:26). It would seem that the physical brutality that Jesus endured exhausted him to such a degree that he was unable to continue carrying such a heavy burden; this required another (Simon) to take the cross the remainder of the way.

15. Matthew 27:33; Mark 15:22; John 19:17.

Father and Son at the Heart of Genesis 22

After considering the parallels above, we can see that Genesis 22 is an extraordinary Old Testament account that anticipates, even rehearses, the final hours of the life of Jesus Christ. There are meaningful images of Christ in this passage. The son Isaac and the substitute ram are two obvious ones. Commentators have suggested that Isaac was old enough that he could have physically overpowered Abraham and avoided being bound upon the wood of the altar. At the very least, he could have escaped on foot, as any young boy could have done over against an old man of nearly ten times his age. Yet Isaac does not do so. Presumably, he discerned the Lord's expectations of him, submitted to the will of God, and placed himself in the hands of his loving father. This is reminiscent of another Son who would do the same in nearly the same area, two thousand years in the future.

Abraham & Isaac and The Father & The Son

The image of Christ in Genesis 22 is central to the meaning of the passage and to the larger message of the Christian gospel that is proclaimed within it. The impact of this chapter echoes throughout the pages of Scripture. Gordon Wenham comments that this is the first time that we read about Abraham performing an act of sacrifice.[16] Since the location of this event is the eventual place of the temple, where regular and repetitive sacrifices would be offered (2 Chr 3:1), this parallel is significant. The offering of the ram as Isaac's substitute, therefore, is a microcosm of the Levitical doctrine of the atonement for the sins of God's people. The New Testament also highlights the Christocentric interpretation of this passage on several occasions.[17] Genesis 22 is impressive in its portrayal of Isaac as a type of Christ.[18] This is altogether crucial to the text and cannot be minimized, compromised, or marginalized.

16. Wenham, *Genesis 16–50*, 117.

17. John 3:16; Romans 8:32; Hebrews 11:17–19; James 2:21–23.

18. In the Greek translation of the Old Testament (Septuagint), the Hebrew word "only" to describe Isaac in verse 2 is translated as "beloved." When Jesus is called the "beloved" Son of God (Matt 3:17; 17:5; Mark 1:11; 9:7; Luke 3:22), this is most likely a reference to Genesis 22. When Jesus is called "only," this refers to his unique status as the "only-begotten" Son of God (John 1:14; 3:16, 18; 1 John 4:9). The Greek word for this unique birth is *monogenēs*, "only begotten." This word is not used in Genesis 22, but it does occur in Hebrews 11:19, referring to Isaac, and even alludes to this

That being said, it is just as important to observe that this chapter
also stresses the significance of Abraham as a father. In fact, the narrative
is told to us specifically from his point of view. It is Abraham who interacts with the angel of the Lord, not Isaac, and it is Abraham who is given
the direct mandate from God to sacrifice his son. The list of descriptions
of Isaac in verse 2 adds to this fatherly point of view. Verse 1 sets the
perspective that we are to have as we read this encounter—this is as much
about the test of *Abraham* as it is about the sacrifice of Isaac. Abraham's
faith faltered in the past, and he had demonstrated some level of doubt;
therefore, it was in need of refinement. This refinement comes as he is
put into a crisis in this chapter. Will he trust in the Lord this time, or will
he attempt to fix this situation on his own, as he tried to do with Hagar
in the past?

Genesis 22 testifies to the faith of Abraham. He trusts the Lord, and
his faith is seen in his obedience to the word of God (Gen 22:12, 16,
18; Jas 2:21–23). Everything that progresses from this point onward is a
direct consequence of Abraham's obedience. Any sorrow that he would
endure at the thought of losing his precious child is due to the fact that
he chose to follow the will of the Lord at the cost of his own personal
desires. The idea that Abraham would suffer for his obedience is unnerv-
ing because it seems irrational. It makes sense for Abraham to receive
blessings for following the will of God, but that does not seem to be the
case here—at least, not at first glance. Abraham obeyed the Lord, and it
nearly cost him everything.

Abraham and Isaac alone

The chapter narrows its focus to this father-son relationship from verse
6 onward, after the servants are left at the base of the mountain so that
Abraham and Isaac can continue on their journey alone. The narrative
strips away any peripheral elements and filters everything down to this
simple, yet profound image of a father taking his son to a place of sacrifice. There are no distractions: servants, other family members, or beasts
of burden. It is just Abraham and Isaac, a father and a son.

As we stated above, the image of Isaac on the altar anticipates Christ
upon the cross. In addition to this, there is the image of a suffering father

---

sacrificial event of Abraham's son. This is further support for the interpretation that
Isaac is a type of Christ.

(Abraham), agonizing over the loss of his son. Similar events will happen again in this area with so much more at stake. Genesis 22 provides a small glimpse of that future, tortuous day. Beyond Mount Moriah, in the far distant horizon of the history of salvation, is another mountain. On this mountain, there would also stand another Father, who again would be asked to do the unthinkable—to sacrifice his *Son*, his *only* Son, *the one whom he loves*. This Father, however, is not given the opportunity to spare his Son. Human parents often allow our children to get away with atrocious acts and wanton behavior with little to no consequence. We simply say, "It's okay," "Don't worry about it," or even, "Just don't do that again." This greater Father could not say any of those things. This Father had to pour out the full force of his holy wrath upon his only Son. He did not withhold an ounce of his righteous judgment, but rather "it was the will of the Lord to crush him" (Isa 53:10). God the Father "made him to be sin who knew no sin" (2 Cor 5:21) and thus his Son became a curse for us (Gal 3:13). While his Son was "stricken, smitten by God and afflicted" (Isa 53:4), we—who had gone astray and turned, each of us, to our own sinful ways (Isa 53:6)—were transformed from children of wrath to objects of his sovereign love (Eph 2:2–4).

Behind the father-son image of Abraham and Isaac is the greater theological relationship of God the Heavenly Father and his one and only Son. Isaac was spared because Jesus was not. Indeed, all of God's elect were spared because God the Father did not spare his only Son (Rom 8:32; cf. John 3:16). Jesus took upon himself our penalty so that we might have "the right to become children of God" (John 1:12) and thus call God our "Abba, Father."[19]

This redemption came at the highest price imaginable. Jesus paid it with his own blood. God the Father also paid in a sense by giving up what was most precious to him, his only Son. The pain of losing his only Son would have been excruciating. It is difficult to imagine, much less to describe. Abraham, however, is given a small glimpse into the broken heart of God the Father at that moment when he lost his Son. A pain so incomprehensible to most is a pain that Abraham understood. Other parents who have also endured such tragic loss may understand the heart of God the Father as well.

19. Romans 8:14; Galatians 4:6; cf. Mark 14:36.

Sorrow of God

The notion of the sorrow of God the Father is related to a very important Christian truth called the *impassibility of God*. A long held belief in the history of the church, this doctrine teaches us that God does not suffer.[20] At first glance, my comments above seem to oppose this doctrine. Many contemporary theologians in our day have done just that. However, a proper understanding of the sorrow of God the Father in Genesis 22 is consistent with the doctrine of divine impassibility. Not only should we agree with the impassibility of God, we should embrace it wholeheartedly as a necessary attribute of God that gives us full assurance that we can find joy from our sufferings.

A fuller understanding of the impassibility of God is to say that God does not suffer—in the sense that he cannot be manipulated, coerced, overwhelmed, or surprised into an emotional interaction that he does not want to have. This is not the same thing as saying that God is without any emotions. God is passionate for his people. He even sent his only Son into this fallen world to offer his life as a ransom because of his love for us (John 3:16). The cross did not coerce God into loving a sinful people; the cross was a manifestation of God's love for his people.[21] Indeed, our Father experiences both joy and sorrow, but he is affected in ways that are aligned, not in conflict, with his holy will, and therefore, he cannot

20. In chapter 2.1 in the *Westminster Confession of Faith*, it states that God is "without body, parts, or passions." The last phase, "[without] passions," is a reference to this doctrine.

21. Many Christians seem to believe that God the Father did not love us prior to the cross. They think that when Jesus died for us, he coerced the Father to love us as he does. Such a thought is not in lines with the Bible. Dr. Robert Strimple, my teacher of theology in seminary, compared the evangelical thoughts of God the Father and Jesus to Roman Catholic beliefs of Jesus and Mary. In popular Roman Catholic piety, Jesus is perceived as holy, full of wrath against believers, and thus unapproachable. However, Mary is merciful and approachable. Therefore, to pray to Mary is the way to appeal to Jesus because Jesus would never deny any request made by his mother. Evangelicals mistakenly view God the Father in the same way. He is holy and full of wrath, but Jesus is gentle and mild. The way to the Father, therefore, is through Jesus. Such a view of God the Father fails to see that he has a sincere and eternal love for us: "God so loved the world that he sent his only Son" (John 3:16). In this passage, "God" refers to God the Father. The reason Jesus died for us is because God so loved us. Think also of Ephesians, which says "he chose us in him before the foundation of the world" (Eph 1:4). Again, the one doing the choosing (predestining) is God the Father; this is why Paul blesses him in verse 3. It is God's love for us that led him to choose us for eternal salvation, not that he saw something in us that was worthy to save.

act against it. Any understanding of God that claims that he is susceptible to being manipulated by his people must be avoided. This is inconsistent with the Scriptures and undermines any hope for joy in times of suffering.[22]

Why is this understanding of God so important? Imagine what life would be like if it were not true. What if God is susceptible to changing his mind and you can change it?

According to those who reject divine impassibility, the answer is clear. The reason why God's people suffer is because we do not pray enough. After all, God suffers with us and his sorrow leaves him open to stepping in to help us in our times of need. If we continue in hardship, it must be because we did not coerce him to act. Maybe if we prayed harder and louder, read more Scripture, or gave more money to the church, our suffering would come to an end. Perhaps we should act like the false prophets of Baal in 1 Kings 18, who "cried aloud and cut themselves after their custom with swords and lances, until the blood gushed out upon them" (1 Kgs 18:28). Maybe then God would help us in our moment of need.

Not only that, but those who reject divine impassibility also cannot attribute any purpose to their suffering. If God can be manipulated, then there is no sense that he is in sovereign control of their lives. If God is capable of being manipulated, then he is just as surprised and shocked by the events that enfold as his people are. If he were not in absolute control, then how can suffering Christian believers be assured that there is purpose in their pain? They could not. They suffer and will continue to suffer, and this agony will ultimately be meaningless. For those who reject divine impassibility, that is what they must say to endure suffering.

Does this sound like the God of the Bible? Absolutely not. The God of the Bible does have emotions, but this does not make him vulnerable nor does it make him weak. He is not a heartless, cold, brute who has no regard for the well being of his creation. In fact, the divine plan that God has established for us is "good and acceptable and perfect" (Rom 12:2), and he is working all things according to this perfect will.

We often think that we know what is best for ourselves and for others. If we were in control of our own lives, then we would rid ourselves of any suffering, pain, or discouragement. In those moments, when I see a struggling individual or family, I tend to think that if I were God, I would

22. For a helpful description of divine impassibility, see Lister, *Impassible and Impassioned*, 2013; Duncan, "Divine Passibility and Impassibility," 1–15.

solve their dilemma with a snap of my fingers. If God is truly working in our lives according to his will, is it not odd for us to struggle through life? After all, if he is in control of everything, then why doesn't he do something about all our suffering? It is so easy to succumb to the path of arrogant Job and accuse God of injustice, all the while thinking that our will is indeed better.

In times like this, we must ask ourselves, "Who is the Creator and who is the creature?" God is totally and completely sovereign; he is in absolute control of everything. He is also all-knowing and all-powerful; I am not. My will is flawed and sinful; his will is perfect and gracious. My inability to see the perfection in his will does not change the fact that he is good and that he works for my good and for the good of all his people (Rom 8:28). Because God, who is the standard of goodness, is the one in control of my life, I can safely sleep at night knowing that God is working everything not just for my good, but my best! God's will is not merely good for me; it is the best for me. Nothing happens that catches him by surprise. If he were not sovereign (that is, if his will was susceptible to change), then he is not in complete control. We no longer have any assurance that there is a divine purpose for the suffering that we must endure.

Yes, in times of heartache, we are called to pray, and to do so fervently. If we are suffering, it is good to pray and to call upon our family and friends to lift us up to the Lord in prayer. However, we pray humbly, submitting ourselves to his will and purpose because his will is perfect. What we desire may not be what is best, but what God desires always is. That is how Jesus prayed as he contemplated the most painful day that anyone would ever have to endure—the day when he would take up his cross. He prayed to his Father that the horrors of the cross would pass from him, but nevertheless, "not my will, but yours, be done" (Matt 26:39; cf. Luke 22:42).

It may seem that divine impassibility has no direct impact upon the fellowship that Abraham had with a sorrowing Father. After all, Abraham's fellowship with God the Father appears to remain unharmed, whether he is sovereign and immutable or not. Though this may be true, what makes fellowship with God such a source of joy is the fact that we fellowship with the biblical God, who is greater than any suffering that we may face. If we believe we can manipulate him, then we claim not only that he is powerless to overcome our pain but also that we are more powerful than him! What joy is there in understanding a being who is so weak, to whom we are superior? There is joy in our fellowship with

God only because it is fellowship with a supernatural Father, one who is all-knowing, all-powerful, and in total and absolute control. Once God the Father determined that his only Son would pay for our sins by dying on the cross, he willingly put himself in a position that guaranteed he would suffer the death of his precious Son. To know such pain draws us into profound intimacy with him, a privilege that only a select few know.

The doctrine of the impassibility of God, when biblically understood, is a blessing. We do well to hold onto it.[23]

The True Father behind the Father

We are not given any specifics on the emotional struggles that Abraham experienced. He reacts to the difficult command of God with extraordinary immediacy and without hesitation. The only clues that we have of Abraham's emotional state are found in those descriptions of Isaac in verse 2 and the *father-son* language scattered throughout the chapter. This suggests that Abraham had a deep affection for his son and that his death would devastate him. There can be little doubt of that.

The New Testament states the astounding love between God the Father and Jesus his Son much more explicitly. The Father speaks of his love for his Son at his baptism: "This is my beloved Son, with whom I am well pleased."[24] The Father made the same statement of impassioned affection at Christ's transfiguration (Matt 17:5; Mark 9:7). Both of these references may allude to Genesis 22:2.[25] Jesus is also aware of the love of the Father and acknowledges it in his priestly prayer in John 17:23–24.

The gospel of John is particularly helpful in revealing the deep affection God the Father has for God the Son: "The Father loves the Son and has given all things into his hand" (John 3:35). He quotes Jesus saying, "The Father loves the Son and shows him all that he himself is doing" (John 5:20).[26] John describes the love that the Father has for his Son

23. The heresy of denying divine impassibility is known as Open Theism. For an orthodox response to the errors of Open Theism, see Ware, *God's Lesser Glory*; Frame, *No Other God*; and Huffman and Johnston, *God Under Fire*.

24. Matthew 3:17; Mark 1:11; Luke 3:22.

25. Recall that in the Greek Old Testament, the word "only" is interpreted and/or translated as "beloved."

26. In New Testament days, a father most likely trained his son in his trade as an apprentice. The son then mimicked the father in his life-career. Jesus describes the intimacy of his relationship with the Father similarly.

who willingly conforms to his Father's desires: "For this reason the Father loves me, because I lay down my life that I may take it up again" (John 10:17).

The salvation of God's people was costly for both the Father and the Son. For the Son, he gave up his very life and shed his own blood. For the Father, he had to give up the Son whom he loves. Romans 8:32 states, "He who did not spare his own Son but gave him up for us all, how will he not also with him graciously give us all things?" In this passage, Paul provides a persuasive argument for God's grace, claiming that God the Father was willing to give up that which is most precious to him, his own Son. If he did not withhold his most precious Son for his elect, then why would he withhold anything of lesser value? As significant as our spiritual blessings are in Christ—i.e., predestination, calling, justification, and glorification (mentioned in verses 29–30)—their value pales in comparison to that which is most precious to the Father, his Son. Therefore, we can be assured that our salvation in Christ is secure.

This argument, however, is only persuasive because there is truly a profound intimacy between the Father and the Son. It is unimaginable that the Father would give up his Son to be a sacrifice. No father could. But that is precisely what this Father did. If the relationship between Father and Son was indeed as intimate as Scripture teaches, then it would be safe to conclude that the only person who suffered as great as the Son at the cross is the Father. I wonder if Paul had Genesis 22 in mind to illustrate the high price that the Father paid for our salvation (Rom 8:32). To have such a perfect unity disrupted by the death of the Son would definitely bring tremendous sorrow to the heart of the Father.

In his work on the atonement, Donald Macleod insightfully comments on the loss of the Father in the cross of Christ. He says that the remarkable unity between the Father and the Son in their Trinitarian bond (John 14:10; 17:21) has direct implications for the Father, who suffers with the Son, but in his own way. He rejects any claim that would suggest the Father somehow also suffered on the cross, but he says that our redemption came at his expense, in his giving up of his beloved son. Macleod asks rhetorically: "If it is true at the human level that where one member of the church suffers all other members suffer with her, must the same not be true of the Trinity?"[27]

Commenting on the popular John 3:16, he says that unless we acknowledge that the Father suffered a major loss when he gave up his Son, the cross could not be an "exposition of *his* love." Macleod says: "If he sacrificed the Son impassively [without suffering a sense of loss] . . . where is the sacrifice for *him*?" He even goes on to allude to our passage in Genesis 22 and observes that analogy between the Father and Abraham:

> Why does the New Testament so often express the relation between the Father and the Son in language reminiscent of Abraham sacrificing Isaac? Abraham was called to sacrifice his son, his only son, whom he loved (Gen 22:2); God so loved the world that he gave *his* only Son (John 3:16; 1 John 4:9). Abraham did not spare his son, his only son (Gen 22:16); God did not spare his own Son, but delivered him up for us all (Rom 8:32).[28]

With this clear, biblical continuity between God and Abraham as fathers, it seems appropriate to observe the analogy between the sorrow suffered by God the Father in the death of his Son and the pain suffered by Abraham in Genesis 22. If the Father did not suffer an earth-shattering loss in the death of his Son, then "we are called to live lives of gratitude (Rom 12:1) for a pity that cost God nothing: the Unmoved Mover was unmoved by the death of his Son on the cross."[29]

Of course, there is an important difference between the pain of God the Father and the pain of any mere mortal man. The Father's relationship with his Son was perfect, without sin. No human father-son relationship can make such a claim. This does not deter from the fundamental point that Abraham *fellowshipped with the sufferings of the Father*. If indeed the eternal, perfect love of the Father and the Son can be manifest in the

27. Macleod, *Christ Crucified*, 50. As further biblical support for the suffering of God as father, Macleod also refers to the prophecy of Hosea, where God is forced to discipline Israel in the exile, "How can I give you up, O Ephraim? How can I hand you over, O Israel? How can I make you like Admah? How can I treat you like Zeboiim? My heart recoils within me; my compassion grows warm and tender. I will not execute my burning anger; I will not again destroy Ephraim; for I am God and not a man, the Holy One in your midst, and I will not come in wrath" (Hos 11:8–9). See Macleod, *Christ Crucified*, 51.

28. Macleod, *Christ Crucified*, 50–51.

29. Macleod, *Christ Crucified*, 51.

unity of believers (John 17:21, 22–23), then similarly, the sorrow of the Father when he lost his Son can also be manifest in the heart of Christian parents who mourn the providential death of their child(ren).

What is it like to lose a child, someone so close to you, your own flesh and blood? I have known many close friends who have had to endure such pain. I can see it in their eyes—the sadness and the heart-break—and it never seems to go away. I cannot even begin to fathom what they are experiencing. Only those who have known such loss could relate and appreciate the sting of such pain and agony. Abraham had a small glimpse of this with the figurative death of Isaac. However, behind the narrative of Genesis 22 lies another father, a greater Father, the true Father. This Father also had a Son, and they shared a perfect unity. Their perfect relationship was upset by the sacrificial death of the Son, a death that would have brought tremendous pain into the heart of the Father.

What I hope you can see is that ultimately, the narrative of Genesis 22 is not about Abraham and Isaac (so the fact that Abraham did not ac-tually lose his son is incidental). The true portrait of the father and son is that of the Heavenly Father and Jesus Christ, his only Son—Christ, who was sacrificially offered so that Isaac could be spared, and God the Father, who endured the agonizing pain of losing his beloved Son.

An Invitation to Fellowship with the Father

Abraham knows the sorrow of the Father. This is a profound and mean-ingful concept. For believers, joy is not determined by our circumstances, our material provisions, or the stability of our physical health. It is not based on our professional success, our personal wealth, the amount in our retirement fund, the size of our homes, the vacation trips we have taken or plan to take, the rules or regulations that have passed as the law of the land, who is sitting in the oval office, or even the size of our churches. Genesis 22 reminds us that our ultimate joy is also not based upon the well being of our children. It *cannot* be because they are frail, fi-nite, and subject to the effects of a fallen world, just like their parents. The joy of believers comes when we know our God in a close and personal way. Parents need to know this, and so do our children.

I think of the daughter of my pastor-friend who wrestled with why God would even place Abraham in such a horrible position. I cannot be certain why. After all, his thoughts are not my thoughts, nor his ways my ways (Isa 55:8). However, if Abraham was given an opportunity to share in the sorrows of the Father, then this is a very special sorrow, as painful as it may have been. It is special *because* it is painful. Abraham was in precious fellowship with the pain of his Heavenly Father as he suffered the loss of his perfect Son. Perhaps such knowledge is not something that my friend's daughter would value since she does not desire to draw closer to God as her Father. Nor can she appreciate the Son's suffering at the cross. What good is this deeper, theocentric understanding of the heart of the Father to someone who does not recognize the price *he* paid for our eternal security? What value is this to one who refuses to acknowledge him as her Heavenly Father? Such a person does not place any worth in *knowing God* because such a person does not *believe in God*. Without faith in the Lord, there is no stable basis to find any definition or meaning in the sorrow we suffer. The loss of a child seems pointless, purposeless, and irrational. Without faith in the Lord, it is difficult to see how such a perspective is incorrect. Nonbelievers have no hope because they have no faith in God.

For those who trust in the Lord, to know the heart of God our Father a little more is truly a profound and meaningful blessing, even when that knowledge is sharing in his grief. Just as we do not truly know the Son unless we know his sufferings, we will not truly know the Father unless we know his grief. Since it is *his* grief, it makes all the difference in the world. For Christians, there is nothing more precious. Such a thought should challenge us at the most fundamental level of our Christian faith. To know the Lord, to know our God, is the greatest blessing there is.

The psalmists would agree. He says in Psalm 42:1 that his soul pants and thirsts for God. Psalm 84:10 says, "For a day in your courts is better than a thousand elsewhere." It is better because in the courts of the Lord, we find the presence of the Lord. The one thing that the psalmist asked of God in Psalm 27 is to "dwell in the house of the Lord all the days of my life" and to "gaze upon the beauty of the Lord" (Ps 27:4).

In our blessed union with the Son, the barriers that separate us from our God are obliterated. In Christ, we have become "co-heirs" with

Jesus (Rom 8:17; cf. Gal 3:29) and can now call *his* Abba Father (Mark 14:36) *our* Abba Father (Rom 8:16; Gal 4:6). We can now see that our Heavenly Father paid a significant price for our salvation: "He gave his only begotten Son" (John 3:16). In eternity, he determined that his Son would be sacrificed for the sins of his people (1 Pet 1:20; Eph 1:4; 2 Tim 1:9). This would have come about even if the events of Genesis 22 had not occurred. But because they did, Abraham was given a glimpse into the greatest sorrow God the Father would have to endure, and Abraham was given a special opportunity to "fellowship" in the suffering loss of the Father.

All mourning parents are given the same opportunity.[30] The precious gift of growing in an intimate relationship with our Heavenly Father should be our greatest treasure and all others a distant second—even something as valuable as our family relationships, including our children. My youngest son celebrates every Father's Day by saying to me, "Dad, you are the second greatest father in the world." For Christian fathers, this is precisely the order that we want our children to embrace. God is the unchallenged and absolute first. We are second best, and we should be grateful for our place.

Final Word of Encouragement

I do not wish this kind of suffering upon anyone. Losing a child is one of the most painful experiences that I have witnessed. Yet the tragic reality is that many have known such pain, and many more will. If you are a person who knows the searing agony of losing a child, this is not the end of your

---

30. John Murray suggests that our union with Christ has a direct impact upon our relations with the other two persons of the trinity. Murray states this boldly when he says, "It is the mysticism of communion with the one true and living God . . . because and only because it is communion with the three distinct persons of the Godhead in the strict particularity which belongs to each person in that grand economy of saving relationship to us. Believers know the Father and have fellowship with him in his own distinguishing character and operation as the Father. They know the Son and have fellowship with him in his own distinguishing character and operation as the Son, the Savior, the Redeemer, and the exalted Lord. They know and have fellowship with the Holy Spirit in his own distinguishing character and operation as the Spirit, the Advocate, the Comforter, the Sanctifier" (Murray, *Redemption*, 172–73). Unfortunately, Murray does not elaborate any further on the union or fellowship that believers have with God as Father and Holy Spirit. His thoughts on those matters would have been invaluable since such union with the Father and the Spirit is not as scripturally clear as union with the Son.

world, even though it feels as if it is. There is a majestic and supernatural way in which your unspeakable loss as parents can be transformed into a divine source of supernatural joy. This does not come by terminating your pain, but by redefining it. This can only happen if we see that such pain is an insight into the heart of our Heavenly Father at the moment of the cross, a pain that you have a chance to share in. The Father has experienced the tragedies and horrors of losing his Son to a fallen and sinful world. As human parents, you have come to know the same pain.

If you are in agony, you have a similar opportunity as Abraham in Genesis 22. If you have not already done so, you can turn to the Lord Jesus Christ and embrace Him by faith, and thus see that you now have a Heavenly Father who also suffered the loss of his Son. Genesis 22 invites you to also share in the sorrowful loss of God the Father and come to know him in a way that only a select few can do. Abraham was one. Sam and Cassie are another. So are Mark and Lucy, James and JiWon, Sean and Stephanie, Greg and LaNita, and many others.

God has given to these beloved parents a very special opportunity. It does not appear to be much of anything because it is covered under a morass of pain and agony. The truth is, however, such suffering provides a very special opportunity. Our Heavenly Father bids them to come and share in his loss, something that only mourning parents can do. The task before this select group is to look beyond the *outward* so that they may encounter the *Omnipotent*, not to be defeated by appearances of *devastation* but to envision an invitation for *devotion*, not to be burdened with mere *earthly frights* but by faith to fellowship with the *everlasting Father*.

7

Joy in a Broken Family

> *How can I give you up, O Ephraim? How can I hand you over, O Israel?*
> *How can I make you like Admah? How can I treat you like Zeboiim?*
> *My heart recoils within me; my compassion grows warm and*
> *tender.*
>
> Hosea 11:8

Many Christian books on the subject of broken marriage usually begin in the same way. First, a troubled couple is introduced and their issues are shared in great detail. Second, the suffering experienced by either one or both husband and wife are described, which leaves the reader sympathetic. Finally, after significant counseling takes place, there is a resolution to the conflict and they can now live happily ever after.

I could start this chapter in a similar manner, illustrating the prevalence of broken marriages, the emotional damage that they cause, and the need for reconciliation. However, I won't do so for several reasons. First, there are so many troubled marriages to choose from that it is not necessary to bring awareness to this problem. It is everywhere. Everyone knows this and it is growing to epidemic proportions. In many churches, the most common issue on the pastor's counseling agenda is marital conflict. Reformed Theological Seminary offers a very helpful class on biblical counseling in marriage and family issues. It is one of the most popular *electives* in our curriculum. I stress that this is an *elective*. It is not a required course for any degree, yet it is consistently packed with students. Many who enroll in this class are not even students; they are members of nearby churches. Such a course is common in other seminaries as well, all of which are very popular. It is not uncommon for troubled couples and families to seek out help from local counseling centers—only to find that the next available session is months away. The high demand for pastors, seminaries, counseling ministries, and training centers in Christian (or even secular) counseling undeniably demonstrates that there is a huge need for marriage and family counseling within our communities. Many are already well aware of this problem; the tricky part is to determine the solution.

Second, I do not need to describe the devastation experienced in broken marriages because sadly, we know it all too well. Even if you personally have not known such pain, you probably know someone close to you who has. It is all around us, like a pervasive stench that will not go away. When a marriage is struggling or tragically comes to an end, many try to downplay the pain, as though this were equivalent to the breakup of a cordial dating relationship, where couples go back to being "just friends." Nothing could be farther from the truth. A troubled or broken marriage is extremely painful, and this pain cannot be avoided.

Third, biblical reconciliation is not the primary focus of my thoughts in this chapter, although I hope that I can also make a small contribution to that discussion.[1] Reconciliation remains an absolutely necessary goal, but it is not achieved as much as we would hope. I don't need to get into all of the well-known statistics on the divorce rate within the church and our society at large. Not only is it appallingly high, but the fact that these numbers have not changed over the years also testifies to the hardness of the human heart. This does not even account for the greater number of marriage relationships that have been reduced to mere coexistence between a husband and wife. No passion, no love, no sacrifice—just agreed upon terms of cohabitation for the sake of their children, their reputations, financial benefits, and other factors.

In spite of the fact that numerous books are constantly being published on this subject and the church is perpetually addressing this issue, the state of marriage is not improving; in fact, it is getting worse.

---

1. For a good biblical treatment on reconciliation, see Sande, *Peacemaker.* The principles of biblical reconciliation found in this book are not just applicable to marital issues but to relational conflicts of all kinds as well (sibling rivalries, church relations, etc.).

This is for you

In this chapter, I am addressing those in troubled marriages who have remained faithful to their sinful spouses and suffered because of it. It is true that in most marital issues, the problem is often caused by a combination of the sins of both the husband and the wife. However, there are times, more often than we would imagine, when one spouse takes advantage of the faithfulness of the other. There are spouses who strive and sacrifice to be true to their marital vows. These spouses' devotion and loyalty are frequently abused by their marital partners who sinfully seek their own selfish pleasures—whether this be in adulterous affairs, pornographic activities on the internet and/or other related businesses (e.g., overindulgent fascination with seductive romance novels), lengthy and unjustified time away from the home, or just frolicking around with friends in excess while ignoring their spouses.

We must remember that in such cases where there is a sinful spouse, there is another who has been sinned against. Whenever such couples seek counsel, the word of instruction from Scripture for the spouse in sin is clear—repent. There is obviously much more to ministering to such a person, but the basic message that needs to be given remains the same. They have sinned, so they need to repent and ask for forgiveness from God[2] and from their spouse.[3]

However, what do we say to those faithful spouses, the ones who sacrificed time, energy, and money for the sake of their helpmates? Imagine a loving wife who has to work extra hours in order to pay off the exorbitant debt her immoral husband has accrued through excessive activities on internet porn and secret rendezvous with women of the night. This wife remains loyal and pays the debt, only to see her husband thank her by engaging once again in ungodly internet sites that rebuild that massive debt. This is a complex scenario that the Scripture does not directly address. Is there any relief or even joy from the emotional trauma that results from such treachery? How do we comfort one who has given up so much and gained so little? Is there any hope for joy at all for one who remains so loving and loyal?

Although this chapter focuses predominantly on broken marriages, it also pertains to the struggles of godly parents who faithfully disciple their children to believe in Jesus but, for whatever reason, these children

2. Psalm 51:7; Matthew 9:6; Mark 2:7–10.
3. Matthew 6:14; 18:21–22; Luke 17:3–4.

become corrupt to the point of rejecting the Christian faith.[4] For believing parents, there is little that is more painful than their children's spiritual struggles. In spite of all their best efforts to raise their kids in the ways of the Lord, they run in the complete opposite direction. The obvious solution for such families is the repentance of these children. However, as the parents wait patiently in hopes that the children will come to their spiritual senses, is there another way for them to find comfort, or even joy?

Learning from the Life of Hosea

It is for believers such as these that I write this chapter. We will do so by turning our focus to the most peculiar marriage in the Old Testament, that of the prophet Hosea.[5] The task of a prophet was not limited simply to the proclamation of "the word of the Lord."[6] The Lord often used relationships and events within their very lives for the express purpose of communicating his divine message to his people. This was the case for Hosea.

Because Hosea was a husband and father, the perspective is naturally masculine. As such, it is difficult to describe scenarios from the point of view of a wife and mother. I have made attempts to be sensitive to both genders. I can only hope that female readers will be able to apply the principles described here and overlook the male-centric angle.

---

4. My interest is in the internal challenges and struggles within the family, particularly marriage. The unusual marriage of the prophet Hosea will be the basis of my comments. His role as a father is also mentioned in the Scripture, but it is not nearly as developed as his role as a husband. I do include a brief section on Hosea's struggles as a father and thus include parents of disobedient children as another group I am considering in this chapter. The principles described can also be applied broadly to relationships outside of marriage in similar lopsided (better yet, one-sided) relationships. For example, sibling relationships, friendships, dating couples, and extended family.

5. My comments focus on chapters 1–3 of Hosea. Obviously, there is so much more that can be said about the prophet and his writings than can be covered in this brief treatment. For further study or detailed comments on the book of Hosea, see Dearman, *Book of Hosea*. This commentary is one of the most helpful on this prophetical book. The introduction to this work interacts with all recent commentaries and related areas of study. Dearman is also insightful as a commentator and exegete of the biblical text, which is difficult.

6. Hosea 1:1; Joel 1:1; Jonah 1:1; 3:1; Micah 1:1; Zephaniah 1:1; Haggai 1:1; Zechariah 1:1; Malachi 1:1; cf. Jeremiah 1:2; Ezekiel 1:3.

According to Hosea 1:2, Hosea was told to take both a "wife of whoredom" and "children of whoredom." This meant that he would not be able to experience the comforts and pleasures of a supportive and loving family. Like all the biblical prophets, Hosea had a difficult life, largely due to the message he was called to proclaim—to tell the stubborn, sinful, stiff-necked people of God to repent of their sins and return to the Lord.[7] Hosea would find no sympathy from his people. Instead, he probably found anger, rejection, and hatred. After a long, hard day of proclaiming the prophetic word, he would return home. Whereas most men would find comfort and support from their wives and children, Hosea did not. He would find the same antagonism from his family as he did from the rebellious community. This was the life of Hosea.

If Hosea's home life, as alluded to in chapters 1–3, were historical fiction (as many scholars believe it was), then it could be appreciated merely as a powerful, even satiric, literary device, and no one would lose much sleep over it. Understanding Hosea's family life as a historical reality makes it easily the most tragic *human* marriage in the Old Testament. I stress that this is a *human* relationship because the prophet tells us that his marriage was meant to be a reflection of a greater one, the Lord's covenantal marriage to his bride, the people of Israel (Hos 1:2).

If Hosea's marriage was tragic, the Lord's was heartbreaking—beyond heartbreaking. As we read about Hosea's family life, we easily (and understandably) take pity on him, praying that neither we nor anyone we know would ever know such pain. We are left with a certain degree of tension, however, because the harsh reality is that we all know similar types of pain.

My hope is that the message of this chapter will refrain you from quickly concluding that this suffering only brings mind-numbing and heart-wrenching agony. We pray that we would never know such betrayal in our personal relationships, but more is happening in Hosea's story than we perceive at first glance. In fact, Hosea can be seen as a blessed husband because he represents a greater Bridegroom who also knew the torment that comes from loving an unfaithful spouse. This can also be the experience of those who share in the prophet's sufferings. According to our theme passage (1 Peter 4:12–13), not only do they share in the sufferings of Hosea but also that of the great Bridegroom whom he represents.

7. See chapter 8, "Joy of a Rejected Messenger" for further descriptions of this.

An Unexpected Arrangement

Using my sanctified imagination, I can visualize Hosea's early years. I suspect that he did what all faithful, young, single men do—pray about his future wife. It really is not that different in our contemporary days. In my undergraduate college years, I had many young Christian friends, and we would often get together for coffee, meals, study sessions, etc. Our conversations somehow always seemed to gravitate back to marriage. For some reason, this was one of our favorite subjects of discussion. It often seemed that if we were not talking about theology or Christian living, we were talking about marriage (at least, what little we knew about marriage as single eighteen to twenty-two year olds). The hardship of marriage was more theoretical in our innocent minds; it was merely fodder for jokes and laughs than serious contemplation on commitment, reconciliation, suffering, sacrifice, and faith. Some of us were in dating relationships, which we mistakenly thought of as comparable parallels. We even used these minor struggles as illustrations in small group Bible studies and words of counseling. In retrospect, I can see now that discussing marriage so frequently was a bit odd, but it was fun to speculate. We were young, idealistic, hopeful, and naïve. The future was an unknown yet exciting horizon, and we could see nothing but the beauty of what our future marriages would be.

I am not certain if the poem of Lady Wisdom in Proverbs 31 was known in Hosea's day, but if he was aware of it, I dare say that it would have inspired thoughts of his future wife. My seminary roommate and I were fascinated by the acrostic organization of Proverbs 31, so we took the English alphabet and used it to create our own acrostic that listed the attributes we were looking for in our future spouses.[8]

Love poems like the Song of Songs were common in the ancient world. Such poems would have shown Hosea (and other young men) that marriage is not merely a practical arrangement for the sake of familial needs, gaining dowries, or making political alliances. There is also an element of passionate love that can only be known in the context of a husband-wife union. Literature such as these ancient biblical texts would have encouraged many young Israelites, including Hosea, to pursue such a spouse.

---

8. For the record, we both married better than our lists!

Choose wisely

One of the dominant themes in the Old Testament is the importance of choosing a godly wife. The Old Testament teaches the importance of Israelites marrying fellow Israelites to prevent the descent into idolatry. This instruction was given to the Exodus generation as they left Egypt (Exod 34:15–16), and as their children entered into the land of Canaan, the same mandate was given to them in Deuteronomy:

> You shall not intermarry with them [the Canaanites], giving your daughters to their sons or taking their daughters for your sons, for they would turn away your sons from following me, to serve other gods. Then the anger of the LORD would be kindled against you, and he would destroy you quickly. (Deut 7:3–4)

The instruction these passages give is clear and unambiguous. The prohibition is not against *interracial* marriages. It is against *interfaith* marriages. In the ancient world, to marry a Canaanite was to marry outside of your community of faith. The biblical mandate was (as it remains today) that marriage is to be "in the Lord" (1 Cor 7:39). Therefore, Hosea would have envisioned that his future, ideal marriage would be to a young, God-fearing Israelite girl.

Lessons from the past

Hosea would have known better than to marry a foreigner, as there are plenty of examples in the history of Israel that illustrate the pitfalls of marrying outside the household of faith. According to Judges 3:5, it was the violation of this mandate that caused Israel's spiritual decline and her eventual exile. Samson, the last judge in the book of Judges, had a propensity to engage with Philistine women (Judg 14–16). Each woman that he became involved with led him closer to his eventual downfall. The adulterous nature of his relationships is heightened when compared to the godly marriage of Othniel, the first and ideal judge.[9] Not only did Othniel marry an Israelite girl, he married a girl from the victorious tribe of Judah.[10] His marriage was portrayed as the model of perfection in the book of Judges, where we are told that his wife was the daughter of the

9. Judges 1:12–13; Joshua 15:16–17; 3:7–11.
10. Judges 1:2, 4, 8, 17–19.

legendary Israelite hero, Caleb.[11] In contrast, Samson married an un-named Philistine woman (Judg 14:1–3), whom he quickly deserted for foolish reasons (Judg 14:15–20), and then engaged in immoral sexual relations with other Philistine women (Judg 16:1, 4).

It is interesting that the book of Judges used the Judge's marriage to evaluate their godliness. This is because Israel's demise came from marrying outside of the covenant community (Judg 3:5). In the postexilic era, Ezra panicked when he saw that the priesthood engaged in this same sinful act (Ezra 9:1–2). He knew that this was the cause of the exile of their forefathers. Although the postexilic Judeans were restored to their homeland, they could be exiled yet again if they continued to violate their covenant like their forefathers. Interfaith marriages were leading them back in that direction (Ezra 9:5–15), so Ezra called for mass repentance and severance of those unbiblical relationships (Ezra 9:3; 10:1–3; cf. 10:10–12; Neh 13:23–31).[12]

Solomon the wise man but foolish king

Hosea would also have been familiar with the stories of Solomon, as Solomon was foundational in the formation of the Israelite monarchy. Solomon was not only famous for his incredible wisdom but he was also the king most responsible for establishing Israel as a national power in that region of the ancient world with her own cultural distinction.

---

11. Judges 1:20; cf. Numbers 13:30; 14:6–9; Deuteronomy 1:35–36.

12. The mass divorce recorded in Ezra 10 is difficult to comprehend in light of other biblical texts that clearly outlaw divorce, such as Malachi 2:10–16 and 1 Corinthians 7:12. In a careful, thoughtful work on the divorce prohibition in Malachi 2, Gordon Hugenberger has successfully demonstrated that Malachi does not prohibit divorce absolutely but rather the kind that violates previously binding vows; see Hugenberger, *Marriage as a Covenant*. In the case of Ezra 10, the previous vow was to "not give our daughters to the peoples of the land or take their daughters for our sons" (Neh 10:30). Hugenberger provides detailed exegetical evidence in Malachi 2:10–16, which shows Malachi would have shared Ezra's concern of interfaith marriages as an act of abomination (see Hugenberger, *Marriage as a Covenant*, 48–83). Thus, he doubts if Malachi "would have countenanced any lesser remedy than the dissolution of these marriages for so grave an offense" (see Hugenberger, *Marriage as a Covenant*, 17). Given the divorce language in the judgment against Israel (Lo-ammi, "you are not my people" in Hos 1:9; see below), an absolute prohibition against divorce in Malachi 2 would find the Lord violating his own holy law, which is a theological impossibility.

Gerhard Von Rod refers to this period of Israel's history as *the Solomonic Enlightenment.*[13]

Despite his wisdom, Solomon brought catastrophic destruction upon Israel through his love of women (1 Kgs 11:1–13). Solomon thought it wise to marry the daughters of regional nations surrounding Israel in order to establish alliances with them. These alliances would strengthen his borders by adding a layer of protection from potential foreign invaders and provide allies in case of war. As politically strategic as this may have been, the religious influence of his numerous wives led to his own spiritual deterioration and eventually the downfall of the nation of Israel. Solomon prioritized worldly stratagems over the godly mandates placed upon the Israelite monarchy by the word of God (Deut 17:14–20). In other words, he chose the "wisdom" of this world instead of the apparent "foolishness" of God, and failed to follow a biblical design for marriage (1 Cor 1:18–31). These are just a few negative examples that would have warned Hosea (and all Israel) of the dangers of marrying outside of the will of God. These truths still stand today.

Marry who?

Hosea, therefore, would have been shell-shocked when he learned of his future bride. Many modern commentators, even the staunchest of conservative scholars,[14] are so appalled at this dreadful choice for a wife that they do not take this as a literal marriage, but rather as an allegory.[15] Whether this marital union is understood as an actual historical reality or a rhetorical metaphor, it communicates the same prophetic message to the ancient Israelites. In this sense, the function/message of the marriage remains unchanged. So Geerhardus Vos says: "The dispute between the allegorists and realists is interesting, but doctrinally, the points of arrival

13. Von Rad, "Beginnings of Historical Writing," 203.

14. See Calvin, *Commentaries on the Twelve Minor Prophets,* 1:43–44, where he says: "That this was done by the Prophet seems very improbable . . . yet it seems not consistent with reason, that the Lord should thus gratuitously render his Prophet contemptible; for how could he expect to be received on coming abroad before the public, after having brought on himself such a disgrace? . . . Their opinion, therefore, is not probable, who think that the Prophet had taken such a wife as is here described." See also Young, *Introduction to the Old Testament,* 245–46, and Keil, *Twelve Minor Prophets,* 1:35.

15. For a survey of various interpretations of Hosea's marriage, see Freeman, *Introduction to the Old Testament Prophets,* 178–82.

on each view coincide."[16] As the simplest, albeit jaw-dropping, interpretation is to understand this as an actual marriage, I proceed on that basis.

Normally, Hosea's father would have set up a marriage for his
son, since arranged marriages were not an uncommon custom in those
days.[17] In Hosea's case, the one arranging his marriage was not his earthly
father but rather his Heavenly Father. With God as his matchmaker, you
would think that he was in safe hands and guaranteed an ideal and loving spouse. If there were ever anyone whom Hosea could trust to choose
a godly wife for him, someone who would love him, care for him, and
respect him, it would be the Lord. However, the one whom God chose for
Hosea was truly unexpected: "Go, take to yourself a wife of whoredom
and have children of whoredom" (Hos 1:2).[18] So, Hosea married Gomer,
the daughter of Diblaim (Hos 1:3).

The Prophetic Message of Hosea

This very eccentric husband-wife union was the basis for the Lord's
prophetic message to his people, which he communicated through his
appointed prophet Hosea. The book of Hosea can be divided into two
major sections, chapters 1–3, which recounts Hosea's marriage, and
4–14, which is composed of a collection of prophetic speeches. Since the
marriage theme is the focus of my attention, particularly the correlation
between the Lord and Hosea, it would help us to be somewhat familiar
with the content of those first three chapters.

16. Vos, *Biblical Theology*, 261. See also Longman and Dillard, *Introduction to the
Old Testament*, 403.

17. We find this practice as early as the days of Abraham, who set up the marriage
of his son Isaac (Gen 24).

18. The inclusion of "have" is common in English bibles, which presumes that
the three children mentioned throughout chapter 1 are identical with these "children
of whoredom." However, the grammar of the Hebrew suggests that Hosea is also to
"take," meaning *adopt*, these "children of whoredom." Therefore, it is possible that the
"children of whoredom" are not Jezreel (1:3–4), Lo-Ruhamah (1:6), and Lo-Ammi
(1:8–9) but rather an unmentioned group of children that Gomer brought into the
marriage from her previous sexual escapades. Either view is plausible, although I find
it awkward to introduce a group of children in 1:2 and then mention an entirely different set subsequently. The grammar, however, is clear. The connection (or lack thereof)
between the "children of whoredom" and the three in chapter 1 should not outweigh
their designation of being "of whoredom," which clearly is intended to represent the
idolatrous nature of Israel.

Hosea 1–3

The book of Hosea opens with God's command to Hosea to marry an adulterous woman: "Go, take to yourself a wife of whoredom and have children of whoredom" (Hos 1:2). Immediately, we are told why Hosea is to do this in the second half of that verse: "For the land commits great whoredom by forsaking the LORD." From this verse, it is clear that there is a direct correlation between Hosea's marriage and the Lord's. The people of God had made a vow to faithfully follow the Lord at Mount Sinai (Exod 19:8; 24:7), but their history reflected their disobedience. They had acted like an adulterous bride by worshiping false gods. Hosea's marriage to Gomer was an earthly reflection of that spiritual reality.

Through the marriage image, the Lord brings his covenant lawsuit against the people. The declaration of their sins (indictment) is represented in the actual adulterous marriage of Hosea; the pending curse (penalty) is seen in the names of his rebellious children (Hos 1:3–9). For Israel, Hosea's marriage was a regular reminder of their sins, which only reinforced his prophetic message that they needed to repent of their idolatrous ways. If they did not, then the curse of the covenant would be enforced. God would no longer have mercy upon them (Hos 1:6), they would be declared "not my people" (Hos 1:9) and suffer the dreaded curse of exile. Thus, the message and life of the prophet are closely intertwined, so much in fact that there is no difference between the two. His personal family life was his message!

His children were of "whoredom" (Hos 1:2). Jezreel is said to belong to Hosea since verse 3 states that Gomer "bore him [Hosea] a son." However, the reference to Hosea is strikingly absent for the other two children, Lo-Ruhamah and Lo-Ammi, in verses 6 and 9 respectively. Gomer "bore" these two children without the indirect object "him"—that is, Hosea. This suggests that Gomer's infidelity resulted in the birth of the final two children. Hosea was daily reminded of his wife's adultery in these two children. He could neither avoid them nor abandon them.

Chapter 2 describes Gomer's adulterous ways in gross and deplorable detail. She is depicted as abandoning Hosea and chasing after her lovers. She gives credit to them for providing her daily provisions of bread, water, wool, flax, oil, and drink (Hos 2:5). Even though Hosea blocks her way to get to her lovers, she is determined to do so anyway (Hos 2:6) and only returns to Hosea as a consolation prize (Hos 2:7). In truth, Hosea was the one who provided for all her needs, but she did not acknowledge his love and fidelity.

As we continue in chapter 2, there seems to be a shift in who the text is addressing. In verses 6–8, the immediate person Hosea addressed was Gomer, but from the middle of verse 8 to verse 13, Israel becomes the new explicit subject of Hosea's prophecy. Throughout chapters 1–3, the parallel between Gomer and Israel is so close that it is not clear who the prophet is describing—is it Gomer or Israel? No place better exemplifies this than in chapter 2. Because of the close correlation between Gomer and Israel, the graphic images of a determined woman who relentlessly pursues her lovers and an ungrateful wife who credits her daily bread to someone other than her devoted husband are designed to apply both to Gomer and Israel interchangeably. Therefore, to describe Gomer is also to describe Israel and vice-versa.

The effect of this identity dynamic also tells us that we are not certain from whose perspective the prophecy is being given. Is it the Lord or Hosea who is preventing his spouse from finding her adulterous partners (verses 6–8)? Is it the Lord or Hosea who is described as providing for his bride who credits his gifts to her lovers (verses 9–13)? This ambiguity is a fruit of the living union between the Lord and his prophet.

Chapter 3 contains images similar to the previous two chapters. It begins with Gomer selling herself off at a marketplace like a common commodity. In this appalling and disgraceful scene, Hosea actually has to buy back his own wife. In summary, it is clear that Hosea married Gomer only by divine mandate. Their marriage started off well, and Gomer began as a loving wife with dreams of building a godly family with Hosea. Together, they had several children, although two of them may have resulted from her unfaithfulness. As a result of this, there was a time when the two were separated (Hos 2), but they were reunited again later (Hos 3).

We are left with an image of the Lord and Hosea as two bridegrooms who have faithfully loved their respective wives. They have cared for them, provided for all of their material needs, and even maintained a safe place for their children to grow. However, their love was not reciprocated. Their wives, who should have expressed gratitude and affection for the love that was showered upon them, responded with abject rejection and flagrant covenantal violation. For Hosea, this continued for the duration of his marriage; we are never told that Gomer changed her sinful ways. For the Lord, this was the case for centuries prior and even continued

after the exile (as the history of the Old Testament tells us). Both know
the pain of rejection, and Hosea is brought into fellowship with the suffering of the Lord. A time will come in the future where Israel will be
justified and cleansed so that she will be a radiant and beautiful bride.
This will only come about because the Lord himself will shed his blood
for her, to sanctify her "so that he might present the church to himself in
splendor, without spot or wrinkle or any such thing, that she might be
holy and without blemish" (Eph 5:27).[19]

Hosea 4–14[20]

Where the theme of the covenant lawsuit was presumed in Hosea 1–3,
it is explicitly stated in Hosea 4–14. This section opens with the Lord
declaring such a "lawsuit" (Hebrew *rîb*; Hos 4:1–3) against Israel. John
Dearman subdivides this section into two major panels that rotate the
themes of sin, judgment, and redemption as in chapters 1–3.[21] The first
panel is Hosea 4:1–11:11; the second is 11:12–14:8. In the first panel, the
Lord declares his "lawsuit" against Israel (Hos 4:1–3), elaborates on her
pending judgment (Hos 4:4–10:15), and describes her restoration using
images of the Exodus (Hos 11:1–11). In the second panel, the prosecution
of the lawsuit continues (Hos 11:12–12:14), the judgment upon Israel is
further depicted, where the Lord is portrayed as a predator and Israel as
his prey (Hos 13:1–16), and the prophecies come to an end with Israel's
redemption by the Lord (Hos 14:1–8). Hosea 14:9 is a closing declaration
of wisdom to the one who understands these oracles.

Hosea/The Lord as Husband to an Immoral Wife

The reason for Hosea's shocking family situation is given in Hosea 1:2.
He is instructed to take (marry) "a wife of whoredom" and have "children
of whoredom" for a very specific reason: "For the land commits great
whoredom by forsaking the LORD" (Hos 1:2). The repetition of the word
"whoredom" in both the description of Hosea's family and the conduct

19. Interestingly, this renewed marriage is not used by Hosea to communicate the
glories of the New Covenant blessings. The marriage image is used exclusively to show
the sins of the people.

20. I provide a brief summary of chapters 4–14 for the sake of completion.

21. Dearman, *Hosea*, 16–21, 145–46, 294–95.

of the land shows that the Lord wanted to demonstrate a correlation between his covenantal relationship with Israel and the family relations of the prophet. Simply put, Hosea's marriage was symbolic of a greater covenantal relationship between the Lord Yahweh and his people, Israel.

This is not the only place in Scripture that the Lord's relationship with his people is compared to a marriage. Paul does the same thing in Ephesians 5:22–33. It is easy to think that the Lord used the husband-wife relationship as an illustration to describe his relationship with his people, but the order is reversed. We have marriage relationships because of the greater spiritual reality that they represent. The purity of the husband-wife bond represents Christ's love for his church, not the other way around. We dishonor the Lord when we break our marriage vows in acts of infidelity or when we reduce our marital union to anything less than a passion-filled relationship.

Israel had a propensity for worshiping foreign deities. One in particular seemed to draw her attention, the Canaanite deity Baal. By worshiping him (Hos 2:13, 16–17), Israel rejected Yahweh as her bridegroom and violated her covenantal vows to him (Exod 19:8; 24:7). To fully express the true nature and effects of this sin, the Lord used the personal relationships in the life of his devoted prophet. Through the promiscuity of Hosea's wife, the Lord illustrated that Israel's idolatry was nothing short of adultery (cf. Exod 34:15–16; Jer 3:6–9). Hosea 3:1 even calls the woman the Lord instructs Hosea to marry an "adulteress."

Prophetic symbolic-action

It was not uncommon for the Lord to use events, people, and circumstances in the life of his prophets to illustrate and reinforce his sovereign message. This is what scholars refer to as "symbolic-action." For example, the prophet Isaiah was told by the Lord to walk around "naked and barefoot" by removing his sackcloth and sandals (Isa 20:2). This served to illustrate the prophetic message against Egypt and Cush; just as Isaiah lived naked and barefoot, "so shall the king of Assyria lead away the Egyptian captives and the Cushite exiles, both the young and the old, naked and barefoot, with buttocks uncovered, the nakedness of Egypt" (Isa 20:4). In a sense, even the names of his children ("Shear-jashub" meaning "a remnant shall return" [Isa 7:3]; "Maher-shalal-hashbaz" meaning "swift is the booty, speedy is the prey" [Isa 8:3–4]) could be understood as symbolic-actions. The prophet Ezekiel was required to lie down on his left side for 390 days, which was to equal the number of years of Israel's punishment (Ezek 4:4–8). He was also told to shave his hair and beard and to burn, strike, and scatter them to symbolize the future destruction that would come upon the city of Jerusalem (Ezek 5:1–17).

Symbolic-actions continued in the New Testament with the apostles. The prophet Agabus took Paul's belt to bind his hands and feet, which symbolized "how the Jews at Jerusalem will bind the man who owns this belt and deliver him into the hands of the Gentiles" (Acts 21:11). There may even be a symbolic-action when Paul says that he bears on his body "the marks of Jesus" (Gal 6:17).

For Hosea, it was not merely one incident or event that became a symbolic-action; his entire life served this function. The consequence of utilizing Hosea's marriage as a symbol would have a life-altering effect upon the prophet. If Israel was somehow able to minimize or ignore the abominable nature of their idolatrous worship of Baal, to continue to do so would be more difficult in light of the prophet's divinely designed family life. The public could not avoid the adulterous nature of Hosea's marriage to Gomer. Everyone would have known about this marriage and the pain that it caused Hosea as a faithful husband. They could now see the sting and suffering caused by a "wife of whoredom" upon the flesh-and-blood servant-messenger of God. In observing his marriage, Israel was faced with her own ugly infidelity to the Lord, who was the truly offended covenant partner.

Perfect start

Scholars have spent a great deal of time debating when Gomer began her whoring ways. Did this marriage have a perfect start or a dreadful beginning? Another way of stating this is, "Did Gomer begin the marriage pure and loyal only to become an adulterous whore later, or was she a 'woman of whoredom' from the outset, who was already living a lifestyle of sinful immorality?" This is difficult to determine. Since a close parallel was established between Yahweh-Israel and Hosea-Gomer, it would be natural to presume that this correspondence also applied to the start of their respective relationships. In that sense, the biblical data seems to lean towards the notion that Gomer began the marriage with the best of intentions, given that Israel did the same.[22] This makes the adultery that the Lord and Hosea faced even more tragic. If Gomer had been an adulteress from the start, then Hosea would never have known the pleasures of a loving home-life, and thus would never have known what he had lost. Since he did have a moment where he knew the joys of a loving wife, he had to live with the dread that he would never know such affection with a woman again.

Internally, within the prophecy of Hosea, the Lord said that he would "allure" Israel and "bring her into the wilderness" (Hos 2:14). The wilderness was mentioned earlier in verse 3 as the place where the Lord would "make her like parched land and kill her with thirst." But in verse 14, the wilderness is also the place where the Lord will renew his covenant with Israel. In alluding to Sinai—where this covenant was inaugurated—Hosea recollected the time when there was harmony between the Lord Yahweh and his bride; Israel depended upon the Lord and he cared for his people by providing for them (Deut 2:7; 8:2–5; 29:5). As Hosea contemplated that future day when the Lord would free Israel from her captivity in exile, he described it using the image of being taken back to the wilderness (therefore freed from exile), where he will "speak tenderly to her" (verse 14). It is as if the Lord were performing a second exodus for Israel and taking her on a second honeymoon. What is significant for our purpose is to see that this wilderness reference alludes to a time when Yahweh's marriage was idyllic and Israel was a faithful bride. A similar allusion to the wilderness as that initial time of joy can be seen in Hosea 9:10; 11:1; 12:9, 13; 13:4–5 (cf. Amos 2:10; 9:7; Mic 6:4–5).

Having said this, it should also be noted that the wilderness image is not exclusively a place of blessing; caution should be taken not to overly generalize the positive descriptions associated with it. As seen earlier, in Hosea 2:3, the wilderness can also be a place of judgment and condemnation. The book of Numbers describes the freedom of the initial generation of Israelites who came out of Egypt only to distrust the Lord. Their lack of faith resulted in the forty-year wandering in the wilderness,

---

22. There are objections to this notion of a happy beginning. Perhaps the most obvious is the fact that Gomer is introduced to the reader as a "wife of whoredom" in 1:2. I take this phrase as retrospectively applied to Gomer after she had committed her acts of whoredom. See Anderson and Freedman, *Hosea*, 162–63, for further defense of this view. It is also possible that this is anticipatory, meaning Hosea was told that Gomer—in spite of all her goodwill and intentions—would become a "woman of whoredom." See Dearman, *Hosea*, 84, 133, for further defense that Hosea married Gomer already in a state of sexual promiscuity.

where they all died; this wilderness episode even included some of the more prominent Israelite leaders (Aaron and Moses).[23] For the Exodus generation, the wilderness was a place where the Lord poured his wrath upon them, but for their children, it was a place where the Lord cared for them and disciplined them as a loving father (Deut 2:7; 8:3–4).

Outside of the book of Hosea, other biblical texts also portray Israel as a faithful bride at the start of her covenantal relationship with the Lord. Jeremiah 2:2 immediately comes to mind, where the prophet Jeremiah says: "I remember the devotion of your youth, your love as a bride, how you followed me in the wilderness, in a land not sown." Jeremiah alludes to the time in the wilderness of Sinai as "the devotion of your youth, your love as a bride." As the newly married bride, Israel is depicted as a faithful and loving wife to the Lord with every intention to remain devout to her husband-God. The obvious parallel between Jeremiah 2:2 and the marriage images in Hosea 1–3 suggests that the Lord may have even drawn upon the writings of Hosea as the inspiration for his prophecy.

In addition to Jeremiah, we find the prophecy of Ezekiel 16, where Israel's relationship with the Lord is described using similar marital images. The prophet said that Israel was once like an abandoned infant, bloody and abhorred, with no one showing her pity or compassion (Ezek 16:2–5). The Lord, however, looked upon her with mercy (Ezek 16:6–8). Through his care and provision, she "flourished" and "grew up and became tall and arrived at full adornment" (Ezek 16:7). Once she reached the "age for love," the Lord "entered into a covenant with [her]" and thus "[she] became mine" (Ezek 16:8). As his new bride, the Lord washed her clean and dressed her with all sorts of extravagant jewels and garments (Ezek 16:9–13). The fame of her beauty spread to the surrounding nations, all due to the "splendor that I [Yahweh] had bestowed on you" (Ezek 16:14). Their relationship was still young, but thus far it was filled with joy and contentment. The Lord rejoiced over his bride, Israel, and Israel over her gracious Lord. This was a time in Israel's covenant history that was worthy of fond remembrance.

Sadly, all this changed (Ezek 16:15–58). Instead of staying true to her devoted bridegroom, Israel trusted in her own beauty and "played the whore" (Ezek 16:15, 17, 26, 28, 29). There is an obvious connection here

---

23. Numbers 14:33; 32:13; cf. Psalm 95:10–11; Hebrews 3:10–11, 17–18.

with Hosea 1–3, as the verb "to act like a whore" (Hebrew *zānâ*), which is so prevalent in Hosea, is also vividly used in Ezekiel 16.[24]

Each of these texts supports the notion that the prophets portrayed the beginning of the Lord's covenant relationship with Israel positively only to have it deteriorate into something detestable. The fact that there was a pure beginning adds to the tragedy of what it becomes by the time of the exile. Indeed, Israel was beloved and cared for by the Lord. Deuteronomy 7:7–8 even states that the Lord's love was not due to anything within Israel herself, but rather because of his own desire to love her—*I love you because I love you.* It is disturbing and heartbreaking to read about how far Israel had fallen from grace by abusing and taking advantage of this divine sovereign mercy by forsaking her Lord. Such treachery is something that Hosea could easily understand since his own marriage followed the same pattern—an initial time of delight degenerating into abomination.

We cannot be absolutely confident about the pure beginning of Hosea's marriage in the same way we can of the Lord's with Israel. To ask such a question is perfectly understandable, and there does seem to be enough exegetical data within the text to formulate alternative opinions. However, these opinions should be held with an open mind, eagerness for discussion, and a level of humility and flexibility. One thing is certain: any dreams that Hosea may have had of possessing a long-lasting and loving relationship with his wife were now shattered. In its place, he would only know the pain of unfaithfulness, the emptiness of loneliness, and the sting of betrayal.

Hosea/The Lord as Father of Rebellious Children

What looked like a family situation that could not get any worse for Hosea certainly did! The difficulties of his marriage are described in detail above—but what about his relationship with his children? The Lord instructs Hosea not only to take a wife but also "children of whoredom" (Hos 1:2). The description of "whoredom" is appropriately applied to the immoral activities of a sexually promiscuous woman, but it is an odd way to describe children. Women (and men) can be "whores," but children cannot. They can, however, be defiant, disobedient, and rebellious.

---

24. A similar passage is Ezekiel 23, where Samaria and Jerusalem are personified as the adulterous women Oholah and Oholiab respectively.

John Dearman provides insightful comments to this end, stating that we should not attempt to be overly precise on the immorality of either Gomer or the children. It is sufficient for us to understand their corruption as an indication of religious/cultic faithlessness.[25]

This suggests that Hosea's children were also living in rebellion against his headship as their father. More importantly, they were living in rebellion against the Lord. Hosea's knowledge of the history of Israel made him sensitive about marrying a godly Israelite woman. That same history also made him aware of the need for godly parenting.

The book of Deuteronomy teaches that faith in the Lord is to be passed on from one generation to the next.[26] Unfortunately, the historical books record several instances where men of faith failed in this area. For example, Judges says that when Joshua and his generation died, "there arose another generation after them who did not know the LORD or the work that he had done for Israel" (Judg 2:10). I have often found it astounding and appalling that such ignorance of Scripture could happen so rapidly—we are talking about one generation! This would be equivalent to my children growing into adulthood not knowing about the cross of Christ and his resurrection. I can only think that the reason for this decline was because the previous generation failed in their mandate to teach the younger Israelites the Word of God. The consequence of this unfaithful parenting is described in Judges, which gives a heartbreaking depiction of that next generation of Israelites. I nearly weep every time I read:

> And the people of Israel did what was evil in the sight of the LORD and served the Baals. And they abandoned the LORD, the God of their fathers, who had brought them out of the land of Egypt. They went after other gods, from among the gods of the peoples who were around them, and bowed down to them. And they provoked the LORD to anger. (Judg 2:11–12)

The high priest Eli did not disciple his sons, Hophni and Phinehas, in the proper mode of offering sacrifices. The choicest part of the sacrifice (the fat), which properly belongs to the Lord (Lev 3:16), they took for themselves. For that reason, the Lord struck them down in his wrath (1 Sam 2:26–35). Even the great Samuel, who serves as a major transition point in the history of salvation (Acts 3:24), failed to raise his sons in

25. Dearman, *Hosea*, 85, 363–68.

26. Deuteronomy 6:7; 20–25; 7:3–4; 11:2, 19; 31:9–13.

the ways of the Lord (1 Sam 8:3). This caused the Israelites to demand a "king to judge us like all the other nations" (1 Sam 8:5). Not only does the eventual high king of the united Israel, David, fail to train his children in godliness (2 Sam 12–13) but also his own son, Absalom, even took his throne in an attempted coup-d'état (2 Sam 14–19). These are just a few examples of failed parenting, which ultimately contributed to the Israelite exile.

Hosea would have been aware of this, but there was nothing that he could do. He was told of the eventual demise of his children from the beginning of the book, and no amount of godly parenting would change the outcome. He could catechize them and diligently teach them the Word of God, talking about it when they sat in the home or when they live in the outside world, when they would lie down or rise up (Deut 6:7). It would not change the course of these children's spiritual decline.

Like his marriage, Hosea's children needed to reflect the covenantal reality of Israel's defiance since it also represented the Lord's relationship with Israel. This is not the case in our day today. We do not live with the knowledge of our children's chilling fate as Hosea did. We are encouraged, therefore, to pray for their well being and their spiritual growth. And by the grace of God, he will answer our prayers, and they will grow to be vibrant and active believers, serving in their local churches and communities for the glory of God. However, no amount of prayer or parental discipleship will guarantee the spirituality of our children. Passages like Proverbs 22:6, which states, "Train up a child in the way he should go; even when he is old he will not depart from it," provides a wise maxim that assures spiritual health *all things being equal*—this is not a prophetic promise. We train up our children in hopes that they grow to be devout young believers, but often (and painfully) they reject their godly upbringing, spurn the covenantal blessings, and live in rebellion against the Lord. All this, in spite of countless hours of prayer for them, family devotionals, consistent Sunday School attendance, constant exposure to the gospel message, and establishing a loving home life. Perhaps nothing stings the heart of a parent more than to see all those years of effort apparently go to waste as their children abandon their household faith in the Lord and turn to their own vices.

You may know such families. Imagine a couple who love the Lord and do their best to raise their children in the ways of God, but for whatever reason their kids grow to be unruly. This is the family that goes out shopping at your local supermarket with children who are running around all over the place, demanding that their parents purchase for them various sweet treats and toys. The parents say no, but the children are relentless. They refuse to take "no" for an answer and make their demands known to the parents loud and clear. In fact, the entire store hears their demands. The parents attempt to restrain these children, but to no avail. They will only be appeased if their demands are met.

Think of other scenarios where the children are teenagers, college students, or young working professionals. If they remain spiritually recalcitrant, it becomes harder to lead them back to the Lord. As teens, the children attend church with us, and disciple them through the preaching of the Word and other means of grace in the church. As college students, they are exposed to hedonistic pleasures, secular philosophies, and religious worldviews that challenge their Christian upbringings. Given their new measure of independence in this environment, we can only hope that they remain true to the faith that was instilled in them. If they wander, we can only pray that they will return to the Lord. As they grow to become adults, we can only encourage them to seek out the Lord and to attend worship services or Bible studies, but we cannot require it or force this upon them. They can no longer be satisfied by toys or a bag of candies; their rebellion is by far more significant. These "children" fight back and can cause bodily harm and/or lasting emotional pain.

Hosea, therefore, is not only portrayed as a husband of a wicked wife but also as a father of rebellious children. The use of both images— husband and father—is powerful in depicting a household in moral and religious chaos. If the image of Hosea as a suffering husband did not communicate God's point to Israel, then it is declared again in the prophet's relations with his children. Israel would have gotten the message loud and clear. Not only is she like an adulterous wife, she is also like an insolent child. In both images, Israel is seen as disobedient, stiff-necked, and in need of utter repentance. In both cases, Hosea had to suffer the real torment and agony of a family life in ruins. Imagine having not only an adulterous wife but sinfully defiant children as well. This was the life of Hosea. Indeed, the cost of being a messenger of the Lord is high.

Although his identity as a father is present in these opening chapters, it is not nearly as dramatic or dominant as the marital image in expressing the sins of the people. His fatherhood is frequently overshadowed by his role as a tragic husband. As seen above, the depiction of Gomer as an unfaithful wife permeates the first three chapters. In chapter 1, where these children of whoredom are most conspicuous, their names, not their disobedience, are used to describe Israel's sin. In fact, the name of the third child (Lo-ammi) is a reference to divorce-language used in the annulment of marriages. Rather than using a parenting imagery, chapter 2 emphasizes the marriage imagery once more in order to graphically depict the nature of Israel's sin. In the same way that Gomer desired to seek out her lovers and swap Hosea for them, so Israel desired to worship Baal with the same intensity. In chapter 3, Gomer sells herself at a marketplace to the highest bidder. Therefore, emphasizing the marital image over against the parental image is warranted, since the text seems to do the same.

Nevertheless, Hosea's suffering is extended to include his role as a father as well as a husband. Hosea 2:4 even specifies the Lord's judgment against these children: "Upon her children also I will have no mercy, because they are children of whoredom." Therefore, the heartaches of Hosea as a father reflect a reality that cannot be denied. He was a father to wayward children, just as God was the Father to wayward Israel.

During these dark and uncertain years, what hope was there? Could joy be found? The answer to this question is a strong, resounding "yes" and "amen" in Christ (2 Cor 1:20).

Hosea, the Suffering Family Man

Suffering in such broken familial relationships is all too common. It is also extremely painful. Unfortunately, this was reality for Hosea. John Dearman comments concerning his suffering, "Those who are interested in such matters as Hosea's feelings about his wife . . . pursue legitimate questions, but we must keep in mind that the literary composition we know as Hos 1–3 may not adequately answer them."[27] He is correct, and any detailed descriptions of Hosea's subjective experience does border on speculation. However, there are a few factors to consider. First, I am not interested in the specifics of the suffering that he experienced—only that he in fact suffered. What he specifically felt is not nearly as significant as the fact that he did feel. Given the fact that nothing—no relationship, no institution, no social program—makes a man more vulnerable to emotional pain than the failure of the husband/wife and father/child relationships, it would have been impossible for him not to know intense agony. Depicting Hosea as the head of a family that was falling apart un-

27. Dearman, *Hosea*, 81.

derscored the instability present in Israel's religious life in a way that no other image could.

Second, the Old Testament psalter does record the agonizing cries of such innocent, righteous sufferers—like Hosea—and does so in great detail.[28] Many of these psalms lack specificity; they do not identify a historical period, their adversaries, a specific circumstance, situation, or a location.[29] This allows anyone to read them and immediately identify themselves with the psalmists. Hosea could have effortlessly sung many of these psalms and adopted the words as his own.

Finally, precise articulation of his emotional distress seems unnecessary since the sorrow from marital infidelity and disobedient children are universal human experiences. Without additional detail, almost everyone who reads this text can share the heartache of the prophet.

Jesus, the True Suffering Family Man

But is it truly the prophet with whom the readers of these chapters identify? Or is it with someone else? Someone greater? If Hosea's suffering as a loving husband/father is a reflection of the greater Husband/Father, then anyone who can identify and share in the tragedies of Hosea can also identify with the greater Hosea. By orchestrating the circumstances of Hosea's life to parallel what is happening in the true reality of Yahweh and Israel, the Lord seems to be saying to Hosea, "It hurts, doesn't it? I know, but now you know as well. You know what it is like to give yourself so freely, graciously, and totally to someone, only to have them betray you, to stab you in the back, to spit in your face. It hurts; I know. It's painful; I know."

Many people who read Hosea may find his circumstances a cause for pity and sympathy. We feel sorry for him and pray that we do not face similar circumstances. I would definitely agree with these sentiments. I also hope that no one ever has to endure such devastating pains, but unfortunately that is not possible. The family is central to the development of our communities and churches, and we need to protect it. In a fallen world, however, those closest to us are the ones who hurt us the most,

28. See chapter 4, "Joy of Singing Psalms of Lament," for more details on this.

29. A few psalms provide a historical setting in their superscription. See Psalms 3, 7, 18, 34, 51, 52, 54, 56, 57, 59, 60, 63, 142.

both in frequency and intensity. Hosea knew this to be true, but so does Someone else.

Consider this thought: Hosea knew a very special kind of joy because the Lord brought him into a relationship that was so much like his relationship with Israel. For that reason—and that reason alone—he can be seen as a blessed man. This is what 1 Peter 4:13 tells us when it declares that we can "rejoice insofar as you share Christ's sufferings."

Paul says something similar in an extraordinary statement in Philippians 1:29: "For it has been granted to you that for the sake of Christ you should not only believe in him but also suffer for his sake." The Greek word for "granted" is *echaristhē*, a third person form of the verb *charizomai*. This is the verbal form of the word used in the New Testament for the amazing "grace" of God, *charis*. Throughout his epistles, Paul constantly teaches that salvation is by the grace of God alone, meaning that we receive all the spiritual blessings of God's kingdom in spite of the fact that we had forfeited the right to receive them. This is because of the person and work of Jesus Christ our Savior. It is by this supernatural grace of God that we are effectually called (Rom 8:29; 2 Tim 1:9; 1 Pet 2:9) and transformed into a "new creation" (2 Cor 5:17; cf. John 1:13; 3:3; Titus 3:5) where the old man has gone and a new man has come (Eph 4:22–25). We can now do what we could not do before—turn in repentance to the Lord (Deut 30:1–10; Rom 10:3–7) and embrace his one and only Son by faith (Rom 4:16). All this is a result of the grace of God. Paul does not equivocate on this point. He is as clear as day.

In Philippians 1:29, however, Paul says something unexpected and bewildering. *Not only is our faith a gracious gift of God, but so is our suffering!* For Paul, the only way that this suffering can be understood as a gift is by seeing it as a way to "share his [Christ's] suffering" (Phil 3:10; cf. 1 Pet 4:13). Paul desired nothing greater than to conform to the image of Christ, and he knew that this could not happen unless he knew the sufferings of Christ as well.[30] In that sense, to know Christ's sufferings is a gracious gift. Paul was not fooled to think otherwise. Neither was Peter and neither was Hosea.

And neither should you. It is easy to buy into the wisdom of this fallen world, which measures joy by ideal circumstances, healthy minds, and significant wealth. It also tells you that the key to joy is a healthy and stable family. But what if all of these things are taken away, and you

30. Ephesians 4:24; Colossians 3:10; cf. Romans 8:29.

no longer have any of them? This is not a hypothetical scenario—it is reality for many. Secular counsel may attempt to say that true joy can be achieved even in such dire straits, but it does not have the foundation to maintain such a conclusion, nor offers a practical way to gain it. It is mere wishful thinking. It cannot provide joy in the midst of suffering because it cannot explain how joy and suffering are intertwined without canceling each other out.

It does not have the gospel, which frequently turns values on their heads. According to the wisdom of God, the first shall be last,[31] one must give up their lives in order to find it,[32] and to be the greatest in God's kingdom requires us to be the servant of all.[33]

We can add to this list—true joy, *a joy unspeakable*, can be found in Christian suffering. In fact, not only can such joy be found in suffering, it is the *product* of Christian suffering (Phil 1:29; 1 Pet 4:12–13). The reason for this supernatural reversal of thought is because "the word of the cross is folly to those who are perishing, but to us who are being saved it is the power of God" (1 Cor 1:18). Jesus is the Creator-King of all the cosmos. He was the first, but he made himself the last. He gave up his life and died so that we can have eternal life and live. He who was the greatest in God's kingdom became a servant of all. And he surrendered his eternal fellowship with God to suffer for the sake of sinners. This call to *fellowship with Christ in his sufferings* is part of the greater call of the Christian to follow in the footsteps of Christ (1 Pet 2:21). We should not allow the world to define joy for us. For Christian believers, our joy is not determined by how much or how little wealth we possess, how steady or unsteady our emotions are, how successful or unsuccessful our careers are progressing, or how stable or unstable our family relationships are. Our joy is determined by how closely we are in fellowship with Christ, who is our joy.

Word of Encouragement

The family is a sanctuary and refuge. At least, that is how it is perceived by many—both in the ancient world and our world today. This is for good reason. In the public arena, we are never truly ourselves, but we can be at home. Among family, we can speak, act, and carry on in ways that we

---

31. Matthew 19:30; 20:16; Mark 9:35; 10:31; Luke 13:30.
32. Matthew 10:39; 16:25.
33. Matthew 18:4; 23:11; Luke 22:26.

would never do in the public sphere. We are free to be ourselves. It is a place of safety and we are happiest there. In many ways, home life has become an idol, a way for us to have a taste of heaven on earth. We strive to protect it and even see God as a means to that end. We can tolerate a lot of stress and pressure in the world as long as we can return to a secure and happy home.

The two relationships that make up the core of family life are the husband/wife and parent/child bonds. Both are sacred. But what if one of these two foundational relationships were not so stable? What if one of these two was filled with distrust, malice, and apathy? What would that do to a person? Life would be difficult, to say the least. Frustration and anxiety may be a common issue to constantly fight off. Regular aspects of everyday life would be a struggle, knowing that you will wake up seeing a person with whom there is an awkward level of animosity. If this type of conflict were present with a distant acquaintance or even a close friend, that would be hard enough, but we are talking about your immediate family. There should not be any walls to separate members of a family. It would be frustrating and painful. Perhaps this is not too difficult to imagine, as I suspect that this is an accurate portrayal of every family in the world—both ancient and contemporary.

But what if *both* relationships were dysfunctional? What would life look like then? It is not terribly insightful to suggest that such a home would have a detrimental effect on a person's emotional well being. In short, life would be hell—and that is putting things mildly.

Again, I don't wish for unnecessary suffering for God's people. Truly I don't. However, suffering in our sin-filled world is unavoidable. So if you are suffering through a broken familial relationship, if you know the sting of loving a spouse who turns his focus lustfully towards others, or one that mistreats you in favor of his own sinful and selfish pleasures, then you are in fellowship with the prophet Hosea—and more importantly, you fellowship in the suffering of Christ, your Savior.

If you know the pain of loving children who rebel against your godly desires and spurn your wise words of counsel, if you know the sorrows of watching your children grow in success in every aspect of their lives, yet refuse to repent of their sins and turn to the Lord for their eternal salvation, then you also are in fellowship with Hosea and, more importantly, with God the Father, who also agonized over the rebellion of his people: "How can I give you up, O Ephraim? How can I hand you over, O Israel? How can I make you like Admah? How can I treat you like Zeboiim? My heart recoils within me; my compassion grows warm and tender" (Hos 11:8).

If you suffer in this way, then you are in fellowship with Christ in his sufferings and therefore can experience a supernatural joy. I do pray for God's people to know this *joy unspeakable* and do so boldly. Paul and Peter knew this, as did the psalmist(s), Abraham, Job, and Hosea. So can you.

8

Joy of a Rejected Messenger

How beautiful upon the mountains are the feet of him who brings
good news, who publishes peace, who brings good news of happiness,
who publishes salvation, who says to Zion, "Your God reigns."

Isaiah 52:7

I WONDER HOW CHRISTIAN parents react when their children tell them that the Lord is calling them to full time pastoral ministry. Some see this as a great honor and are blessed to know that the Lord would call them to such noble work. Others, however, are not as eager, and react with some hesitancy and reluctance. During one specific time when I was going through a difficult stretch in my pastorate, I recall praying a prayer that I now confess with some embarrassment, "Heavenly Father, please do not call any of my sons to the pastoral office, for I do not want them to ever endure what I am going through right now!" The Lord has sanctified my heart since that time, and now I eagerly wait to see if in fact any of my three boys will be so blessed to receive a calling to serve the Lord as an ordained minister. The weight of the burden at that moment, however, was real and brought about my warped perspective.

My parents also reacted similarly for the same reason when I informed them about my desire to pursue a life of pastoral ministry. I was a sophomore in college. I really did not enjoy my classes and lacked a deep conviction about what to do with my life. However, I loved going to Bible studies. I joined three different campus small groups, regularly attended my church college group's weekly Bible study, and even joined a study group led by my pastor on the *Westminster Shorter Catechism*. If you are wondering—yes, I did attend my college classes, but I loved studying the Word of God more. It was a passion that has remained with me my entire Christian life. I simply could not get enough.

As I prayed about my future, it became clearer to me that this was what I wanted to do for the rest of my life. The Lord was calling me into the ministry. When I shared this with my parents, they did not share my enthusiasm. Rather, they saw my future life as a pastor as filled with nothing but hardship and poverty. Like any loving parent, they did not want that for me. They asked me to reconsider my plans to attend a theological seminary after graduation and to consider the reality of the life I was choosing to live.

In hindsight, I realize now that they only wanted me to be certain of my call because they had witnessed the pressures and sufferings that were so common in the life of the other pastors they knew. Although they ended up giving in and allowed me to pursue seminary training, they did so with some trepidation and remained this way until my ordination, after which they felt there was no turning back. Until that day, my mother would regularly remind me, "Law school is only three years. Law school is only three years!" I have served as a minister for over twenty years, and I must confess that there have been moments during that time when I have whispered to myself, "Law school is only three years."

Proclaiming the Gospel Hurts

Pastoral ministry is not for the faint of heart.[1] It is a wrestling match every week, and sometimes more frequent than that. The most vulnerable moment for pastors, ironically, is also the most critical aspect of his ministry—the preaching of the gospel of Jesus Christ. They are called to preach a message that reminds God's people of their total depravity, their inability to turn to the Lord of glory, and their wholehearted need for the sovereign mercy and grace of God alone. Not only that, pastors are called to share that the sins of their people deserve eternal condemnation, and that attempting to stand before the Lord on their own merits would only lead to their judgment before the throne of God. But if they repent and

---

1. For a very real (almost skeptical) description of the challenges of pastoral ministry, see Tripp, *Dangerous Calling*.

trust in the Lord for their salvation, the Lord promises to forgive them of their sins[2] and give to them an inheritance "that is imperishable, unde-filed, and unfading, kept in heaven for you" (1 Pet 1:4). Any proclamation short of this gospel does not honor the call of preachers and effectively makes their ministerial work useless.

Throughout the history of salvation, you will find preachers who proclaim this bold but necessary message—from the days of Adam, to the Old Testament prophets, and to the days of the New Testament apostles. It is a message filled with grace, beauty, and hope, but it is also direct, discomforting, and confrontational. It is a call for people to sur-render their sense of moral entitlement and humbly acknowledge their need for Jesus Christ as their Savior. Unsurprisingly, those who were called to deliver this message throughout redemptive history were not always well received. For there to be forgiveness of sins, the people must willingly acknowledge that they are sinners who have truly offended the Most Holy God. It challenges people to regard themselves as fallen and worthy of eternal condemnation when our inclination is to think the op-posite—that we are right and everyone else is wrong. How many times have you seen a professional athlete or Hollywood celebrity caught in an immoral situation claim, "Those who know the *real* me know that I am a good person." Sinful humanity does not see themselves as fallen but rather as moral and good. We have a strong sense of this desire to always be right and fight to maintain our superiority over others at all cost, even at the expense of harming those around us. For that reason, even the most faithful of God's people have found this "good news" of the gospel difficult to stomach. It is the aroma of life for some, but the stench of death for others (2 Cor 2:15–16).

Messengers of the gospel had a deep love for their own people, and since they did not want to see their destruction, they were eager for their repentance. For that reason, they proclaimed this message boldly and courageously, even putting themselves in harm's way. They often faced intense opposition, risked losing their friendships and their reputations, and put their own lives in extreme circumstances. Yet they were called to proclaim this message nonetheless and endure the subsequent fallout of rejection. Not only can you find such messengers in the history of re-demption but also in the history of the church.

2. Jeremiah 31:34; 33:8; Psalm 103:3; 1 John 1:9.

This is the picture of one such messenger who also came to share this gospel of repentance and hope, who also was rejected by his people. In fact, he was "despised and rejected by men; a man of sorrows, and acquainted with grief; and as one from whom men hide their faces he was despised, and we esteemed him not" (Isa 53:3). Because of the message he preached, he was beaten, battered, bruised—and ultimately executed for crimes that he did not commit. Indeed, he knew pain as a rejected messenger in ways that we will never know.

Yet insofar as we also preach that "good news" and endure similar rejection, we also share in his sorrows and thus draw closer to him as fellow messengers in his likeness. This definitely applies to modern pastors who proclaim a message of repentance of forgiveness of sins on a weekly basis to their church communities. This also applies to all believers who boldly share the good news of the gospel to friends and family around them. The task to share the message of Christ is not limited to only a select few ordained leaders. Rather, we—the entire body of Christ—are called to this work, and sometimes at a great risk to ourselves. Whenever we share this good news to those who respond in hostility towards us, we share in the sufferings of the Son who spoke the final word in these last days (Heb 1:1–2) to a people who also reacted with fiery abhorrence.

The Prophets as God's messengers

The proclamation of this good news did not begin with the New Testament apostles. It actually began in the Old Testament, communicated by chosen messengers of the Lord. These were the Old Testament prophets, and they functioned as authoritative spokesmen who represented the Lord to Israel and communicated his divinely revealed word. Exodus 4:16 provides a good illustration of the prophetical function. The Lord sent Moses and Aaron to Egypt and said, "He [Aaron] shall speak for you [Moses] to the people, and he shall be your mouth, and you shall be as God to him." Aaron's role as a prophet is stated explicitly in a related passage in Exodus: "And the LORD said to Moses, 'See, I have made you like God to Pharaoh, and your brother Aaron shall be your prophet'" (Exod 7:1).

Covenants of the ancient world

In the ancient world, it was customary that whenever a king conquered a smaller city-state, the ruler of the defeated city would be incorporated into the larger, growing empire of the triumphant king. This did not necessarily mean that there would be a mass deportation, where the inhabitants of these defeated cities were redistributed and replaced by peoples from other regions.[3] Instead, they were divided into provinces, and the defeated king became a vassal who continued his reign, but under the jurisdiction of the greater-suzerain. There were times when both the northern kingdom of Israel and the southern kingdom of Judah were vassal states under the authority of a foreign ruler until their eventual exile (in 722 BC and 605 BC respectively).

This suzerain would require the vassal king to swear a loyalty oath in the form of a treaty where he would agree to certain terms that were dictated by the great king. This treaty was then written down and a copy was given to each contractual party member in order to keep the others accountable to their agreement.[4] At times, the vassal would violate these terms, which would cause the great king to send his royal messengers to communicate his disfavor. These messengers would confront the rebellious vassal, remind him of the oaths that he had made, and warn him that the negative sanctions of the treaty would be enforced unless he changed his ways and conformed to the tenets of their original agreement once again.

3. The practice of mass deportation began during the Neo-Assyrian empire (circa 744–612 BC) under the reign of Tiglath-Pileser III (2 Kgs 15:29; 16:7, 10; 1 Chr 5:6, 26; 2 Chr 28:20). For a helpful summary of the history of the ancient world, see Charpin, "History of Ancient Mesopotamia," 823.

4. The Ten Commandments (Exod 20:1–17) has been recognized as a small version of this treaty. This was the reason why there were "two tablets of the testimony" (Exod 32:15). One copy was for the Lord, the other for Israel. Safeguards were also put into place to prevent any tampering or changes to this treaty (Deut 4:2; cf. Rev 22:18–19). See Kline, *Structure of Biblical Authority*, 113–30.

Israel breaks the covenant

Many of the great biblical covenants are examples of this ancient genre where the Lord Yahweh functioned as the great suzerain and Israel as the vassal nation (also Israel's kings as vassal monarchs).[5] In the book of Exodus, after having been redeemed from enslavement in Egypt, the Lord led them to Mount Sinai where he gave them his holy law. He called out to the people from the mountain through Moses and said:

> Thus you shall say to the house of Jacob, and tell the people of Israel: You yourselves have seen what I did to the Egyptians, and how I bore you on eagles' wings and brought you to myself. Now therefore, if you will indeed obey my voice and keep my covenant, you shall be my treasured possession among all peoples, for all the earth is mine; and you shall be to me a kingdom of priests and a holy nation. These are the words that you shall speak to the people of Israel. (Exod 19:3–6)

Having heard these words, Israel responded by affirming their desire to obey the Lord:

> All the people answered together and said, "All that the LORD has spoken we will do." And Moses reported the words of the people to the LORD. (Exod 19:8)

In their excitement at receiving the holy law of God, Israel shouted in exuberant enthusiasm that they would conform to this standard. Unfortunately, their time in the wilderness tells a very different story, revealing their inability to live up to their commitment to obey God's covenant. As a result, that entire generation (with the exception of Joshua and Caleb) died in the wilderness.

A second generation of Israelites survived that time of judgment in the wilderness. Afterwards, they entered and conquered large portions of the land of Canaan. As Israel began to settle in that land, the Lord renewed the covenant to instruct them how to live as a holy people there. This renewed covenant was the book of Deuteronomy. The record of Israel's history in Canaan, however, showed the same tendency towards covenant violation, just like their forefathers in the wilderness. They

---

5. There are examples of this loyal-oath in the Old Testament. Exodus 20 was mentioned earlier. The book of Deuteronomy is a larger example of this ancient genre; see Van Pelt, *Biblical-Theological Introduction to the Old Testament*, 137–52 for further details on how Deuteronomy is patterned after ancient treaty documents.

frequently and consciously disobeyed the mandates of the covenant of God.

The Message of the Prophets

In each of these two generations, the Lord followed the norms of the ancient world and sent his divinely appointed messengers, "my servants the prophets."[6] For the first generation, this was the paradigm-prophet Moses; for the second generation and throughout Israel's tenure on the land, it was the Moses-like prophetic office bearers (Deut 18:15, 18; cf. Num 12:6–8).[7]

A quick glance at the message of these emissaries of the divine King does not sound very "good." It shows why they were so rejected and scorned by the people of God.

Prosecutors of the Mosaic Covenant

The first thing that the prophets did was to preach a message of warning and judgment. In doing so, they were essentially prosecuting a lawsuit in accordance with the terms of the covenant. The prophets used the history of Israel as evidence against the nation to support the legal claims of the Lord, highlighting the covenant violations of the people.[8]

They reminded God's people of the many extraordinary acts God performed in their history to redeem them from their many enemies (Egypt, Canaan, Moab, Edom, Philistia, etc.). The prophets often

6. 2 Kings 17:13; Jeremiah 7:25; 35:15; 44:4.

7. Once the monarchy was established, the prophets spoke their messages directly and primarily to the king (e.g., Nathan in 2 Sam 12; Elijah and Elisha in 1 Kgs 17–2 Kgs 8). As Israel grew increasingly sinful and idolatrous, the recipients of the prophets' message included the Israelite community at large and even the nearby nations. This expansion coincided with the transition from the oracular (speaking) prophets from the tenth and the ninth century BC to the writing prophets of the eighth century BC (Hosea and Amos to the northern kingdom of Israel, Isaiah and Micah to the southern kingdom of Judah). See Wright, *Mission of God*, 454–500.

8. In the Hebrew canon, the "historical books" (Joshua, Judges, 1–2 Samuel, and 1–2 Kings) are also categorized as the "former prophets." The "latter prophets" are traditionally considered the prophetical books, namely Isaiah–Malachi. The reason for this categorization and organization may be due to the fact that the ancient historiographers were prophets who specifically recorded the history of Israel to serve this legal purpose.

reiterated the stipulations of the covenant and the expectation that they were to obey them in light of who God is and all that he had done for them. The prophets declared that the people failed to conform to his holy standard and thus brought an indictment against them; they formally charged Israel with covenant violation. Therefore, Israel justly deserved to receive the wrath of God—namely, the exile.[9]

When you peruse the prophetic literature, you frequently find strong, explicit descriptions of the sins of God's people, words of condemnation (indictment), and declarations of the coming wrath (judgment). Consider the opening lines of Isaiah 1:2–4, 7–8:

> Hear, O heavens, and give ear, O earth; for the LORD has spoken: "Children have I reared and brought up, but they have rebelled against me. The ox knows its owner, and the donkey its master's crib, but Israel does not know, my people do not understand." Ah, sinful nation, a people laden with iniquity, offspring of evildoers, children who deal corruptly! They have forsaken the LORD, they have despised the Holy One of Israel, they are utterly estranged. . . . Your country lies desolate; your cities are burned with fire; in your very presence foreigners devour your land; it is desolate, as overthrown by foreigners. And the daughter of Zion is left like a booth in a vineyard, like a lodge in a cucumber field, like a besieged city.

Or Jeremiah 2:11–13, 15–17:

> Has a nation changed its gods, even though they are no gods? But my people have changed their glory for that which does not profit. Be appalled, O heavens, at this; be shocked, be utterly desolate, declares the LORD, for my people have committed two evils: they have forsaken me, the fountain of living waters, and hewed out cisterns for themselves, broken cisterns that can hold no water. . . . The lions have roared against him; they have roared loudly. They have made his land a waste; his cities are in ruins, without inhabitant. Moreover, the men of Memphis and Tahpanhes have shaved the crown of your head. Have you not brought this upon yourself by forsaking the LORD your God, when he led you in the way?

Or Ezekiel 3:5–7:

> For you are not sent to a people of foreign speech and a hard language, but to the house of Israel—not to many peoples of

9. Leviticus 26:21–39; Deuteronomy 28:25, 33–34, 41–44, 47–57; 63–68.

foreign speech and a hard language, whose words you cannot understand. Surely, if I sent you to such, they would listen to you. But the house of Israel will not be willing to listen to you, for they are not willing to listen to me. Because all the house of Israel have a hard forehead and a stubborn heart.

This is just a small sample of the countless instances where the prophets conducted the lawsuit of the Lord against his wayward people.[10] It is no wonder that these messengers were hated by the people of God.[11] They constantly reminded them of what they did not want to know— their rebellion against the Lord and their pending destruction.

Heralds of the New Covenant

Happily, the prophets were also called to proclaim the blessed promises that God made to Abraham. These promises come to their fullest realization in the coming of the New Covenant.[12] To assure Abraham that he would be true to his word, the Lord even took upon himself a self-maledictory oath by passing between two halves of sacrificial animals (Gen 15:9–21). By partaking of this ancient practice, the Lord swore that he would receive the death-curse of the covenant (symbolized by the cutting up animals) if he did not fulfill the promises that he had made (cf. Jer 34:18–20). This ritualistic act assured Abraham (and Israel) that absolutely nothing would prevent him from keeping his covenantal commitments—not the abhorrent sinfulness of his people and not the apparent victory of their enemies that resulted in a temporary displacement from their homeland.

The blessings promised to Abraham are mentioned throughout the Pentateuch and reiterated in Deuteronomy 30:1–14. The importance of this passage is evidenced by the fact that the latter prophets constantly

---

10. Another example of this lawsuit is found in Hosea 1–3. See chapter 7, "Joy in the Broken Marriage/Family."

11. 2 Chronicles 36:16; Daniel 9:6; cf. 1 Kings 19:10, 14.

12. Jeremiah 31:31; cf. Hebrews 8:8, 13; Luke 22:20; 1 Corinthians 11:25; 2 Corinthians 3:6. Recall that the promise that God made to Abraham was that he would become a "great nation." In order to be a nation, several factors were needed: 1) innumerable descendants, 2) a homeland, 3) law, and 4) leadership (king). Therefore, the promise(s) of the Abrahamic covenant can be seen as both singular and plural. See chapter 6, "Joy of a Mourning Father."

allude to it in their description of the blessings of the New Covenant.[13] There are two aspects to the promises found here. First, there will be an *internal renewal* within the hearts of God's people. The Lord will circumcise their hearts so that they can do what they could not do prior—repent, believe, and obey the commands: "And the LORD your God will circumcise your heart and the heart of your offspring, so that you will love the LORD your God with all your heart and with all your soul, that you may live" (Deut 30:6; cf. verses 2, 8, 10–14).

Second, there will be *external blessings*, culminating in a return to a prosperous land that will be greater than that of their forefathers (verses 3–5, 9) along with the blessing of victory over their enemies (verse 7; cf. Gen 12:3a). This anticipated homeland would be greater than the previous version because this one will be "a heavenly one" (Heb 11:16) with an eternal city "whose designer and builder is God" (Heb 11:10). In other words, the prophets preached the coming New Heavens and New Earth[14] with the New Jerusalem at its center.[15]

Both the new land and new city will be revealed at the return of the Messianic Son of David (Ps 2:7; 110:1; Matt 1:1). Geerhardus Vos states this well when he says: "The prophet now knows that, not repair, but regeneration of the present lies in the womb of the future. But the main thing to be observed is that this rebirth is not equivalent to a new setting up of the past, not even in an idealized form. . . . God made use of the impending destruction of the Mosaic theocracy to create room for something far transcending the original structure."[16] In other words, as Israel grew increasingly more and more sinful, the prophets preached more and more of the blessings of the New Covenant.

Loved the false word, hated the true word

Although you would think that Israel would love this message of the Abrahamic/New Covenant and receive it with joy, there is no clear record in the biblical texts that suggests they did. Perhaps this is because they wholeheartedly accepted a different message, one spun by false

---

13. Isaiah 59:19–21; Jeremiah 31:31–34; 32:37–41; Ezekiel 11:16–20; 34:24–28.

14. Isaiah 65:17; 66:22; 2 Peter 3:13; Revelation 21–22.

15. Revelation 21:2; cf. Isaiah 2:3; 60:14; Jeremiah 31:38–40.

16. Vos, *Biblical Theology*, 189.

prophets.[17] The prophet Jeremiah, in particular, had to deal with these pseudo-messengers who constantly asserted that even though the people of God had committed dreadful sins against the Lord, there would still be peace in the city (Jer 7:1—8:3; 26:1–24); at worst, there would be a minimum period of two years when a foreign power may suppress them, after which would be a quick return and restoration (Jer 28:1–4). This fueled a latent thought in the minds of God's people—that the Lord would not dare bring destruction upon his own beloved city of Jerusalem, since it is the location of "the temple of the LORD, the temple of the LORD, the temple of the LORD" (Jer 7:4). This caused further issues for Israel by lulling them into a state of moral and religious complacency.

This contrasted with the true, divinely sanctioned message of Jeremiah. He warned Israel that this was a false message. He insisted they cannot engage in religious formalism while committing atrocities against the Lord and expect no consequences. In fact, Jeremiah said that the Lord would bring full destruction upon the city by means of an invading force from the north who will remove them from their homeland.[18] This would not be for a period of two years, as the false prophets had said, but rather seventy years (Jer 25:11–12; 29:10) and possibly longer.[19] Instead of peace, there would be the "storm of the Lord," "His wrath," and "a whirling tempest" (Jer 23:19). When compared to Deuteronomy 13:1–5 and 18:20–22, it becomes clear that these prognosticating charlatans were textbook examples of false prophets. Not only did they prophesy by the false god Baal, they also committed adultery and even strengthened the hands of evildoers, so that no one turned from their evil practices (Jer 23:13–14; cf. Deut 13:2). They claimed to have visions from the Lord but did not, and thus they spoke lies (Jer 23:25b; cf. Deut 18:21–22) and acted presumptuously (Deut 18:20). They lacked the necessary prerequisites to be true prophets, namely entrance into the heavenly council of God (Jer 23:18, 22; cf. Num 12:8; Isa 6:1–4; Ezek 1:1–28).

The temptation to give in to the will of the masses is overwhelming. Think of men such as Pontius Pilate. He knew that Jesus was innocent of any wrongdoing, yet out of fear of the Jews, he ordered his torture

17. Jeremiah 3:9—24:10; 26–29; cf. 7:1—8:3.

18. Jeremiah 3:18; 6:22; 10:22; 16:15; 23:8; 31:8.

19. Daniel 9:24–27 interprets this as seventy-times-seven years, meaning an unspecified amount of time. Apparently, the exile continued until the coming of the true Son of David, Jesus Christ.

and crucifixion nonetheless.[20] Many preachers in our contemporary day also avoid preaching about the sinfulness of humanity and our need for repentance for similar reasons—they fear that such a message of doom and gloom will not appeal to the people; it may even offend them. We are not told what motivated the false prophets of Jeremiah's day to do what they did, but it is not difficult to suspect that they also desired to be in the good graces of the populace, fearful of their mob-like tendency when hearing words of judgment.

Compare these false prophets to the true prophets of God. They chose to proclaim the revealed word of the Lord without compromise, even if it meant rejection by their own people and even their own family members (Jer 11:19). Meredith Kline, in his work on the formation of the prophets, says that these divinely appointed messengers—though frail, imperfect sinners—were empowered by the Spirit of God, and thus renewed their moral compass so that they could follow the will of the Lord and not the will of the people. This did not mean that they achieved some sense of moral perfectionism, rather: "The prophets underwent such spiritual transformation that they could assume a stance over against Israel and the nations . . . and carry out their commission under the constraint of a consuming emotional-ethical sympathy with the holy righteousness and truth of God."[21]

Only when someone's heart is totally in line with the will of the Lord can they possess the internal fortitude and the moral stamina to confront those whom they love so dearly with the ugliness of their transgressions and call them to repentance.

Jeremiah in Fellowship with Christ

In addition to Hosea, Jeremiah is another wonderful example of a prophet who endured tremendous hardship because of his prophetic call. We are not given much detail on his career (although more so than other prophets). What we do have is a large amount of materials that reveal his internal state of mind. The book of Jeremiah, therefore, is not so much a sequential narrative of historic events in the life of the prophet (and the last days of the southern kingdom of Judah), but rather a wondrous insight into the psyche of a prophetic messenger. Of all the prophets within

20. Matthew 27:21–24; Mark 15:15; Luke 23:14; John 18:38; 19:12–13.

21. Kline, *Images of the Spirit*, 61.

the Old Testament canon, Jeremiah—above all others—demonstrates the struggles and anguish that these ancient messengers had to suffer. Their struggles are similar to those of the New Testament apostles; they are also similar to modern preachers whose ministries are "built upon the foundation of the apostles and the prophets, Christ Jesus himself being the cornerstone" (Eph 2:20).

This message of condemnation was painful for Jeremiah to deliver and brought him conflicting emotions. He often lamented over the fate of his homeland[22] and, at times of weakness, he felt "deceived" by the Lord (Jer 20:7a).[23] It seemed that Jeremiah was under the impression that proclaiming this prophetic word would make him a hero among the people and thus beloved by them. It is like the man who sees a building on fire and runs up and down every floor, into every room, telling everyone that their lives are in danger and they have to evacuate as quickly as possible. He would not have made a gentle request, "I hate to inconvenience you, but I just wanted you to know that there is a fire in the building. It's not bad, but you may want to consider leaving the building for a short time. I'm sure everything will return back to normal soon." No! He would holler at the top of his lungs, "Get out or you will die!" Is this a harsh message? Probably, but no one would fault him for it. Such a man would easily be highly esteemed by the people, by the press, and on social media.

However, the complete opposite happened to Jeremiah. Not only was he hated (Jer 20:8a, 10a), his fellow Israelites even sought to destroy his life (Jer 20:10b). He was falsely accused of being a Babylonian collaborator, so he was beaten and imprisoned (Jer 37:13–15). He was thrown into a cistern and left to wallow in mud and die (Jer 38:3–6). For this reason, he saw his own prophetic word to be a "reproach and derision all day long" (Jer 20:8), but Jeremiah had no choice but to deliver it. He said that if he attempted to remain silent, the word of the Lord became like a "burning fire shut up in my bones" (Jer 20:9–10). He thus found himself between two difficult decisions. If he preached this true word, he would be rejected by his close friends (Jer 20:10); if he remained silent, those words would flare up within him like fire and burn until he finally pronounced them. Either way, Jeremiah seemed doomed.

22. Jeremiah 20:7–18; cf. 11:18—12:6; 15:10–11, 15–21; 17:14–18; 18:19–23.

23. This expresses the genuine struggle within the prophet—not an actual theological reality.

His life reflects his message

Jeremiah's suffering can also be seen in the numerous symbolic-actions that were used throughout his prophetic ministry. No one exemplified the use of symbolic-actions more than Jeremiah. A symbolic-action describes instances when the Lord uses a particular event, people, and circumstance in the life of his messenger to illustrate and reinforce his divine message. In the case of Jeremiah, he was called to purchase a loin-cloth only to bury it, rendering it unusable; the "spoiling" of the loincloth paralleled how the Lord will "spoil" the pride of his people (Jer 13:1–9). He was also commanded to wear an animal's yoke-bar (Jer 27:2), which corresponded to the way in which the Babylonian king, Nebuchadnezzar, would place Judah and the surrounding nations under "the yoke." He was prohibited from marrying—and thus having children—since nothing but destruction would come upon the inhabitants of the land (Jer 16:1–4).[24] All these acts made an impact upon the prophet's life and brought an intense level of distress. What would he have experienced? Loneliness, confusion, frustration, and anger.

Jeremiah and Isaiah 53

What is truly intriguing is not *Jeremiah's* sufferings per se, but how he reflects the sufferings *of others* in Scripture. This is particularly true for the suffering servant of Isaiah 53. In Jeremiah 11:19, the prophet is described as being like a "gentle lamb led to the slaughter." This echoes the description of the suffering servant in Isaiah 53:7 who was also "like a lamb that is led to the slaughter" (cf. Ps 44:11, 22). In Isaiah, the servant is a messianic figure who is "despised and rejected by men; a man of sorrows, and acquainted with grief" (Isa 53:3). In Jeremiah, the suffering servant is the prophet Jeremiah himself, whose "joy is gone; grief is upon me; my heart is sick within me" (Jer 8:18). Since the New Testament interprets the suffering servant of Isaiah as fulfilled in Christ (Acts 8:32–35; 1 Pet 2:21–25), so the suffering servant of Jeremiah should also be seen in the same way, where the prophet's own suffering anticipates the greater suffering of the greater Jeremiah.

Jesus and Jeremiah shared other similarities that strengthen the Messianic-like nature of the prophet's ministry. According to Jeremiah

24. See Thompson, *Book of Jeremiah*, 71–75 for more examples of symbolic-actions in Jeremiah.

11:21–23, he was called to preach to his hometown of Anathoth, where the people abhorred his message. Not only did they attempt to prevent him from carrying out his prophetic task of proclaiming the divine word, they also warned that he would do so at the risk of his very life. Some of the persecution and rejection Jeremiah faced was not merely from his fellow countrymen, but also from childhood friends or even members of his own family. Both Jeremiah and Jesus "came to his own, and his own people did not receive him" (John 1:11).

Jeremiah 24 depicts the prophet falsely accused of crimes, facing a blood-thirsty mob eager to condemn him to death, and standing before royal officials who see his innocence yet succumb to the will of the masses and imprison him nonetheless. This sequence of events is later reenacted in the history of redemption, in the city of Jerusalem; only it is the Lord himself, in his incarnate form, who endures these trials during the final days of his earthly life as recorded in the New Testament gospels.[25] The prophet is called to experience and share in the same rejection and oppression that the true suffering Servant would experience centuries later (John 1:29, 36).

Connection between Jeremiah and the Lord

Interestingly, within the book of Jeremiah itself, there are moments when the actions and thoughts of Jeremiah cannot be clearly distinguished from those of the Lord. For example, Jeremiah 4:19–22 records the tormenting cries of an anguished speaker, who laments over the sins of the city of Jerusalem:

> My anguish, my anguish! I writhe in pain! Oh the walls of my heart! My heart is beating wildly; I cannot keep silent, for I hear the sound of the trumpet, the alarm of war. Crash follows hard on crash; the whole land is laid waste. Suddenly, my tents are laid waste, my curtains in a moment. How long must I see the standard and hear the sound of the trumpet? "For my people are foolish; they know me not; they are stupid children; they have no understanding. They are 'wise'—in doing evil! But how to do good they know not." (Jer 4:19–22)

---

25. See chapter 6, "Joy of a Mourning Father" as another example of a reenactment narrative of the passion of Christ with the divine call to sacrifice Isaac in Genesis 22.

Who is this speaker? Probably Jeremiah, but not necessarily; it could be the Lord himself. The text does not make this clear. The inability to determine the one who cries for Jerusalem should be taken as exegetical data whereby this ambiguity is by divine intent.[26] What this demonstrates is the radically close correlation between the great Suzerain and his suffering messenger. Tremper Longman says, "It is probably best, therefore, to understand these verses (Jer 4:19–21) as the prophet's lament followed by an answer from God (Jer 4:22), *but the ambiguity does remind us of the close connection between God and his spokesperson.*"[27]

This ambiguity of speakers is only one example of several that illustrates how the prophet and the divine Sovereign share similar experiences. The Lord even said that in turning against Jeremiah, these people have, in reality, turned against the Lord himself (Jer 12:8). Both the Lord and Jeremiah weep and mourn for the people.[28] David Bosworth insightfully says that in the book of Jeremiah, the Lord weeps more than the prophet, and that the few occasions of the prophet's weeping embody the tears of the Lord. Therefore, he suggests, the book of Jeremiah is not about the "weeping prophet" but the "weeping God."[29] The unveiling of the heart of Jeremiah, then, is also an unveiling of the heart of the Lord.

The overall effect of this shared suffering between the Lord and his prophet portrays Jeremiah as a righteous sufferer, one called by the Lord to experience and know his suffering. Although our theme passage (1 Pet 4:12–13) does not explicitly refer to the prophet Jeremiah, the principle Peter espouses can appropriately be applied to him: he "fellowshipped" with the Lord in his suffering and is now currently continuing to fellowship with him in glory. For this reason, he should be considered a man who was endowed with extraordinary grace. Jeremiah could claim to have a deep union with his Suzerain since they knew similar agony—being rejected by those whom they loved so dearly. To not have such heartache would deny Jeremiah the richness of this fellowship. So Jeremiah can say that he had a "joy that is inexpressible and filled with glory" (1 Pet 1:8).

26. For another example, see Jeremiah 8:18–9:11.

27. Longman, *Jeremiah, Lamentations*, 50. Emphasis added.

28. Jeremiah weeps in Jer 9:1; 13:17; the Lord in Jer 9:10; 14:17; cf. Luke 19:41.

29. Bosworth, "Tears of God in the Book of Jeremiah," 24–46.

The Suffering of Ancient Messengers

Jeremiah was not alone. Indeed, the prophets as a whole measured the cost of their calling and were willing to pay the price for the sake of their mission to the people of God and the nations. The price that they paid was high—they were rejected by their own people and suffered because they had a deep love for them. Rejection of any kind is painful, even when it is from strangers. We all have an innate desire to be welcomed, accepted, and loved. When you are cast off by your own family, friends, and community, this is suffering of an entirely different magnitude.

Rejection of the Old Testament prophets

2 Chronicles 36:15–22, which form the final words of the Hebrew canon, provide a brief summary of the history of Israel. It describes how the Lord, out of compassion for his people, sent a series of prophetic messengers to call them to repentance. However, "they kept mocking the messengers of God, despising his words and scoffing at his prophets, until the wrath of the LORD rose against his people, until there was no remedy" (2 Chr 36:16). Jesus also condemned Israel for such heinous acts of violence against these well-intentioned prophets: "O Jerusalem, Jerusalem, the city that kills the prophets and stones those who are sent to it" (Luke 13:34; cf. Matt 21:33–46; Luke 11:47–54).

Several factors become clear within the prophetical books: 1) the false message of the false prophets is antithetical to that of the true prophets of the Lord, 2) the people are enamored with the positive optimism of the false prophetic word, which by comparison depicts the words of the true prophets as increasingly negative, and 3) the true prophets suffered greatly in body and spirit at the hands of the people.

Yet what choice did the prophets have? To withhold this message would provide comfort in their earthly lives, but torment unto their souls (Jer 20:9), since the result would be the destruction of their beloved people. Of minimal solace for the prophets was that, although the people eventually rejected their message, at least they had the chance to hear the message of repentance.

The good news that these ancient Israelites needed was precisely a call to repentance. They did not want it nor did they appreciate it. Still, they needed it desperately. The prophets proclaimed this message, and they did so at great discomfort to themselves.

Rejection of Moses

The prophets were following the pattern that was set for them by the paradigm-prophet Moses (Deut 18:15–18). We don't immediately think of Moses as a messenger who suffered at the hands of his people, but that was his life. Acts 4:23–29 provides an inspired commentary on Exodus 2:11–25, which recounts the time when Moses killed an Egyptian task-master for mistreating his fellow Hebrew. According to Luke, by killing the Egyptian, Moses thought his people would understand that God was giving them their long-desired redemption and rally around him as their leader. However, they did not understand this. The following day, when Moses attempted to reconcile two quarreling Hebrews, they pushed him aside and rejected his leadership. The lack of the people's understanding is used by Luke as an example of a larger pattern of disobedience, which was characteristic of Israel's history.

For Luke, as horrible as the rejection of Moses may have been, this was nothing compared to the rejection of the greater Moses, Jesus Christ (Acts 4:52). Moses was a shadowy copy of the true, righteous Messenger (Deut 34:10–12), who was sent to the people with sincerity and devout affection only to be met with scorn, disdain, and violence.

This is not the only place where we are given an insight into the psyche of Moses. Consider also Hebrews 11:24–28:

> By faith Moses, when he was grown up, refused to be called the son of Pharaoh's daughter, choosing rather to be mistreated with the people of God than to enjoy the fleeting pleasures of sin. He considered the reproach of Christ greater wealth than the treasures of Egypt, for he was looking to the reward. By faith he left Egypt, not being afraid of the anger of the king, for he endured as seeing him who is invisible. By faith he kept the Passover and sprinkled the blood, so that the Destroyer of the firstborn might not touch them. (Heb 11:24–28)

According to this passage, Moses demonstrated an outstanding act of faith by refusing to be known as the son of Pharaoh's daughter. Instead, "he chose to be mistreated along with the people of God rather than to enjoy the fleeting pleasures of sin" (Heb 11:25–26). The suffering that Moses endured was caused by his desire to identify with a community of faith. He had a choice: to be recognized as a member of the household of Pharaoh and prosper, or be identified as a member of the household of God and suffer. For Moses, it was an easy decision to choose God.

What is even more intriguing is realizing how, for the author of the book of Hebrews, "choosing . . . to be mistreated with the people of God" in verse 25 is equivalent with the "reproach of Christ" in verse 26. The abuse experienced by the people in Egypt was not due to any sin on their part; a new pharaoh arose who did not know Joseph and felt threatened by the growth of foreigners within his borders (Exod 1:6–10). The reproach that they knew was equivalent to the reproach that Christ knew: both suffered unjustly. This was the same reproach that Moses knew, and in an amazing way, this was more valuable to him than the earthly riches of Egypt. No amount of wealth, fame, or glory could have caused Moses to abandon the Lord because "he considered the reproach of Christ greater wealth than the treasures of Egypt" (Heb 11:26).

The author of Hebrews makes another intriguing correlation. The "reproach of Christ" is "greater wealth than the treasures of Egypt." This is truly a remarkable statement. Would anyone consider suffering of any kind a "treasure"—much less a "greater treasure"? Probably not. The author of Hebrews does, but only the kind of suffering that can be called a "reproach of Christ." He even says that to know this Christ-like reproach is more valuable than all the wealth of the wealthiest nation. Moses chose righteous suffering, Christ-like suffering, because this suffering is a treasure that is more valuable than any (even all) earthly riches.

Behind Moses was a greater Prophet, who also chose disgrace instead of riches. Moses was probably unaware that his experience in Egypt reflected the suffering of a coming Messianic Prophet, who would be "like Moses, whom the LORD knew face to face" (Deut 34:10). We are told that "he left Egypt, not fearing the king's anger; he persevered because *he saw him who is invisible*" (Heb 11:27). Later, the author of the book of Hebrews describes Jesus, the true Moses, in a similar way, as someone "who for the joy that was set before him endured the cross, despising the shame" (Heb 12:2). Moses and Jesus both knew rejection. In fact, Moses knew it because his ministry reflected—and even anticipated—the greater suffering of the greater Moses. By faith, Moses fellowshipped with his greater counterpart and thus could know something much more profound than sorrow: Moses knew Christ.

Rejection of the apostles

Not only did the Old Testament prophets face rejection and hardship for the message they preached, so did the New Testament messengers—the apostles. One way of understanding the book of Acts is as a record of these Spirit-empowered messengers of the gospel who were following the path of Jesus Christ. Just as Jesus was baptized before beginning his ministry, so his appointed apostles were "filled with the Holy Spirit" (Acts 2:4) prior to their ministry. As a result, they boldly proclaimed this gospel message to the harshest of critics who brought about their suffering.

In Acts 3–4, after healing a man lame since birth, Peter and John began to preach concerning the resurrection of Christ. Several Jewish leaders arrested them, finding it annoying that they would preach about the person whom the Jews had sent to the cross. However, this did not deter either Peter or John from their mission. They continued to proclaim the name of Jesus because "there is no other name under heaven given among men by which we must be saved" (Acts 4:12). They did this even after they were further threatened.

Stephen, one of the original seven deacons (Acts 6:5), faced similar opposition. Several wise men of the Jews instigated the masses and stirred up antagonism against him after he outwitted them in dialogues on wisdom. This led to Stephen's courageous proclamation of Christ before the Jewish council of leaders. His words were powerful, piercing the heart, and beautifully portrayed Jesus as a righteous sufferer, like Joseph, who was sold into slavery by his brothers, and like Moses, who was rejected by their rebellious forefathers. The Jews, like their fathers, were "stiff-necked," "uncircumcised in heart and ear," and "resisted the Holy Spirit." According to Stephen, their fathers rejected God's righteous prophets and their children rejected the true Prophet, Jesus Christ. As Stephen faced the hostility of his fellow Jews, he saw a beatific vision of the glory of God and Jesus seated at his right hand (Acts 7:55). He was quickly seized and stoned, uttering words reminiscent of his Savior prior to his death (Acts 7:59–60). Stephen's execution triggered a day of "great persecution against the church in Jerusalem" (Acts 8:1), led by Saul of Tarsus (Acts 8:3). The church's only crime was committing to the gospel of Jesus Christ and to boldly proclaim him. Thus, the book of Acts portrays the church experiencing the same sufferings as Jesus.

Saul, the bitter enemy of the church, was soon confronted by the resurrected Christ. From this point on, he was never the same (Acts 9).

He who had fervently been a *persecutor of* the gospel soon thereafter became *persecuted for* the gospel. Saul the executioner was now transformed to Paul the Apostle, the most influential preacher to the gentiles. This new call, however, came at a very high price, as Paul would come to know tremendous suffering, some of which is recorded in Acts 11–28 and summarized in 2 Corinthians 11:23–28. He would come to know:

> Imprisonments, with countless beatings, and often near death. Five times I received at the hands of the Jews the forty lashes less one. Three times I was beaten with rods. Once I was stoned. Three times I was shipwrecked; a night and a day I was adrift at sea; on frequent journeys, in danger from rivers, danger from robbers, danger from my own people, danger from Gentiles, danger in the city, danger in the wilderness, danger at sea, danger from false brothers; in toil and hardship, through many a sleepless night, in hunger and thirst, often without food, in cold and exposure. And, apart from other things, there is the daily pressure on me of my anxiety for all the churches. (2 Cor 11:23–28)

The book of Acts can be understood as the Acts of the Spirit-empowered apostles, but it is difficult not to think of the righteous, innocent sufferings of Christ as well, who permeates the message they preached. You can also see the sufferings of Christ reflected in their very lives, which can be understood as a New Testament symbolic-action. For that reason, Paul can say: "I bear on my body the marks of Jesus" (Gal 6:17). You can almost envision the scars and gashes on his body that he accumulated over the years of gospel service.

Regarding Galatians 6:17, the great Dutch biblical scholar Herman Ridderbos beautifully comments that these are called the "marks of Jesus"—not because they are the same wounds that Jesus received, "but because in these tokens his fellowship in suffering with Jesus becomes manifest."[30] Ridderbos goes on to apply this Christ-like suffering to believers: "This demonstrates also that what the believers must suffer at the hands of the world's enmity is the same thing that Jesus had to undergo—not the same in its fruit, but in its nature."[31] Similarly, Paul says in 2 Corinthians 4:10 that we are always "carrying in the body the death of Jesus, so that the life of Jesus may also be manifested in our bodies." We are not called to be crucified as Jesus was, nor do our afflictions provide any basis

30. Ridderbos, *Galatia*, 228.
31. Ridderbos, *Galatia*, 228.

for our redemption. That was accomplished by Christ alone. Rather, we are called to suffer unjustly as he did and thus intimately commune with him in a way that we could not otherwise.

Filling up what is lacking in Christ's affliction

The most remarkable statement by Paul in this regard is in Colossians 1:24, where the apostle says:

> Now I rejoice in my sufferings for your sake, and in my flesh I am filling up what is lacking in Christ's afflictions for the sake of his body, that is, the church. (Col 1:24)

Filling up what is lacking in Christ's afflictions? Is this possible? Does Paul truly expect us to think that the redemptive work of Christ left something undone that his church must complete? That hardly seems to be the case. Clearly, Paul does not mean that there is some further work of redemption that the church must accomplish apart from Christ. No way! Christ's sufferings accomplished complete and total redemption "once for all."[32]

The statement is jarring—that there is something that is lacking and, in some amazing way, Paul's sufferings in his flesh completed "the affliction of Christ." Specifically, Paul says that it was his *joy* in his suffering that completed it. Jesus's sufferings served a purpose; he did not suffer merely for the sake of suffering, without a goal. He did so for the good of his body, the church. He not only suffered so that the church could know eternal life (John 17:3) but also so the church could overcome the suffering that he knew they would experience as his disciples. When the church can rejoice in the suffering that marks the life of the Christ-like disciple, this "fills up what is lacking in Christ's afflictions."

We have seen numerous examples of the close relationship between the sufferings of Jesus and those of his disciples. Hebrews 4:15 says we have a high priest in Christ who is able to sympathize with our weaknesses. Peter (1 Pet 4:12–13) and Paul (Phil 1:29; 3:10) differ from Hebrews by redirecting our focus; instead of the Lord sharing in *our* sufferings (Heb 4:15), we are called to share in *his* sufferings (1 Pet 4:13). This suffering is unavoidable. Even Jesus said as much: "In this world you will have tribulation" (John 16:33).

---

32. See Romans 6:10; Hebrews 7:27; 9:26; 10:10; cf. John 19:30.

Christ may not have rejoiced at the thought of the cross, but we can rejoice because we are called to know the sufferings of Christ, whom we long to know.[33] In Christ's suffering, we have triumph over the *penalty* of sin—which is death—but we also have triumph over the *power* of sin—which is suffering. His suffering, therefore, redefines how we are to understand our suffering in Christ. This is not misery that leads to utter hopelessness or dark days of depression. Instead, it is a suffering that gives us full fellowship with Jesus, who is our joy. Until we know this joy in his sufferings, his affliction has not achieved its complete goal. For Paul, this suffering was the source of his joy. He said the church could know the same because, "Now I rejoice in my sufferings *for your sake.*" We can also know the same joy.

The Suffering of Contemporary Messengers

The struggle and anguish that the Old Testament prophets endured was truly difficult. They have a kindred spirit in modern, contemporary preachers, who have continued this long, enduring tradition of messengers—from the days of Moses, to the speaking prophets of Nathan, to the writing prophets of Hosea, Isaiah, and Jeremiah. All of them were called to proclaim a similar message, and so they faced the same difficulties. If indeed it is true that the "feet of those who bring good news" is "beautiful" (Isa 52:7; Rom 10:15), it is only perceived as such after an initial period of loathing and revulsion. The prophetical books, therefore, serve as a reminder of the great necessity of the ministerial call to the proclamation of the gospel message and the sober reality of the consequences that may result from it.

Suffering in preaching the gospel

The Christian gospel is scandalous to the sinful mind. To the humble and broken, it is a message of life and hope. However, to the arrogant and able, it is an offending message. To those outside of the church, this gospel is contrary to the greatest virtue of our day—the celebration of the indomitable spirit of humanity. Christian pastors preach the fallen, sinful nature of humanity. Yes, they preach the beauty of a New Heavens and New Earth that is only found in Christ, but this message presumes

33. Matthew 26:38–39; Mark 14:34–35; Luke 22:42.

accepting our fallen nature, our offense of a holy God, and the need for a substitute to atone for our sins. The situation is better in the church, but even there Christians struggle to remember the truths of the gospel—we sin and do so everyday and against everyone. We need Jesus or we die.

Pastors constantly face challenges. They are tempted to compromise their call to preach a message of repentance and faith for more light-hearted sermons that offer daily "practical" advice on how to manage the wear-and-tear of life. We must remember that the wear-and-tear of life comes from living among sinners. To preach a message of repentance is not only practical—it is absolutely necessary. We must hold fast to this message and not surrender to those who would challenge the call of preachers to proclaim faith and repentance in Christ as the foundation of life. As Paul said, "[It is] him we proclaim, warning everyone and teaching everyone with all wisdom, that we may present everyone mature in Christ" (Col 1:28).

Suffering in sharing the gospel

It is not only leaders in the church who must hold onto this message; all Christians are called to share this message with those around them: friends, neighbors, coworkers, and even family. This is not a popular message and it may not find an initial appeal. But what other message can we share? This is the exact question the disciples asked Jesus when many took offense at his teachings and left him, "Lord, to whom shall we go? You have the words of eternal life, and we have believed, and have come to know, that you are the Holy One of God" (John 6:68–69). For the sake of those around us whom we love so dearly, we are called to share this message of the gospel. It is truly a message of hope and life to those who turn to Christ by faith, but to the stiff-necked and arrogant it is foolishness of the highest degree.

As we share this message, we will face opposition, ridicule, and slander. For some, they may risk even more—perhaps their own lives. These sacrifices are reflections of the price that was paid by our great Shepherd-Pastor Jesus Christ, who suffered greater than anyone in the history of salvation. To endure such suffering for the cause of the gospel is to know the sufferings of our Savior. That alone is a "greater wealth than the treasures of Egypt" (Heb 11:26).

As I prayed about the possibility of the Lord calling one (or more) of my sons to ministry, I came to realize something—I don't want them to suffer, but I do long for them to know Jesus. There is nothing glamorous about suffering pain for the sake of suffering. What would be the point of that? However, I do long for them to know Jesus in a personal and profound way. And if knowing Christ's suffering is the only way for them to draw closer to their Savior, then so be it. With utter humility, fear, and compassion, I entrust these young men to the Lord to do with as he pleases. What they will gain is nothing short of a glorious *joy unspeakable*.

Finale

From Glory to Glory

> *And we all, with unveiled face, beholding the glory of the Lord, are being transformed into the same image from one degree of glory to another.*

2 Corinthians 3:18

BY NOW, I HOPE you have found comfort in the message of this book. We live in a fallen world that detests the message of the Christian gospel, so all those who identify with the cause of Christ are subject to the assaults of this hostile environment. Suffering—not health or wealth—will come because we are disciples of Christ. This is a suffering, however, that is worthy of praise—unlike suffering due to sin, which should lead us to repentance. Righteous suffering is filled with glory because it is not ordinary. According to 1 Peter 4:12–13, this is Christ's sufferings, and fellowship with the sufferings of Christ is a blessing, not a curse. In fact, Peter says that we cannot have a *joy unspeakable* unless we share in a full knowledge of Christ. This means we are called to know his suffering as well as his glory. We should never pray for this suffering because that would be foolish. However, when it comes (and it will come), we should be prepared to understand what it is.

Many in the history of salvation have shared in this righteous suffering, and we cannot describe them all in detail. We will, however, meditate upon just a select few heroes of faith in hopes that this will instill in you a new and profound way of reading the Bible. As the writer of the book of Hebrews reflected upon these heroes, he says: "And what more shall I say? For time would fail me to tell of . . ." (Heb 11:32). I echo his words.

What more shall I say? For time would fail me to tell of . . .

- *The seed of the woman (Gen 3:15)*. We interpret this as fulfilled in Jesus Christ, but Revelation 12:13 describes the apocalyptic vision of the serpent in Genesis 3:15 as fully grown into "a great red dragon" (Rev 12:3; cf. 12:9) that hungered for the unborn child of a woman. He failed and ultimately was thrown down into the earth. Frustrated in defeat, this dragon now wages war "on the rest of her offspring" (Rev 12:17). The reference to "offspring" is an allusion to Genesis 3:15 and the "seed" or "offspring" of the woman. Remarkably, Revelation 12:17 does not interpret this "offspring/seed" as Christ, but rather as those in Christ, "on those who keep the commandments of God and hold to the testimony of Jesus." The suffering of the elect-children of God is the suffering of Christ as they wage their war against the draconic beast, that serpent of old.

- *Abel and Joseph (Gen 4; 37–50)*. Genesis describes several conflicts between the seed of the woman and the seed of the serpent in sibling rivalries. The first was that of Cain and Abel (Gen 4). 1 John 3:12 encourages us to not be like Cain: "Who was of the evil one and murdered his brother. Why did Cain murder Abel? Because his own deeds were evil and his brother's righteous." The first righteous sufferer was Abel (Matt 23:35; Luke 11:51), and Hebrews says: "Through his faith, though he died, he still speaks" (Heb 11:4). Another sibling rivalry was that of Joseph (Gen 37–50) who was wrongfully persecuted by his older brothers for no sin on his part. Joseph still clung onto the Lord and saw his divine sovereign plan for good (Gen 50:20). These two cases testify of faithful men who suffered unjustly. The image of Christ is not difficult to see in these narratives, but we can also see the joy that they came to know because of whom they were in fellowship with. We can see the joy that we who share the sorrow of such betrayal can gain as well. Jesus knew it, and so do we.

- *Ruth (Ruth 1–4)*. Ruth was truly "a woman of excellence" (Ruth 3:11; Prov 31:10), but she was also a "Moabitess" (Ruth 1:22; 2:2, 6, 21; 4:5, 10). She was a faithful follower of the Lord, but she was never truly accepted by her mother-in-law, Naomi, until she bore a son to continue her family line. She had sacrificed ties to her own Moabite family, her homeland, and rejected her gods—all for the sake of Naomi—and followed her god, but she was still looked down upon as a foreigner by the Israelites.

- *The Son of Man (Dan 7:13–14, 27)*. The apocalyptic vision of "one like a son of man" is understood by the New Testament writers as Jesus Christ.[1] This figure has not always been interpreted messianically, but rather as "the people of the saints of the Most High" (Dan 7:27). Just as Genesis 3:15 has an individual and corporate understanding, so does the "son of man" in Daniel 7:13–14 as well. In both texts, it is possible that the corporate interpretation was the way they were originally understood by their ancient Israelite readers. It took the fullest revelation of the New Testament to help us realize that they are truly references to Christ. He is the true "seed of the woman" and "Son of Man." However, in our union with Christ, we also can be understood as the "seed of the woman" and "son of man." In Daniel 7, these "saints of the Most High" are persecuted by a bestial creature that represents the world empires opposed to the dominion and authority of the Lord (Dan 7:24–25). Just as the world persecuted our Savior, so we share in that suffering by being persecuted as well.

In each of the examples listed above, believers suffered because of their faith and trust in the Lord. They suffered innocently, righteously, and unjustly. They were sinners in need of the accomplished redemption of Christ, but the circumstances of their suffering were not brought on by any sin on their part. As such, they exemplify the Christ-like suffering that the New Testament (particularly 1 Pet 4:12–13) refers to, and the *joy unspeakable* that can come from it.

From Glory to Glory

Throughout this book, I have tried to show the amazing way in which our suffering in the Lord can be a source of Christian joy. Peter teaches this in 1 Peter 4:12–13. Because of our union with Christ, not only is suffering to be expected, but we can also rejoice in the midst of it because we "share

1. Matthew 24:27, 30; Mark 14:62; Luke 24:7; Acts 7:56; Revelation 14:14.

Christ's sufferings." I am always struck by the incredible comfort that this passage gives me, knowing Christ is my heart's greatest desire. This is the lesson that we are taught by heroes of the faith throughout the history of salvation.

The psalmists gave us songs of lament that capture more than the cries of God's people—they are the laments of Christ himself. By singing them, we join a choir of believers with Jesus as our choirmaster because his sufferings made it possible to have such songs written for us. Job instructs us that to have a life of suffering and have Jesus is by far better (wiser) than having all the wealth of this world without him. Abraham shows us that mourning parents can share in the sorrows of the greater Father who lost his greater Son. Hosea teaches us that a family devastated by betrayal and rebellion can still be a place where joy can be found because Jesus also knew such pain. The prophets remind us that people will hate us for sharing the message of the gospel, but they first hated Jesus who shared the same message.

My humble desire is to encourage us to appreciate the fact that when we "share Christ's sufferings," we come to know Jesus in a way that we could not otherwise. Peter described the life of Christ as going from suffering to glory. We are called to share in that same Christ-centered movement (1 Pet 1:10–11). What is significant is not the fact that we transition from *suffering* to glory, but that we transition from *the sufferings of Christ* to *the glory of Christ*. We are really transitioning from a *lesser-glory* to a *greater-glory*—or better yet, from *great-glory* to *greatest-glory*. Yes, our suffering can be a form of "glory" when it is understood in Christ.

There will come a time, at the second coming of Christ, when we will experience nothing but sheer glory. Paul provides one of the most well-known passages that describes this glory:

> For I consider that the sufferings of this present time are not worth comparing with the glory that is to be revealed to us. For the creation waits with eager longing for the revealing of the sons of God. For the creation was subjected to futility, not willingly, but because of him who subjected it, in hope that the creation itself will be set free from its bondage to corruption and obtain the freedom of the glory of the children of God. (Rom 8:18–21)

He insists that not only we, but creation as well, are waiting for our resurrection. That great day of resurrection glory is also the occasion for the renewal of the entire cosmos. The Bible speaks of this day as the

coming of the "new heavens and the new earth" (Rev 21:1; Isa 65:17–18).
Isaiah describes this as a day when:

> No more shall there be in it an infant who lives but a few days,
> or an old man who does not fill out his days, for the young man
> shall die a hundred years old, and the sinner a hundred years
> old shall be accursed. They shall build houses and inhabit them;
> they shall plant vineyards and eat their fruit. They shall not
> build and another inhabit; they shall not plant and another eat;
> for like the days of a tree shall the days of my people be, and
> my chosen shall long enjoy the work of their hands. They shall
> not labor in vain or bear children for calamity, for they shall be
> the offspring of the blessed of the LORD, and their descendants
> with them. (Isa 65:20–23)

The book of Revelation also describes this as a place where God
"will wipe away every tear from their eyes, and death shall be no more,
neither shall there be mourning, nor crying, nor pain anymore, for the
former things have passed away" (Rev 21:4).

But greater than all of this is the blessing of being with Jesus. I once
tried to describe heaven to my children by making a picture collage. I
cut out pictures of ice cream cones, candy canes, amusement parks, and
family picnics—the message being that heaven will be like this. I thought
that these images would express the amazing joy of the eternal kingdom
in ways that children could understand. After looking at my collage, one
of my kids asked, "Where is Jesus?" Where *was* Jesus? I realized at that
moment: not only can children appreciate (and need) a message focused
upon Christ, they desire it. They want to be with him. What makes heav-
en such a desirable place is not only that death, pain, and suffering will
be absent, but that *Jesus will be there*! So Jesus says, "Behold, the dwelling
place of God is with man. He will dwell with them, and they will be his
people, and God himself will be with them as their God" (Rev 21:3). Even
children know this.

Scripture makes this point clear: there is a future glory that awaits
us. But we do not need to wait for this future glory for our current joy,
because our current suffering can be a source of joy. Yes, this will not
compare to the blessings that await us in the eternal Kingdom, when our
Lord returns to gather his people to him for all eternity. Truly, in the presence of God, there will only be eternal praise and heavenly joy because
we will have a pure and holy knowledge of Jesus. But you do not need to
wait until that time to have a glorious joy; you can have it right now by

fellowshiping with Jesus in his suffering. As long as we know this, we can have a *Joy Unspeakable,* full of grace and truth. That is my prayer for you.

Final Prayer

Father in Heaven,

I rejoice that we can call Jesus Christ our Lord and Savior, for I know that we cannot do so unless you first showed your abundant mercy and grace upon us. Thank you, that we can look at our sins that haunt us from day to day without fear of condemnation because your Word tells us that "there is therefore now no condemnation for those who are in Christ Jesus" (Rom 8:1). There is no condemnation because of the death and resurrection of your only Son. Thank you, Father, for giving us Jesus. Thank you for his enduring and all-atoning sacrifice for our sins. Thank you for imputing upon us his righteousness and placing upon him our sins so that "for our sake he made him to be sin who knew no sin, so that in him we might become the righteousness of God" (2 Cor 5:21). Thank you that this "righteousness of God" comes to us by faith, and not by our works.

Now, as your disciples, you call for us to live a life of obedience filled with love and gratitude to you as our faithful Father. Yet to do so in this fallen world is truly difficult. On some days, I fall and suffer, for "the spirit indeed is willing but the flesh is weak" (Matt 26:41; Mark 14:38). On others, I am rejected by this world and again suffer. Either way, it seems that suffering will be the hallmark trait of life on this earth. When such trials come, give me wisdom to discern suffering that I bring upon myself by my sins from those that come as a result of my desire to remain faithful to you. If I suffer for my iniquities, forgive me, Father, and give me the strength and humility to overcome my sinful desires and conform to the image of your blessed Son.

If suffering for obedience, give to me the grace and wisdom to see this truly as "fellowship" with Christ's suffering. The world tells me something else: they mock you, scorn your Word, and even try to convince me that you simply do not exist. But persevering is difficult and I am tired. I'm tired of suffering all the time. In the midst of the emotional and physical pain, I am tempted to wallow in self-pity, fall into depression, and even lash out at you, questioning your sovereign goodness. I am not alone. Your church is constantly barraged by evil and sins that surround us. We are often betrayed by friends and family, even when we come with the best of intentions and share your gospel message. Help us, Father, for on our own, we cannot discern our suffering. Help us to see it for what it truly is—a blessing from you. And what an extraordinary blessing that is! We rejoice to know Jesus in the fullness of his life and we long for that more than anything else—to know Jesus. Although we are confident that a day will come when all pain and suffering will end and we shall know nothing but eternal bliss and harmony with you, help us to see that our current sufferings in Christ gives us a source of joy today. A "joy unspeakable." Thank you, Father, that we can experience such joy, something that is not of this world, something that is a product of heaven.

I ask this not just for myself, but also for your church. Until you return and take us to eternal glory, pour mercy upon your children that we may come to know Christ.

I ask this in the name of Jesus Christ,

Amen

Appendix

Reading Questions

Chapter 1–Introduction: A Layout of the Land

1. What is the purpose of this book?

2. Why is the book of 1 Peter helpful for those enduring hardships?

3. How does the Bible comfort suffering that results from sin?

4. Explain how suffering helps us trust in the Lord.

5. How does the Word help us in our suffering?

6. Is fatherly discipline painful? If so, how?

7. How does Christian suffering produce Christ-like virtues?

8. How does Christian suffering demonstrate the power of God?

9. How does Christian suffering encourage missions?

10. How does Christian suffering witness the reality of the gospel?

11. How does Christian suffering purify our faith?

12. How does Christian suffering glorify Jesus Christ?

13. You have often heard it said that the suffering we endure now does not compare with the glory that will be revealed in the last days. Does this really bring you comfort and joy?

14. How does 1 Peter 4:12–13 differ from other biblical instruction on finding hope in suffering? What do you think of this principle?

Chapter 2–The Inconvenient Truth

1. What is the "inconvenient truth" about the Christian life?

2. In this chapter, the question is asked: "What is the true reality of life?" How would you answer this question?

3. How is complacency a distractor in the Christian life? Do you struggle with this in your life? Your church? Discuss.

4. How is Matthew 7:21 relevant to suffering in the Christian life?

5. Faith is needed during times of suffering. Of all virtues, why faith? Explain how Psalm 73 illustrates this.

6. How is our "new-birth" related to Christian suffering?

7. How is our identity as spiritual sojourners related to suffering in the Christian life?

8. In light of our identity as spiritual sojourners, how should we live our lives?

9. Describe the correlation between spiritual warfare and suffering in the Christian life.

10. Describe the connection between our union with Christ and Christian suffering.

11. Describe union with Christ and the Christian's new-birth, spiritual sojourning, and spiritual warfare.

Chapter 3–The Surprising Source of Joy

1. Do you find the command in 1 Peter 4:13 shocking? Why or why not?

2. What are three significant factors to keep in mind in order to understand how Peter correlates joy and suffering?

3. What does "sharing in the sufferings of Christ" *not* mean?

4. Who can "share in the sufferings of Christ"?

5. How does 1 Peter describe the suffering servant of Isaiah 53? How is this related to our union with Christ?

6. Explain how the movement from suffering to glory is comforting for Christians.

7. Explain how sharing in the sufferings of Christ brings joy to believers.

8. Is it helpful for the church to preach/teach a Christ who knows suffering? Why or why not?

Chapter 4–Joy in Singing Songs of Lament

1. The ancient title of the book of Psalms is "Book of Praise." Why is this title ironic?

2. Why do you rarely hear a psalm of lament used in the church?

3. Explain how celebrating a psalm of lament is an act of faith and not a complaint.

4. Describe the movement within the book of Psalms.

5. Are the psalms prophetic? Explain.

6. What lessons do we learn from Luke 24?

7. Who is the singer of the psalms?

8. Did the psalmist know joy?

9. How can psalms of lament bring joy?

Chapter 5–Joy in the Perfect Storm of Job

1. What is the argument of Job's three friends? What is right and wrong with it?

2. What is the argument of Job? What is right and wrong with it?

3. What are some wise principles to consider when contemplating about righteous suffering?

4. How is Job introduced to us?

5. Describe the "perfect storm" of Job.

6. According to Job 1–2, why did Job suffer?

7. In essence, what was the accusation made against Job? Is this unreasonable?

8. Psalm 44:20–21 is bold. How does this bring joy?

9. Is Jesus similar to Job, or is Job similar to Jesus? Is this difference significant?

10. Did Job know joy?

11. How can the book of Job bring you joy?

Chapter 6–Joy of a Mourning Father

1. We are told that Sarah, Abraham's wife, is barren in Genesis 11:30. Why is that significant in light of the promises God made with Abraham?

2. What was at stake in the birth of Isaac?

3. There are two different kinds of crises Abraham had to face in Genesis 22. What are they?

4. Describe the pace of the narrative in Genesis 22. What effect does this have?

5. How is Isaac described in Genesis 22? Is this significant?

6. What other event in the history of redemption does Genesis 22 seem to anticipate?

7. From whose perspective is the narrative told in Genesis 22? Is this significant?

8. Who can share in the pain of the loss of a child?

9. How can Genesis 22 bring joy to those mourning the loss of a child?

Chapter 7–Joy in a Broken Family

1. For whom is this chapter written? Do you know of people who could identify with the message of this chapter?

2. Why was the Lord's choice for Hosea's wife so surprising?

3. Describe the literary organization of the book of Hosea and the message within it.

4. Describe the theological reality behind Hosea's marriage. Why is this important?

5. Describe the struggles of Hosea as a husband and as a father.

6. Who else can identify with Hosea's struggles?

7. How can understanding Hosea bring joy to those struggling with family issues?

Chapter 8–Joy of a Rejected Messenger

1. Share a time when you shared the gospel with negative results.
2. Describe the function of the Old Testament prophets.
3. Describe the message of the Old Testament prophets.
4. How did Israel respond to the prophetic word? Whose word did Israel like?
5. What are some modern "false prophetic words"?
6. Describe the life of the prophet Jeremiah.
7. Describe how Jeremiah could identify with the Lord.
8. Describe how Moses could identify with the Lord.
9. Describe how the New Testament apostles could identify with the Lord.
10. Describe how you can identify with the Lord.

Bibliography

Adams, Jay E. *The Grand Demonstration: A Biblical Study of the So-Called Problem of Evil.* Santa Barbara: EastGate, 1991.

Anderson, Francis I., and David Noel Freedman. *Hosea.* Anchor Bible Commentary. Garden City, NY: Double Day, 1980.

Bosworth, David A. "The Tears of God in the Book of Jeremiah." *Biblica* 94 (2013) 24–46.

Brueggemann, Walter. *The Message of the Psalms.* Minneapolis: Augsburg, 1984.

Calvin, John. *Commentary on the Book of Genesis.* Grand Rapids: Baker, 1993.

———. *Commentary on the Book of Psalms.* 3 vols. Translated by James Anderson. Reprint. Grand Rapids: Baker, 1993.

———. *Commentaries on the Twelve Minor Prophets.* Translated by John Owen. Reprint. Grand Rapids: Baker, 2005.

———. *Institutes of the Christian Religion.* 2 vols. Edited by John T. McNeil. Translated by Ford Lewis Battles. Philadelphia: Westminster, 1960.

Carson, D. A. *How Long, O Lord: Reflections on Suffering and Evil.* Grand Rapids: Baker, 2006.

Charpin, Dominique. "History of Ancient Mesopotamia: An Overview." In *Civilizations of the Ancient Near East*, edited by Jack M. Sasson, 807–29. Peabody: Hendrickson, 2000.

Clowney, Edmund P. *The Message of 1 Peter.* Downers Grove: InterVarsity, 1988.

Currid, John. *Why do I Suffer?: Suffering & the Sovereignty of God.* Berkshire: Christian Focus, 2004.

Dearman, J. Andrew. *The Book of Hosea.* New International Commentary of the Old Testament. Grand Rapids: Eerdmans, 2010.

Delitzsch, Franz. *The Book of Job.* Commentary on the Old Testament. Edited by C. F. Keil and F. Delitzsch. Peabody: Hendrickson, 1996.

Duncan, J. Ligon. "Divine Passibility and Impassibility in the Nineteenth Century American Confessional Presbyterian Theologians." *Scottish Bulletin of Evangelical Theology* 8.1 (1990) 1–15.

Elliott, J. H. *A Home for the Homeless: A Sociopolitical Exegesis of 1 Peter, Its Situation and Strategy.* Philadelphia: Fortress, 1981.

Ferguson, Sinclair. *The Grace of Repentance.* Wheaton: Crossway, 2010.

Frame, John M. *No Other God: A Response to Open Theism.* Phillipsburg: P&R, 2001.

Freeman, Hobart E. *An Introduction to the Old Testament Prophets.* Chicago: Moody Press, 1968.

Futato, Mark. *Transformed by Praise*. Phillipsburg: P&R, 2002.

Gaffin, Richard B. *Resurrection and Redemption*. Phillipsburg: P&R, 1987.

―――. "The Usefulness of the Cross." *Westminster Theological Journal* 41 (1979) 228–46.

Griffith, Howard. *Spreading the Feast: Instruction and Meditations for Ministry at the Lord's Supper*. Phillipsburg: P&R, 2015.

Gunkel, Hermann. *An Introduction to the Psalms*. Completed by Joachim Begrich and translated by James D. Nogalski. Macon: Mercer University Press, 1998.

Huffman, Douglas S., and Eric Johnston, eds. *God Under Fire: Modern Scholarship Reinvents God*. Grand Rapids: Zondervan, 2002.

Hugenberger, Gordon. *Marriage as a Covenant: Biblical Law and Ethics as Developed from Malachi*. Grand Rapids: Baker, 1998.

Jobes, Karen. *1 Peter*. Grand Rapids: Baker, 2005.

Keil, C. F. *The Twelve Minor Prophets*. Grand Rapids: Eerdmans, 1967.

Keller, Timothy. *Walking with God through Pain and Suffering*. New York: Dutton, 2013.

Kierkegaard, Søren. *Fear and Trembling*. London: Penguin Books, 1985.

Kline, Meredith G. *Images of the Spirit*. Eugene, OR: Wipf and Stock, 1998.

―――. *The Structure of Biblical Authority*. Grand Rapids: Eerdmans, 1972.

Lee, Peter. "The Surprising Source of Joy: A Biblical Foundation for Christ-Centered Suffering." *Reformed Faith & Practice: The Journal of Reformed Theological Seminary* 3:3 (2018) 3–31.

Lewis, C. S. *The Screwtape Letters*. Westwood, NJ: Barbour Books, 1990.

Lister, Rob. *God is Impassible and Impassioned: Toward a Theology of Divine Emotion*. Wheaton: Crossway, 2013.

Longman, Tremper. *Jeremiah, Lamentations*. Peabody: Hendrickson, 2008.

―――. *Job*. Commentary on the Old Testament Wisdom and Psalms. Grand Rapids: Baker, 2012.

Longman, Tremper, and Ray Dillard. *An Introduction to the Old Testament*. Grand Rapids: Zondervan. Second edition, 2006.

Macleod, Donald. *Christ Crucified: Understanding the Atonement*. Downers Grove: InterVarsity, 2014.

McCartney, Dan G. *Why Does It Have to Hurt?: The Meaning of Christian Suffering*. Phillipsburg: P&R, 1998.

McDonald, Lee Martin. *The Biblical Canon: Its Origin, Transmission, and Authority*. Peabody, MA: Hendrickson, 2007.

Miller, C. John. *Repentance: A Daring Call to Real Surrender*. Fort Washington: CLC, 2011.

Murray, John. *Redemption: Accomplished and Applied*. Grand Rapids: Eerdmans, 1955.

Piper, John, and Justin Taylor, eds. *Suffering and the Sovereignty of God*. Wheaton: Crossway, 2006.

Provan, Iain, et al. *A Biblical History of Israel*. Louisville: Westminster John Knox Press, 2003.

Ridderbos, Herman. *The Epistle of Paul to the Churches of Galatia*. Grand Rapids: Eerdmans, 1953.

Sande, Ken. *The Peacemaker: A Biblical Guide to Resolving Personal Conflict*. Grand Rapids: Baker, 2004.

Sproul, R. C. *Surprised by Suffering*. Wheaton: Tyndale House, 1989.

Thompson, J. A. *The Book of Jeremiah*. New International Commentary of the Old Testament. Grand Rapids: Eerdmans, 1980.

Tripp, Paul David. *Dangerous Calling: Confronting the Unique Challenges of Pastoral Ministry*. Wheaton: Crossway, 2012.

Van Pelt, Miles. *A Biblical-Theological Introduction to the Old Testament: The Gospel Promised*. Wheaton: Crossway, 2016.

Von Rad, Gerhard. "The Beginnings of Historical Writing in Ancient Israel." In *The Problem of the Hextateuch and Other Essays*, 166–204. Philadelphia: Fortress Press, 1984.

Vos, Geerhardus. *Biblical Theology*. Grand Rapids: Eerdmans, 1948.

Ware, Bruce A. *God's Lesser Glory: The Diminished God of Open Theism*. Wheaton: Crossway, 2000.

Warfield, B. B. "On the Biblical Notion of 'Renewal'" in *Biblical Doctrines*. Grand Rapids: Baker, 1932.

———. *Perfectionism, Part Two*. New York: Oxford, 1932.

Watson, Thomas. *The Doctrine of Repentance*. Edinburgh: Banner of Truth, 2009.

Wenham, Gordon. *Genesis 16–50*. Nashville: Thomas Nelson, 1994.

Wolterstorff, Nicolas. *Lament for a Son*. Grand Rapids: Eerdmans, 1987.

Wright, Christopher J. H. *The Mission of God*. Downers Grove: InterVarsity, 2006.

Young, Edward J. *An Introduction to the Old Testament*. Grand Rapids: Eerdmans, 1949.

Scripture Index

11:13–20	101	18	172
12:1–25	101	18:2	5
13:14–15	101	22	77, 87, 90, 91
15:20–35	101	22:1	87, 90, 91
18:5–21	101	26	117
19:4–22	101	26:3	117
20:5–29	101	26:4	117
21:22–26	101	26:5	117
22:22–30	101	26:8	117
28—31	100	27	81, 147
28:13–20	107	27:4	147
28:15–17	120	32	81, 93, 119
28:18–19	122	34	172
31	101	37:4	113
31:24–28	107	38	93, 119
32—37	97, 101	42	91, 92
35:10	94, 117	42:3	92
38—42	97, 101, 103, 119	42:8	94
38:4	97	44	117, 118
42:2–6	114	44:1–3	117
42:6	102	44:1–8	117, 118
42:7–9	101	44:4–8	118
42:7	102	44:9–26	118
42:10–17	116	44:9–22	118
42:10	102, 114	44:9–16	118
42:12	105	44:11	190
42:13	105	44:17–18	118
		44:20–21	118, 211
		44:22	190

Psalms

		44:23–26	118
		51	26, 81, 93, 119, 172
1	81	51:3	26
2	81	51:5	26
2:2	83	51:7	150
2:7	82, 83, 186	51:10	26
3	172	52	172
3:1–2	81	54	172
4:1	81	55	88
5:1–2	81	55:12–14	88
6:2–3	82	55:14	88
7	172	56	172
7:1–2	82	57	172
10	90, 91	59	172
10:1	90	60	172
13	90, 91	61:2	5
13:1–2	90	63	172
13:1	90, 91	73	24, 119, 210
13:2	90	73:1–3	119

Jeremiah

Isaiah

John

Acts